Contents

Naked Statues, Fat Gladiators, and War Elephants

Frequently Asked Questions about the Ancient Greeks and Romans

Garrett Ryan

Prometheus Books

Guilford, Connecticut

Prometheus Books

An imprint of Globe Pequot, the trade division of
The Rowman & Littlefield Publishing Group, Inc.
4501 Forbes Blvd., Ste. 200
Lanham, MD 20706
www.rowman.com

Distributed by NATIONAL BOOK NETWORK

British Library Cataloguing in Publication Information Available

Library of Congress Cataloging-in-Publication Data

Names: Ryan, Garrett, 1986– author.
Title: Naked statues, fat gladiators, and war elephants : frequently asked
  questions about the ancient Greeks and Romans / Garrett Ryan.
Description: Lanham, MD : Prometheus, [2021] | Includes bibliographical
  references and index. | Summary: "Most books on the Roman Empire deal
  with famous figures or events, but Naked Statues, Fat Gladiators, and
  War Elephants focuses on things that seldom appear in history books:
  myths and magic, barbers and birth control, fine wine and the daily
  grind. This book, based on questions Roman historian Garrett Ryan, PhD,
  gets asked most often on Quora and the popular Reddit forum
  AskHistorians, reveals the nitty gritty details on how Romans and Greeks
  lived in a series of short and engaging essays, organized into six
  categories: daily life, society, beliefs, sports and leisure, and
  legacies"—Provided by publisher.
Identifiers: LCCN 2021002666 | ISBN 9781633887022 (paperback) | ISBN
  9781633887039 (epub)
Subjects: LCSH: Civilization, Classical—Miscellanea.
Classification: LCC DE71 .R93 2021 | DDC 938—dc23
LC record available at https://lccn.loc.gov/2021002666

Preface

$\mathcal{A}$ few years ago, when I was teaching at the University of Michigan, I brought one of my classes to the Detroit Institute of Arts. As we were finishing our tour of the Ancient Greek and Roman Galleries, a student approached me. Leaning forward conspiratorially, he murmured: "Dr. Ryan—I have to ask—why are so many Greek statues naked?"

This book answers that question and dozens more. If you've ever wondered when the Romans started wearing pants, whether the Greeks believed their myths, what the ancient world's best-paying jobs were, or how lions were captured for the Colosseum, you've come to the right place. Mysteries and magic, gladiators and assassins, fine wine and war elephants: this book has 'em all.

My answers are nothing more and nothing less than pithy summaries of current scholarship, spiced with anecdotes from ancient sources* and garnished with the finest illustrations the public domain could provide. They do not pretend to be comprehensive—there's only so much that can be said in a few sprightly pages—but I sincerely hope that they inspire deeper reading.

No answer assumes more than the most basic knowledge about the Greeks and Romans. Since a bit of context goes a long way, however, I've included a very short history of the classical world in the appendix at the end of the book. If you'd like to begin with the big picture, I encourage you to read that first. Otherwise, plunge right into the questions.

---

* Many of the best anecdotes are in the footnotes, which provide interesting details that I couldn't conscionably cram into the main answer. Sources are cited in the endnotes.

I
DAILY LIFE

• 1 •

Why Didn't the Greeks or Romans Wear Pants?

*Y*ou are walking on a busy street in Classical Athens. It is a summer morning—hot, but not too hot to run errands. White walls glitter in the sun. A murmur of Greek drifts through the dusty air. The mouthwatering aroma of honey cakes, stacked in a nearby stall, competes with the unmistakable stench of a city without a sewage system.

Most of your fellow pedestrians are men. Most of these men are not quite half-naked. Some have a cloak wrapped around their torsos. The rest stroll by in loose, knee-length tunics. The few women in sight are wearing longer tunics, fastened at the shoulders with long pins.* Female and male, the clothes of the poor are the off-white of uncolored wool. The more prosperous are plumed in every shade of yellow, green, and brown.[1]

Now transport yourself to a street in early imperial Rome. Although it is nearly noon (or sixth hour, as the Romans call it), the street is still dark, shadowed by the towering apartment buildings on either side. The cobbles underfoot are slick with foul-smelling muck. Smoke spills from the door of a tavern across the street, carrying the scent of roasted chickpeas. A multilingual hubbub fills your ears, and harried pedestrians rush past, all wearing clothes very different from anything in Athens.

A few men are wearing togas. An unfolded toga is a vast woolen expanse up to twenty feet across. Immersing oneself in this sea of cloth is such a complicated process that aristocrats often have a slave whose

---

* In a pinch, these could be pressed into service as weapons. A crowd of Athenian women once killed a man with their brooches.

2

From left to right: a Greek man wrapped in a cloak (*himation*), a Greek woman in a tunic (*chiton*), a Roman man in a toga, and a Roman matron in a mantle (*palla*). *Images from the public domain*

primary duty is to crease and drape it. Since walking in a toga is equal parts art and ordeal—any failure to keep one's left arm at just the right angle spells death for all those careful folds—most of the men on our street have left their togas at home and are going about their business in short tunics. Some of the women are swathed in the traditional mantle of the Roman matron. The rest wear full-length tunics in a riot of colors.

Both Greek and Roman clothing was draped over the body. Whether linen, wool, or cotton,* draped clothes were well-suited to a Mediterranean climate and conveniently adaptable to changes in the social situation or weather. They tended, however, to be uncomfortable in the cold and damp. Some, like the toga, required constant attention to wear correctly. All lacked pockets.†

This, it would seem, was a world crying out for pants. Yet with only a few exceptions—such as the eccentric Emperor Elagabalus, who

---

* The most common fabrics in the classical world were wool and linen. Since wool was warmer, more durable, and easier to dye, it was typically used for outerwear. Linen—more breathable, simpler to clean, and less friendly to lice—was preferred for undergarments and everyday use. Cotton (grown in Egypt) only became common during the Roman imperial era.

† Equivalents could be improvised: Greek women often drew a portion of their tunics over their belts to create a large pocket, and Roman men stashed leftovers in recesses of their togas. Coins, however, had to be kept in purses suspended from the belt or neck. Alternatively, since the world was yet innocent of germ theory, they could be tucked into a corner of one's mouth.

gloried in his silken slacks*—the Greeks and Romans regarded pants as barbaric. To the Athenians, they recalled the Persians, who had invaded Greece in overwhelming numbers and baggy trousers. The Romans associated them with the tattoo-streaked and beer-swilling peoples of the north, especially the Germans.[2]

In the end, however, the Romans buckled. The process began among the legions. The knee-length tunics legionaries wore, designed for the heat of a Mediterranean summer, were unpleasantly breezy in northern winters. Inspired by barbarian cavalrymen, soldiers stationed in chilly climes began to squeeze into short breeches of wool or leather. Soon, some took the natural next step of wearing full-length pants. Their commanders followed suit: a third-century emperor shocked respectable opinion by wearing such pants (and a floppy blond wig) while leading his troops.[3]

Over the course of the fourth century, as soldiers in politics made military clothing fashionable, civilians began to trade their own tunics for trousers. By the century's end, the practice had become so widespread that pants were banned from the city of Rome by imperial edict. Any man found so scandalously attired was to be arrested, stripped of his property (and presumably his pants), and sent into perpetual exile. The cause, however, was already lost. Within a few decades, senators were wearing trousers even in the emperor's presence.[4]

Having glanced at the advance of pants, we must confront a more profound question: did the Greeks and Romans wear underwear?

Most women certainly wore the proto-bras we call breast bands.† Though fitted versions with shoulder straps existed, these were usually

---

* Roman emperors were persistent sinners against fashion. Some contented themselves with clothes dyed purple, the classical world's most expensive, and therefore most prestigious, color. (Use of the finest shade of purple, a dark and shimmering crimson the color of dried blood, was sometimes restricted to the imperial family; Nero once set up a sting operation to catch merchants who handled contraband dye.) For others, robes worth more than most villas were too subtle. Caligula liked to costume himself as Zeus, complete with a golden beard and gleaming thunderbolt. Commodus came to the Colosseum in lion skins.

† The evidence for panties is skimpy. There were certainly panty-like garments: some Roman women wore swimsuits in the baths, and female athletes and entertainers appeared in a proto-bikini. (The future empress Theodora, who began her career as a burlesque actress, had a routine that involved strutting onstage in the ancient equivalent of a G-string.) Normally, however, women wore only shifts beneath their street clothes. These had hazards of their own: one Roman poet devoted an unkind epigram to a lady enduring a wedgie from an overtight undertunic.

simple strips of cloth wrapped around the torso. Since small breasts were considered attractive, women often used the bands to flatten their chests.* If we can believe ancient poets, they also served as makeshift pockets for everything from love letters to vials of poison. Breast bands were even reputed to have medicinal properties: a used band wound round one's head was said to relieve headaches.[5]

Greek men apparently had nothing but sunburn and self-assurance beneath their tunics. In the Roman world, a few traditionalists wore loincloths under their togas, and men might sport a sort of Speedo in the baths. Most, however, dispensed with underwear, preferring breathable undertunics of linen or silk. Though comfortable, these garments were not conducive to modesty. A late antique author tells the story of a visitor who sat across a fire from Saint Martin of Tours. The man eased back on his chair, spread his legs—and accidentally gave the saint an expansive view of his genitals.[6]

By the fourth century, when Saint Martin was flashed, Roman clothing was well on its way to becoming medieval. Imagine yourself on a street in late antique Constantinople. Let's say, for the sake of ambience, that it is a crisp autumn afternoon, with a salt-smelling breeze in the air and church bells serenading the mellow light. A pompous court official glides past in a slim version of the traditional toga. Lesser men bustle by in knee-length tunics with broad sleeves and as much embroidery as they can afford. The women's tunics are longer, though equally billowy and bedizened. A few of the wealthiest pedestrians flaunt garments of clinging silk. A few of the most pious bear Christian tattoos on their hands. But none at all, you feel quite certain, is wearing underwear.

---

* In some contexts, breast bands were erotic; a character in one Greek comedy slowly loosens hers to tease her husband.

• 2 •

How Did They Shave?

$\mathcal{H}$adrian was the most enigmatic of the Roman emperors. He was an accomplished poet, architect, and flutist. His favorite form of relaxation, however, was lion hunting. He led the empire's greatest scholars in academic discussions. But he was equally comfortable leading legionaries on forced marches. He was a generous friend and just judge. Yet he was also arrogant, suspicious, and—when the mood struck—murderous. Most paradoxically of all, he had a beard. For centuries, almost every prominent Roman had been clean shaven. Hadrian's cheeks, however, were proudly and profusely hirsute the full length of his twenty-one-year reign. The beard may have been a sign of his fascination with the Greeks, a throwback to the Roman past, or a nod to Zeus. Or perhaps, as one Roman author speculated, the emperor was just trying to cover his acne scars.[1]

Whatever Hadrian's reason for being bearded, it was more than a personal quirk. Beards were taken very seriously in the classical world. First and foremost, they were a badge of masculinity.* They were also a way of advertising status: it was the calling card of a gentleman to be neatly groomed, and a sign of poverty to be stubbled or scraggly. The state of one's beard was a convenient emotional index, since those in mourning (and those trying to win sympathy in court) left their facial hair untrimmed. Beards, finally, bespoke culture—barbarian, Roman, or Greek.[2]

---

* Young Roman men celebrated their first shave as the beginning of maturity, immortalizing the occasion by dedicating their wispy whiskers to the gods. After his first shave, Nero collected the clippings in a golden box and enshrined them in a temple of Jupiter.

Hadrian and his majestic beard. *Classical Numismatic Group Inc. (www.cngcoins .com)*

During the Classical period, Greek men were almost always bearded. Although fashions varied, the most popular style was a full beard with a shaved upper lip.* Shaving clean was considered effeminate—until the reign of Alexander the Great. Among the great conqueror's many peculiarities (which ranged from an obsession with the *Iliad* to the conviction that he was a literal son of Zeus) was an insistence on regular shaving. We don't know whether Alexander wished to emphasize his youth or was simply cursed with patchy facial hair.

---

* Mustaches were illegal in Sparta. Every year, upon assuming office, the chief Spartan officials issued an edict ordering all citizens to obey the laws and shave their upper lips.

We do know, however, that his immense prestige made beardlessness trendy.[3]

After Alexander's death, and despite prickly pro-beard legislation in several cities, the clean-shaven look spread rapidly through the Greek world. Not everyone, however, adopted the new fashion. Intellectuals, in particular, continued to pride themselves on their beards; one philosopher claimed that, if forced to choose between shaving and death, he would gladly perish. There was a lingering sense that beards were just more dignified than scraped cheeks. In the imperial era, a visitor to a remote Greek city found every man bearded in the traditional manner, save a single wretch who shaved—it was said—to impress the Romans.[4]

The Romans had started off as hairy as the Greeks. But in the middle of the second century BCE, the Roman elite, probably inspired by contemporary Greek fashion, began to shed their whiskers. The great general Scipio Aemilianus, conqueror of Carthage, was remembered as the first Roman to shave daily, and all the famous figures of the late Republic and early empire followed his example. Julius Caesar, who was rather vain, always appeared in public with a comb-over and precisely cleaned cheeks. Augustus took a few moments each morning to have his face shaved and hair trimmed by three barbers working in tandem. Ambitious men throughout the empire followed the example of the aristocracy, banishing beards to the fringes of respectability.[5]

Then our friend Hadrian appeared on the scene. Thousands of statues and millions of coins proclaimed his bearded majesty; local trendsetters sprouted in his wake; and after four centuries of tough love, the Romans embraced their beards again. For the next two hundred years, until the tide was reversed by the clean-shaving Constantine, fashion-forward Romans boasted beards of every length and style, usually following the example of the reigning emperor. Sometimes, the beard of the hour was neatly trimmed, like Hadrian's. In other periods, it looked more like the full philosopher's beard adopted by Marcus Aurelius or the rough stubble affected by the military emperors of the third century.

For many Greek and Roman men, managing even the brushiest of beards must have seemed easier than shaving. The standard ancient razor consisted of a bronze or iron blade, often sickle-shaped, mounted on a short handle. Even for those few who owned adequate mirrors,* it was difficult to shave oneself cleanly with such a blunt instrument. As far as we can tell, few ventured to try. Wealthy men had their slaves shave them. The rest went to barbers.

Although a few jet-setting hairdressers coiffed aristocrats in lavish salons, most barbers were humble tradesmen working out of small shops or in the open air. A man in search of a shave would be seated on a low stool. His shoulders were wreathed with linen. His cheeks were softened with a splash of water. And then he watched with grim apprehension as the barber stooped over him, razor in hand. Since they were difficult to keep sharp, ancient razors tended to tug and tear as they were dragged over cringing flesh. They also were prone to drawing blood. Although customers puffed out their cheeks to minimize the risk of gouging, all but the best barbers sometimes shaved a little too close to the skin.† Worst of all were the dreaded barber's apprentices, who tended to have more enthusiasm than skill and were sometimes only allowed to use blunted razors.[6]

For those who wished to be rid of their beards but dreaded the ordeal of shaving, there were a few alternatives to the razor. One Greek tyrant, terrified of having his throat cut, trained his daughters to singe off his stubble with red-hot nutshells. More conventional methods included plastering oneself with depilatory pine resin and painstakingly tweezing offensive follicles. The same means, along with the equally unpleasant trick of tearing hair loose with rough pumice, were employed to obliterate body hair.[7]

Some women clearly shaved (or rather, waxed, pumiced, and plucked) their legs; a Roman poet, for example, advised ladies to be sure that their legs were smooth before meeting a prospective lover. The classical equivalent of a bikini wax also seems to have been fairly common.‡ It is less clear whether women who did not belong to the urban elite bothered with such things. Most probably didn't, not least because their legs were almost always covered by their clothes. Ancient authors shed little light on the matter, since they were much more interested in the scandalously shaved legs of men.[8]

---

* Although glass mirrors began to appear in the Roman era, most mirrors in the classical world were small disks of polished bronze. Only the rich had large hanging mirrors.

† A Roman author helpfully suggested using cobwebs to bind shaving cuts.

‡ The inhabitants of one Greek city reputedly worshipped Dionysus as "the denuder of genitals." Why that particular chore required a divine patron is difficult to say.

Particularly in the Roman world, many men removed some or all of their body hair. Emperor Otho, for example, was noted for the pains he took to keep himself smooth all over. This practice presented traditionalists with a bristling thicket of problems. For a vocal minority, shaving any body hair was a willful rejection of masculinity. At least once, a heated public debate took place between a bewhiskered philosopher and a freshly plucked orator over the morality of hair removal. Moderates were willing to concede that some parts of the body could be decently denuded. Gentlemen, they acknowledged, could and should tidy up their armpits.* But only a reprobate would stoop so low as leg shaving.[9]

---

* Many Roman baths had a professional plucker of armpits (and other troublesome crevices) on duty at all times.

What Kinds of Pets Did They Have?

𝒯he ruined city of Termessos is engulfed by its tombs. They carpet the hills on every side—sarcophagi in heaps, sarcophagi in rows, grass-grown, broken, and bare. Most are massive and hulking. But a few, half-hidden by their ponderous cousins, are more modest. One of these, a gray stone chest with a peaked lid, bears a short epitaph. The final line is still clear: "I am the dog Stephanos; Rhodope set up a tomb for me."[1]

Dogs were the classical world's favorite pets. The largest, conventionally called Molossians, were deep-chested mastiffs. Originally bred to hunt boars, these dogs were used to guard homes and sometimes to pull carts.* Another large variety was the "Indian" hound, said to result from a cross between a male tiger and a female dog (the breed was rare, it was thought, because the tigers often ate the dogs after mating with them). The slim and swift Laconian hound, which ran down deer and hares, was long the premier midsize breed. Over the course of the Roman era, however, it was overtaken by the equally slim and still swifter vertragus, an ancestor of the modern greyhound. The best-known small breed was the Maltese dog, a stub-legged, long-haired little creature whose most useful quality was being able to fit in a handbag.† The names given to dogs tended to reflect their appearance. Molossian and Laconian hounds had macho monikers like Courage,

---

* One eccentric Roman emperor reportedly harnessed four huge dogs to a chariot when he wanted to drive around the grounds of his estates.

† They did have a single practical attribute: letting a Maltese nestle on one's stomach was said to relieve indigestion. The ancient Maltese dog, incidentally, seems to have looked more like a Pomeranian than a modern Maltese (to which it is not directly related).

A Maltese dog on a Roman tombstone. *Grave Stele for Helena, AD 150–200. The J. Paul Getty Museum, Villa Collection. Digital image courtesy of the Getty's Open Content Program*

Lancer, and Whirlwind. Lapdogs, on the other hand, tended to be called things like Fly, Pearl, or Smidgen.[2]

Many wealthy Greeks and Romans kept a Maltese dog or three. They appear on Greek vases, leashed to their masters' banqueting couches. In the Roman world, they became fashionable accessories for elite ladies, who carried them in the folds of their tunics. Often, they were outrageously spoiled: a Roman poet describes how one doting owner commissioned a painting of his lapdog Missy. Favorite hunting dogs were equally pampered. In one of his works, a Greek historian enthuses at length about his greyhound, which lay beside him as he wrote and accompanied him to the gymnasium every day. Alexander the Great named a city after his faithful hound Peritas.*[3]

However attached they were to their dogs, wealthy families delegated feeding, walking, and other chores to slaves and dependents. One ancient author describes how a somber stoic philosopher was put in charge of his patron's yippy lapdog, with comedic results (the dog kept getting tangled in the philosopher's beard). Dogs were normally fed some combination of table scraps and stale bread, though favored hounds might receive baked doggy treats. Despite an understanding of basic medical procedures—male dogs were sometimes neutered—veterinary care was rudimentary. It was thought, for example, that a dog could be cured of mange by having it sleep next to a person every night.[†] Ancient dogs seem, however, to have had about the same lifespans as their modern descendants: some breeds, according to Aristotle, could live up to twenty years.[4]

Cats were much less popular than dogs. They entered the classical world from Egypt, where they had long been sacred animals and treasured pets.[‡] The Greeks and Romans, however, tended to regard them as hunters of vermin, not companions. Even as mousers, cats seem to have been less common than ferrets and tame snakes until the Roman imperial era. In upper-class houses, at least, their unpopularity might be explained by the abundance of tame birds.[5]

One Greek philosopher had a goose that followed him wherever he went. Another was in the habit of conversing with his pet partridge. Wealthy Romans kept peacocks for their beauty, nightingales and blackbirds for their song, and ravens and parrots for their ability to speak. Indian parrots were especially prized and often trained to greet guests and perform other tricks. A Greek historian lived for twenty years with a parrot that could sing, dance, and address his visitors by

---

* In return for all this pampering, pet dogs often displayed remarkable loyalty to their masters. In the early first century, for example, after a Roman aristocrat was executed for treason, the man's dog refused to leave his body, even bringing it scraps of bread. When the corpse was flung into the Tiber, the dog leapt in after it and tried to nose it out of the water.

† This would have succeeded only in giving that person scabies.

‡ When a Roman soldier in Alexandria accidentally killed a cat, he was lynched by an Egyptian mob.

name. Other parrots were taught to hail Caesar and, inevitably, to curse. It seems to have been a party trick to get the house parrot drunk and make it repeat dirty words. This, however, was a risky business; once a parrot starts swearing—one author laments—it never stops.[6]

Some Greeks and Romans, to the dismay of most other Greeks and Romans, insisted on keeping large snakes as pets. The cold-blooded emperor Tiberius was a famous snake enthusiast. Alexander the Great's mother was another. Snakes seem to have been popular among the Roman aristocracy, who draped them over their shoulders and allowed them to glide among the dishes at banquets.* Equally unwelcome guests were the monkeys (probably Barbary macaques) kept as pets by many Roman notables, which had a habit of wreaking havoc at the dinner table.[7]

The most exotic and impressive pets belonged to Roman emperors. Lions were particular favorites. Domitian once forced a senator he disliked to fight the fiercest of his pet lions (unfortunately for the emperor, the senator was a skilled hunter and defeated the beast). Caracalla was accompanied at all times by a lion named Scimitar, which he caressed like a Bond villain while sitting on his throne. One of his successors liked to unleash his pack of tame and defanged lions on unsuspecting party guests as a joke.† Bears were another favorite imperial pet. Valentinian I owned man-eating she-bears named Goldflake and Innocence, who lived in a cage by his bedroom and lived on a hearty diet of political prisoners. A like-minded predecessor reportedly enlivened banquets by having men thrown to his pet bears.‡ Some emperors kept whole zoos in their palaces. Nero allowed herds of tame and wild animals to wander the grounds of his Golden House, and a later emperor was said to have owned elephants, elk, lions, leopards, tigers, giraffes, hyenas, hippopotami, and a solitary rhinoceros.[8]

Although most of the animals in imperial menageries can hardly be called pets, some were much more than symbols of power.

---

* Since these pet snakes are never described in detail, their species is uncertain. The non-venomous and relatively docile four-lined snake is a plausible candidate. If one author's story about a giant child-eating snake in Rome is more than an urban legend, it is conceivable that some reckless Roman purchased (and then lost) a reticulated python from India.

† A few aristocratic Romans also owned lions, but most were discouraged (or so a poet suggests) by the expense involved in feeding and training them.

‡ Not all Romans were so bloodthirsty. One young emperor cherished a pet chicken named "Roma." Another liked to watch puppies playing with piglets.

Caracalla's lion, for example, slept in his bedroom, and supposedly tried to save his life the day he was assassinated. Valentinian was so fond of one of his bears that he couldn't stand to see her in a cage and finally released her in a remote forest. Sometimes, man's best friend eats his enemies.

Did They Use Any Form
of Birth Control?

A black rain once swept over the hills of eastern Libya. Where the ebon drops fell, it was said, silphium grew. It was a tall and striking plant with black roots, a single thick stalk, and shocks of golden leaves. And as the residents of Cyrene, a nearby Greek colony, soon discovered, it had many uses. It fattened the local sheep.* Its stalks and leaves, diced and dipped in vinegar, graced banquets. The fragrance of its flowers scented perfumes. The real prize, however, was its resin. Besides improving the flavor of any food it was sprinkled on, silphium resin had a host of medicinal uses, including (but not limited to) stripping hair, soothing eyes, salving bites, slaying warts, and staving off the ill effects of poisoned arrow wounds. Above and beyond all these, it was a potent contraceptive. For this, silphium was commemorated on coins, celebrated in song—and picked to extinction. Nero got the last stalk.†1

Even before the disappearance of silphium, the use of contraceptives was limited in the classical world. The vast majority of free Greeks and Romans were married, and it was generally agreed that the purpose of marriage was to produce children. The pressure to procreate was heightened by the terrible toll of childhood diseases: couples who limited themselves to a few children risked losing all of them. Most women, accordingly, bore children as long as they were able, at intervals determined by abstinence and breastfeeding. Since women typically breastfed their children for about two years, and since they were

---

* Silphium-fed beef and mutton were praised for their flavor. Goats that grazed on silphium, however, were afflicted with hiccups.

† Or so one author claims. Other references suggest that silphium survived a little longer, and a few optimistic scholars think that it may still flourish in some remote Libyan valley.

16

A stalk of Silphium, as depicted on a coin from Cyrene. *Classical Numismatic Group Inc. (www.cngcoins.com)*

encouraged to avoid intercourse during this period (on the theory that sperm would somehow spoil their milk), their pregnancies were often spaced several years apart without any use of contraceptives.[2]

Some women, however, were motivated to limit their fertility more drastically. For prostitutes, for the unmarried, and for many slaves, children were a liability. Desperately poor parents often found themselves unable to feed another hungry mouth. And on the other end of the social scale, aristocratic families sometimes sought to preserve their wealth and status by producing only one or two heirs.

Short of abstinence, the most basic form of contraception was an offbeat version of the rhythm method. Women were assumed to be least fertile in the middle of their menstrual cycle. But since this is actually the period of greatest fertility, couples who coupled in keeping with this theory were prone to parenthood. A more reliable alternative was nonvaginal intercourse.* Conception might also be evaded with some good old-fashioned coitus interruptus—especially effective, according to one author, if the woman held her breath.[3]

There is no evidence for condoms in the classical world. Vaginal barriers and suppositories, however, were common. Virtually any substance that seemed like it might catch, cool, or otherwise stymie sperm was pressed into service. Bits of pomegranate rind and small sponges soaked with oil or resin seem to have been especially popular. A less invasive approach required one or both partners to smear their genitals with crushed juniper berries, cedar resin, or olive oil. Like some of the suppositories, these substances had real contraceptive properties and may have been at least partially effective. One suspects, however, that they did little to enhance the experience for anyone involved.[4]

Oral remedies were also widespread. Although some featured the bracing undertones of copper ore or the musky aroma of roasted mule testicles, most consisted of plant extracts stirred into water or wine. Besides the late lamented silphium, common ingredients included pennyroyal, willow, and two plants with evocative names: squirting cucumber and death carrot. Taken in proper doses, some of these extracts actually may have worked. The same cannot be said for the contraceptive amulets many women wore, which incorporated everything from weasel liver to the contents of a hairy spider's head. If all else failed, there was always magic. One spell for preventing pregnancy entailed catching a frog, convincing it to swallow seeds soaked in menstrual blood, and releasing it, bewildered, back into the wild.[5]

Even if fortified with mule testicles or death carrot, a woman who wanted to avoid pregnancy could take additional precautions immediately after intercourse. Sperm, it was thought, might be chilled to sterility with postcoital cups of cold water, obliterated by a dose of pulverized

---

* The tyrant Pisistratus was forced to flee Athens due to a scandal arising from his practice of having anal sex with his wife.

beaver testicle,* or expelled from the womb with a timely and vigorous sneeze.[6]

Since Greek and Roman doctors understood conception as a gradual process, no clear distinction was drawn between contraception and what we would call early term abortion. In the first few days and weeks after conception, women might attempt to prevent sperm from settling into their wombs by going for bumpy carriage rides or jumping and kicking up their heels. But once this initial period had passed, abortion was both controversial and dangerous.† Herbal teas were the safest method, but suppositories—which could damage the uterus—were more effective. Surgical methods were attempted only as a last resort.[7]

In most cases, women with unwanted pregnancies avoided the hazards of abortion and carried to term. Shortly after birth, the baby's fate would be decided by its father (or, in the case of an enslaved woman, by the mother's master).‡ If the child was healthy and legitimate—and especially if it was male—it had a good chance of being accepted into the family. But if the father refused to acknowledge it, the baby was usually exposed—carried outside and left to its fate. Exposure was not necessarily a death sentence. Babies were often brought to public places, such as temple gates, where they had a reasonable chance of being found.§ Sometimes, a rattle, ring, or other token would be left with them, by which they might be identified later. Survival, however, was not always a blessing. Many exposed children were picked up by slave traders and raised to be prostitutes or beggars. Only a fortunate few would be adopted by free families.[8]

---

* Beaver testicles were in high demand as contraceptives. A folktale claimed that cornered beavers, knowing why they were being hunted, would bite off their own testicles and throw them in their pursuer's path. (In case you're wondering, beavers don't actually do this—and even if they wanted to, they can't reach their testicles with their teeth.)

† Most ancient doctors thought that a fetus assumed human characteristics after about forty days. Despite criticism in some philosophical and medical circles, termination of a pregnancy past this point was accepted almost everywhere until the third century CE, when abortion was banned by imperial edict.

‡ In Sparta, fathers presented their newborns to a council of elders. Healthy children (one test involved bathing them in wine) would be raised. Those that seemed sickly, however, were left to die in a lonely valley.

§ Babies were also left on the outskirts of cities, often near garbage dumps. Sometimes, infants saved from such places were given names like Stercorius ("dung-heap boy") by their literal-minded rescuers.

Like the savagery of the Roman arena and the vast inhumanity of ancient slavery, infant exposure reveals the chasm that separates us from the classical world. For most Greeks and Romans, life was a struggle, and having a family required hard choices. These decisions may have been calculated, but we should never assume that they were easy.

How Likely Were They to Survive Surgery?

The arrow was about a yard long, with a wicked barbed head the size of a dagger. Glinting against the coppery sky, it whistled through the dust, kissed the edge of a gilded shield, and punched through Alexander's breastplate. With a cry, the conqueror fell. As his men hurled themselves at the wavering enemy lines, Alexander was dragged to the rear, wheezing and dripping blood. When his breastplate was cut away, it was discovered that the arrow had driven through his sternum and grazed a lung. The arrowhead, bedded in bone, refused to budge. According to one tradition, Alexander's bodyguard cut it free with the tip of his sword. Most ancient authors, however, gave the credit to his doctor, who extracted the arrowhead through a careful incision and stanched the hemorrhage that followed.[1]

Alexander, lucky as always, survived. Many Greeks and Romans who underwent surgery were less fortunate. Since ancient doctors had no understanding of germ theory, they never sterilized their surgical instruments. And since human dissection was taboo,* they tended to have a patchy understanding of anatomy. The conscientious tried to compensate by dissecting animals; the great Galen anatomized apes, pigs, goats, ostriches, and at least one elephant.† But even Galen was never able to make full use of a cadaver and envied the physicians on the emperor's campaign staff, who were allowed to cut up the occasional barbarian.[2]

---

* Human dissections, however, occasionally took place. For a short period, doctors in Hellenistic Alexandria were even allowed to vivisect criminals.

† Galen often demonstrated his skill by dissecting and vivisecting in public, asking members of his audience to call out the organ or body part he should flense next.

Galen was one of the classical world's celebrity doctors, a high-rolling, fast-talking, and fanatically competitive tribe that catered to the rich and famous. These men proposed and opposed trendy cures, gave dueling surgical demonstrations, competed at festivals,* and occasionally poisoned each other. Most doctors moved in less exalted social circles. In the city of Rome, many were freedmen specializing in things like pulling teeth or removing bladder stones. Despite their lack of formal medical education—there was no licensing process—some of these men were highly skilled. Quite a few, however, were not. On many a tombstone, claimed a Roman author, was the inscription: "A gang of doctors killed me."[3]

Quackery notwithstanding, ancient doctors were capable of sophisticated surgical procedures. Their basic tools were those of modern surgery: probes, scalpels, forceps, and even a syringe known as the pus extractor. Operating conditions, however, were primitive. Although herbal sedatives like mandrake or poppy juice were sometimes administered, patients remained conscious through even the most agonizing procedures. The mark of a good surgeon—one ancient author blithely remarks—is that he is unmoved by screams of pain. Surgeries, unsurprisingly, were completed as quickly as possible. Once the slicing and dicing were done, the incisions were pinned or stitched shut and salved with resin or honey (which, we now know, have mild antiseptic properties). Some wounds were covered with moistened cloths; others were bandaged with linen.[†4]

Surgeons often were called upon to treat combat wounds. Although battlefield medicine is attested as far back as the *Iliad*, we know the most about the doctors in the Roman imperial army, the only classical military with a medical staff and hospitals. Roman soldiers wounded in battle received temporary field dressings from medics attached to their units and then—whenever possible—more careful treatment from the legionary doctors. Stab wounds and gashes were cleaned, cauterized, and bandaged. Arrows were plucked out with forceps, pried loose with an exotic instrument called "the spoon of Diocles," or (if deeply embedded in an arm or leg) pushed out with a thin rod via an incision on the other side of the limb. Poisoned arrows were treated in the same way,

---

* One medical festival, at Ephesus, had contests for devising new or improved surgical instruments, diagnosing case studies, and—apparently—performing surgery live

† There was a wide range of bandage techniques and styles, some with colorful names like "the eye" and "the long-eared hare."

but with a bit more haste.* Lead sling bullets, which could be embedded as deeply as any arrow, were wiggled loose like teeth or fished out with ear probes. Mangled limbs were lopped off.† Such rough-and-ready treatment was surprisingly survivable. Once, for example, an arrow struck a Roman soldier between the nose and right eye and passed completely through his head, the tip protruding from the back of his neck. Incredibly, an army doctor managed to pull the arrow out through his neck without killing him or even (we are told) leaving a scar.[5]

In civilian life, most surgeries were minor. The most common procedure was tooth pulling. Although the Greeks and Romans used dental powders and toothpicks to clean their teeth, cavities were rampant. Only the rich could afford golden dental crowns and bridgework; for everyone else, dentistry meant pliers and plucking. Eliminating varicose veins, the classical world's best-attested elective surgery, was even more unpleasant, since every vagrant vessel had to be cut out or cauterized. Cicero claimed to be the first man bold enough to endure the procedure without being tied down. Less common cosmetic surgeries included male breast reductions and a primitive form of liposuction.[6]

The most serious operation performed with any frequency was trepanation, the cutting away of diseased or fractured sections of the skull. Our sources describe the procedure in excruciating detail. First, the skin was peeled back, exposing the skull. Small holes were drilled around the targeted area, and a chisel was used to snap the bridges of bone between (the patient's ears, it was suggested, should be plugged with wool to muffle the chipping and cracking). The broken bits were carefully removed, often with a special instrument that protected the brain membrane. Then the edges of the skull were filed smooth, the wound was covered with oil-soaked wool or astringent plaster, and the patient was allowed to stagger home.[7]

Trepanation was more or less survivable. Death by infection, however, was common in the wake of any serious operation. One of Marcus Aurelius's sons, for example, died shortly after a growth was removed from his neck. A later emperor was killed by a bladder stone operation. Against this evidence, we have descriptions of dangerous surgeries that succeeded. Galen once saved a gladiator who had been

---

* One author recommends dog blood as an antivenin.

† A Roman officer managed to be wounded twenty-three times in battle, crippling all four of his limbs. Undeterred, he had his missing right hand replaced with an iron claw and continued to serve with distinction.

almost completely disemboweled.* Later, he performed the even more impressive feat of removing the infected breastbone and pericardium above a slave boy's beating heart. But Galen—as Galen himself was well aware—was exceptional. For even the most skilled physicians, invasive operations must have often resulted in the patient's death. Many Greeks and Romans would have sympathized with the poet who joked that his doctor had finally realized where his skills lay, and become an undertaker.[8]

---

* Galen reports that the man survived but felt cold for the rest of his life.

· 6 ·

What Were the Greatest Delicacies?

*T*he Mediterranean moray is not an attractive fish. Its sinuous body oozes mucus. Its eyes are beady and cold. It lurks in holes and slinks among stones, lacerating prey with crooked teeth. Yet despite combining all the malice of a predator with every unloveliness of the worm, the moray was a delicacy in the classical world. The Roman elite were particularly susceptible to its slippery charms. Morays swam in the ornamental ponds of villas, surfacing to snatch bits of meat from jeweled hands.* The most alluring eels became cherished pets, called by name and adorned with necklaces and earrings. Lesser specimens were eaten with rich sauces and considerable gusto.[1]

Only the wealthy could afford to sample the dubious delights of morays. For the vast majority of Greeks and Romans, almost every meal was bread or porridge† flavored with oil, honey, or herbs. Depending on the season and availability, this might be complemented with goat cheese, beans, or a bit of pork or chicken.‡ In the countryside, the monotony of this diet was relieved by hunting and fishing. Religious festivals—which featured communal barbeques of sacrificed animals—were the main sources of dietary variation in cities, especially in the

---

* Vedius Pollio, a confidant of the emperor Augustus, had slaves who displeased him thrown into a pit of ravenous morays. Then he ate the morays.

† By some estimates, cereals—the wheat, barley, and other edible grains that could be made into bread or porridge—accounted for 75 percent of all the calories commoners consumed. Although barley was common, especially in Greece, wheat was always the grain of choice. Whether wheat or barley, the quality of bread varied considerably from the heavy black loaves gnawed by the poor to the fine white rolls that graced the tables of the rich. A shopping list from Pompeii mentions three grades of bread, the cheapest being "bread for slaves."

‡ Early in Greek history, geese were the principal poultry. When chickens were first imported from the east, they were valued more for their cockfighting pluck than for their eggs.

That's a moray! *Marine mosaic from the House of the Faun in Pompeii, now in the National Archaeological Museum of Naples. Author's photo*

Greek world. Besides a proliferation of pork during the Roman era, the only real change over time was the introduction of new crops, most notably peaches, apricots, and lemons.[2]

Elite cuisine, by contrast, was characterized by vast variety and rapid changes in fashion. Although many cities had taverns, there were no fine restaurants. The Greco-Roman elite dined at home, on dishes prepared by large and exactingly trained staffs of kitchen slaves. They reclined on couches as they ate, leaning on their left elbows, using knives, spoons, and toothpicks but never forks. As a result, their entrées were served in small pieces and frequent hand scrubbing was necessary. Only the Romans, however, used napkins.*

Since the democratic ethos discouraged ostentatious displays of wealth, elite banquets in Classical Athens were relatively modest. The meal often began with loaves of fine wheat bread served with small

---

* Pieces of coarse bread served the Greeks as napkins. Since Roman banquets featured slaves with basins of scented water for handwashing, the Romans' napkins were used mostly to protect the host's couches during dinner and to bring home leftovers afterward. A few napkins were made of asbestos, which gave them the useful property of being washable in fire.

portions of shellfish, vegetables, and other appetizers. The main course followed. Although goat kid and lamb were acknowledged delicacies, a truly luxurious Athenian banquet centered on fish. Gourmands canonized a complicated hierarchy of fishes, from the humble anchovy to the lordly tuna. Most expensive of all were the freshwater eels of Lake Copais:* at a time when a skilled laborer earned a drachma for a full day's work, a single Copaic eel could cost twelve drachmas.[3]

As might be expected, there was little fine dining among the Spartans, whose signature dish was a bitter black soup made of blood and vinegar. The culinary hotspots of the Greek world were the prosperous cities of Sicily, which produced history's first cookbooks. The fad for gourmet dining was taken to extremes in the courts of the Hellenistic monarchs. To take one notorious example, King Ptolemy VIII (otherwise notable for marrying both his sister and his niece) wrote learned treatises on delicacies, and—having become so obese from constant banqueting that he could barely walk—came to be called "the potbelly" by his less-than-adoring subjects.

Yet even the banquets of kings like Ptolemy were outdone by the Roman elite. Early in Roman history (or so the Romans later liked to think), rich and poor alike had been content with simple foods. But as they conquered the Greeks—who, they noticed, ate much better than they did—the Roman elite began to import Greek chefs and Greek recipes and to infuse both with a Roman spirit of competition and display. The result was a dining culture of sometimes incredible extravagance.

Every aspect of a Roman banquet was calculated to impress. A dining room typically centered on three couches arranged in a U-shaped pattern.† The setting was as lavish as the host could afford to make it. Mosaics carpeted floors; walls glowed with frescoes; gardens beckoned through tall windows. The emperors, of course, did it best. The main banquet hall in Nero's preposterously opulent Golden House was

---

* Lake Copais, a marshy freshwater lake about sixty miles north of Athens, was drained in the nineteenth century. Its eels were so venerated in antiquity that especially large specimens were wrapped in laurels and offered to the gods.

† The Greeks apparently acquired the habit of reclining during banquets from the Near East. Although couches were never universal—Greeks in some regions preferred chairs, and informal dining everywhere was probably done seated—they became prestigious. The Romans borrowed the practice of reclined dining from the Greeks (possibly via the Etruscans) early in their history. The habit stuck: as late as the eleventh century, the Byzantine court still feasted on couches.

crowned by a star-spangled rotunda that rotated as guests reclined beneath. Other dining rooms in the palace had ivory ceilings fitted with pipes that drizzled perfume and panels that released showers of rose petals.* In warm weather, the emperors and their wealthiest subjects held banquets among the plashing fountains and manicured greenery of their villas. One senator liked to dine from dishes floating in the fountain beside his garden couch, surrounded by bushes trimmed into the letters of his name.[4]

A Roman banquet began with a round of appetizers—salads, snails, and sardines were all popular—washed down with honeyed wine. The dinner that followed typically included between three and seven courses, carried on glittering silver platters.† The variety of foods was immense: birds of every feather and shellfish of every shell; schools of fish, freshwater and salt; orchards of fruit, gardens of vegetables; and meats from aurochs to wild boar. By modern standards, the flavors were strong: often dishes were dosed with pepper, doused with honey, and served with *garum*, a condiment made from sun-ripened fish guts.

Foods were displayed, disguised, and dismembered to shock and awe guests into a state of proper appreciation for their host's wealth. At one tasteless banquet described in a Roman novel, the dishes included a boar filled with live birds, a pig stuffed with sausages tied to look like entrails, and a cake shaped like the tumescent fertility god Priapus. From the dazzling variety of foods on offer, guests would sample dishes that struck their fancy, belching occasionally to signal their appreciation.‡ After hours of leisurely nibbling, the pageantry ended with a dessert of honeyed cakes, fruits, and nuts.[5]

The Romans relished a wide range of delicacies. They adored dormice, nocturnal rodents fattened for months in special containers

---

* A later emperor was said to have smothered several of his guests by allowing too many rose petals to plummet at once.

† Besides the house slaves who served the meal, every guest brought a personal attendant, who would stand behind his or her couch throughout the meal, filling goblets, whisking away flies, and proffering bowls of rose-scented water between courses. Even more slaves worked behind the scenes in the kitchens. We know from inscriptions, for example, that the imperial palace had dozens of skilled cooks working under the direction of a pompous head chef.

‡ Occasional belching was considered polite, and a little light spitting was expected. Overt flatulence was less acceptable, though some doctors claimed that refraining was injurious to one's health. Although the vomitorium (in the sense of a room dedicated to regurgitation) is a myth, some Romans did induce vomiting between courses or after meals. A few were gluttons, but most were acting on the widely held belief that periodic purging was good for the digestive system.

before being roasted, dunked in honey, and served as hors d'oeuvres. The Roman palate was also pleased by the udders, womb, and reproductive parts of female pigs—one emperor, in fact, was rumored to have been assassinated with a poisoned sow womb. Among the more exotic meats, elephant trunk and elephant heart were particularly valued. The heads of birds made up a whole class of delicacies (flamingo tongue was a special favorite). Peacock was eaten with such eagerness that farms dedicated to raising them sprang up throughout Italy. Oysters grown in Lucrine Lake by the Bay of Naples were always welcome. Until pollution ruined the taste, the most valued fish were sea bass from the Tiber. Later, sturgeon (but not yet caviar) was recognized as the premier freshwater delicacy. The most prestigious of all fishes, however, was the unassuming bearded mullet.*[6]

Roman dinners could be stupendously expensive. When most men earned between five hundred and one thousand sesterces a year, leading senators might spend a million or more on a single banquet. One emperor is said to have lavished six million sesterces on a dinner for twelve people, during which each guest received a slave, crystal goblets, rare perfumes, and a carriage trimmed with silver.† At an even more extravagant dinner staged by the short-lived emperor Vitellius, a gargantuan platter was brought out, heaped with delicacies from every corner of the empire: lamprey milt and pike livers, the brains of pheasants and peacocks, and glistening fans of flamingo tongues. The culinary merits of this dish may have been questionable, but the message was clear. Food was power.[7]

---

* Cooking mullet was both art and science. Some chefs reportedly thought that only kissing the fish on the mouth before baking could prevent the stomach from bursting in the oven.

† Another emperor was said to have given each of his guests a eunuch as a party favor.

· 7 ·

How Much Wine Did They Drink?

*W*ine was a pleasure. Whole genres of poetry celebrated its delights, and some could think of no nobler fate for the souls of the just than blissful and eternal drunkenness.

Wine was a panacea. The Spartans bathed their children in it to toughen their skin, and the philosopher-emperor Marcus Aurelius warded off insomnia with an opiated cup each night.

Wine was a staple. Homer's heroes received shipments of it as they camped beneath Troy, and every one of imperial Rome's four hundred thousand soldiers was given a half-pint daily.

And wine was a vice. St. Augustine reflected gravely on his mother's youthful alcoholism, and Alexander the Great always regretted killing one of his best officers in a drunken rage.[1]

Modern oenophiles would be unimpressed by Greek and Roman wine. If aged more than a year, it usually spoiled. It contained galaxies of grape skin and pips, which had to be filtered out when it was served. And since it was stored in vases lined with pitch or resin, it tended to taste and smell like turpentine. This would be masked only partly by the honey, herbs, spices, perfumes, and/or marble dust that the Greeks and Romans added to their cups. If nothing else, ancient wine was affordable. A sign painted outside one Pompeii bar advertised a cup of ordinary wine for one *as* (that is, about half the price of a loaf of bread), a better wine for two, and a fine wine for four.[2]

Tastes varied over time. Homer's heroes drank honey-sweet red wine flavored with goat cheese and barley. The Athenians of the Classical era preferred varieties produced on the Aegean islands, including a few salted with seawater. The Romans—history's first true wine snobs—relished white wines from the hills of central Italy, which were aged for decades in vases stamped with the year and vintner. A few Italian vintages, like that of 121 BCE, became so iconic that they were preserved for centuries. Less discriminating Romans settled for wines artificially "aged" by being exposed to a smoky fire.[3]

It has been estimated that the average Roman man drank about a liter of wine every day—the equivalent of one and one-third modern bottles.* Although this rate of consumption may have been possible in the well-supplied city of Rome, most Romans—and for that matter, most Greeks—probably drank less. Everywhere, moderation was the rule: it would have been unusual to have more than a cup or two of watered wine with a normal meal. A Roman poet suggested that a pint (about two-thirds of a modern bottle) was more than sufficient for a pleasant dinner. Some individuals, however, drank much, much more. Socrates could knock back a half-gallon of wine without difficulty, and a man once impressed the Emperor Tiberius by draining two and a half gallons of wine in a single pull.[†4]

Although the alcohol content of most ancient wines was probably around 15 percent,[‡] potency varied considerably. Slaves and farm laborers were given a barely alcoholic "wine" made from shredded grape skins. On the other end of the scale, a few Italian varieties were reputedly flammable if aged long enough. No self-respecting Greek or Roman, however, drank pure wine. That was for degenerates and barbarians.[§] At least one Greek city, in fact, made drinking wine neat a crime punishable by death. Avoiding strong wine was not only a means of demonstrating self-control; it was also a matter of personal safety. Consuming unmixed wine—it was assumed—led inexorably to drowned semen, mental decay, and premature aging (in approximately

---

* This is less extreme than it might sound. Men in eighteenth-century Paris, for example, drank about the same amount. During the sixteenth century, workers at the Arsenal of Venice guzzled an incredible five liters (1.3 gallons) of wine every day.

† Tiberius was far from the only emperor to take a personal interest in epic drinking. The libertine emperor Lucius Verus owned a crystal goblet so large that no man could empty it. Aurelian, a later emperor, used to amuse himself by watching a jester chug an entire cask of wine through the ancient equivalent of a beer bong.

‡ The alcohol content was so high because the Greeks and Romans harvested grapes when they were ripe and full of sugar and because they allowed fermentation to reach its natural conclusion—that is, to continue until all the sugars were consumed or alcohol killed the yeast, which occurs at about 15 to 17 percent alcohol by volume.

§ Barbarians were notoriously bibulous. The Gauls (perhaps not incidentally, ancestors of the French) were said to be so addicted to wine that they invaded Italy to get more of it.

that order). These anxieties are epitomized by the inscription on a Greek tombstone: "I, Asclepiades . . . lived for 22 years. I drank a great quantity of undiluted wine, spat blood, and choked to death."[5]

The civilized way to drink wine was to mix it with water. Authorities disagreed about the ideal proportion. In most cases, however, the wine consumed at social gatherings was probably between two-thirds and three-fourths water, which would have reduced the alcoholic content to about that of modern beer. Those who lived dangerously might venture a blend that was half water, though this was considered almost barbaric.*[6]

Most Greeks and Romans, paradoxically, only drank strong wine when they were sick. Ancient doctors were fervent believers in the medical properties of wine, prescribing it for everything from fevers to flatulence. Wine was treated as an emetic: one prominent Athenian doctor encouraged drinking to the point of vomiting. A more easygoing physician urged his patients to consume wine only until they were quite drunk and cheerful.[7]

For the healthy, heavy drinking was almost always social. Public inebriation was acceptable, and even encouraged, on certain religious occasions: only at festivals, proclaimed Plato, was it proper to get drunk. Festivals honoring the wine god Dionysus were especially prone to excess. During one, empty wineskins were inflated, lubricated with oil, and laid out in an open place. Those who were themselves well-lubricated enough to try would then attempt to dance or hop on one leg atop the slippery skins. Processions could be equally wine soaked: during a grand parade, one Hellenistic king honored Dionysus with a float carrying a thirty-thousand-gallon wineskin sewn from leopard pelts. This colossal container was designed to leak, so that men costumed as satyrs could collect the wine and distribute it among the spectators.[8]

The best-known contexts for social drinking, however, were the private banquets that the Greeks called symposia. A symposium typically involved one or two dozen men, sprawling on couches around the perimeter of a room. After they had eaten dinner, servants carried away the tables on which the meal had been served and replaced them with new boards bearing bowls of fruit, nuts, and other desserts. Then the *krater*, the wine-mixing bowl, was set in the center of the room. The

---

* When a Spartan wanted a strong drink, he ordered it "Scythian style"—an homage to the barbarian Scythians, who guzzled unmixed wine from skull goblets and wiped their mouths with napkins made from their enemies' skins.

guests donned their myrtle or ivy garlands (which were thought to delay drunkenness) and selected a master of ceremonies. For the remainder of the evening, this man would determine the topics of discussion, the games to be played, and—crucially—how much water would be mixed into the communal wine. Once that decision had been made, servants blended the designated amounts of water and wine in the *krater*, and the first of many rounds was drunk. When not imbibing, the guests at a symposium talked and watched the entertainers. These were almost always young women, usually slaves. Some tumbled, juggled, and mimed; others were expert players of the flute or cithara. Many were trained dancers, capable of everything from the ancient equivalent of ballet to striptease.

The Roman drinking parties tended to be more hierarchical: it was not unusual for different wines to be served to guests of different ranks. Unlike their Greek counterparts, women could attend, though they were expected to refrain from heavy drinking.* Wine was served in large mixing bowls, chilled by snow in the summer and heated with miniature boilers in the winter. Contrary to Greek practice, however, the bowls were brought out at the beginning of the banquet and rounds of drinking alternated with courses of food. As at symposia, there were musicians and dancing girls (troupes from Spain were especially popular). Sometimes, the guests would listen to orations and other compositions, often read by a trained slave. If they were unlucky, the host might insist on reciting his own poems. The more elaborate banquets featured skits performed by famous actors or the tales of a professional storyteller. Less pretentious gatherings enjoyed the convolutions of contortionists, the quips of clowns, or the grappling of gladiators.[9]

At both Greek and Roman drinking parties, the ideal was a generously defined moderation. Guests at a symposium were supposed to drink enough to be social, but not so much that they lost control. A Greek poet advised drinking as much as one could without having to lean on a slave the whole way home. Another poet suggested that no symposium should collectively consume more than three *kraters* of wine. Such guidelines were not always heeded. Some symposia degenerated

---

* That at least some women were full participants is suggested by an epitaph in which a husband praises his wife for knowing how to have fun and drink wine. Interestingly, ancient doctors assumed that women were more resistant to drunkenness than men. Old men, by contrast, were thought to be particularly susceptible, both because their bodies were "dried out" and because they tended to like strong wine.

into drunken brawls, during which clay chamber pots were hurled at opponents' heads. Others just drank to the point of insanity: the guests at one symposium managed to convince themselves that the room in which they were drinking was actually a ship, and that the ship was sinking. When they began to throw furniture out the windows to save the vessel, they were arrested and only released after promising to drink less.[10]

Like the Greeks, the Romans seem to have preached moderation more often than they practiced it. Roman banquets often lasted eight hours. Some, we are told, went on for days. Such protracted partying took a serious toll on the participants. After one very long night, for example, Mark Antony vomited into a fold of his toga at a public meeting; he eventually felt compelled to write a pamphlet defending himself against charges of being a hopeless alcoholic. Antony, however, was far from the only prominent Roman notorious for overindulgence in wine. In the early years of his reign, for example, Nero would drink heavily, disguise himself as a slave, and sally out into the streets of Rome. Shadowed by gladiator bodyguards, the emperor and a band of drunken companions would break into shops, attack pedestrians, and generally wreak havoc.[11]

The wine-soaked atmosphere of Greek and Roman banquets gave rise to a rich bouquet of drinking games. The most straightforward of these was competitive drinking. In the typical Greek version, two or more contestants would drain progressively larger cups. The only rule was that each cup had to be finished in a single gulp; anyone who paused for breath was disqualified. According to one ancient author, Alexander the Great caught the fever that killed him after emptying the "Bowl of Hercules," a gargantuan goblet that held more than two gallons of wine. At another drinking contest over which Alexander presided, no fewer than forty-one men were said to have dropped dead of alcohol poisoning. Roman drinking contests seem to have been comparatively sedate. Sometimes the host threw dice, and the guests had to match the number of cups they drank to the score of the throw. A variation entailed drinking as many cups as the number of letters in the host's name. Since a Roman's full name might be twenty letters long or more, this could be a daunting task.[12]

Besides competitive chugging, the most popular drinking game in Classical Greece was *kottabos*. The goal of the game was to hit a small target with dregs or drops of wine thrown from one's cup. In

A *kottabos* player whirling his cup. Note that he has another very large cup in his left hand for sipping wine as he plays. *Red-figure Attic kylix now in the Louvre. Photo by Bibi Saint-Pol, Wikimedia Commons*

the best-known version, the target was a small bronze disk poised atop a stand about seven feet tall. This stand was set up in the middle of the room, and party guests took turns whipping wine at it from their couches. To throw, a guest twisted his index finger around the handle of his cup, and then whirled it around with a motion of his forearm. A successful shot would knock the disk from its perch and send it clattering onto a metal platform built into the stand. An alternative (and probably easier) version of *kottabos* involved aiming at small clay cups floating in a large bowl of water.*[13]

---

* Sometimes, the dancing girls played with the diners: one Greek vase shows a naked courtesan named Smikra—that is, "Slender"—whirling a *kottabos* cup.

Another popular drinking game at symposia centered on riddles. One guest posed a riddle—for example: "a dead donkey struck me in the ear; what was I doing?"—and prompted the other guests to respond. A correct answer—in this case, "listening to a flute" (Greek flutes were often made from the leg bones of donkeys)—might be rewarded with a piece of cake or a kiss from one of the dancing girls. Those who guessed incorrectly, however, were sentenced to drink a great deal of wine, sometimes mixed with saltwater. Equally difficult, at least once one had passed the point of coordination, was a game that involved trying to stop a spinning coin with the touch of a finger. Although similar games may have been played at Roman banquets, the Romans typically preferred to gamble. Despite its illegality, Romans of all classes bet heavily on dice games, especially once wine had massaged their inhibitions. One emperor was so addicted that he wrote a book on the subject.[14]

At both Greek and Roman banquets, those who lost at dice or any other game of chance were compelled to pay a penalty, which might involve dancing naked, giving one of the flute girls a piggyback ride around the house, or a solo round of heavy drinking. The stakes were a bit higher at the drinking parties of the Thracians, the Greeks' barbaric northern neighbors. An unlucky guest, chosen by lot, was given a small knife and hanged from a noose in the center of the room. As the other guests watched, the man flailed with his knife, trying to cut the rope before he lost consciousness. If he failed, he was allowed to suffocate.[15]

Sometimes, the guests at a symposium formed a staggering conga line and erupted into the streets, trying to crash another party. Usually, however, the revelers wobbled home, accompanied, guided, or carried by a trusted slave. The hateful morning after was spent appeasing hangovers. Some victims clung to garlands of freshly cut ivy and myrtle. Others guzzled honey, chewed cabbage, or crunched almonds.* Still others pressed amethysts to their skin, rolled in mud, or performed calisthenics. The rest found it kindliest to simply sip more wine.[16]

---

* The personal doctor of the (alcoholic) Roman prince Drusus, who liked to partake with his patient, always ate five or six bitter almonds just before a banquet to stave off drunkenness.

· 8 ·

How Did They Keep Track of Time?

The planet's habits haven't changed. Then as now, the Earth took a little less than twenty-four hours to rotate on its axis, and a little more than 365 days to complete a revolution around the sun. Then as now, the rhythms of the days and round of the seasons were known to be fixed natural patterns. Then as now, there were technologies and techniques for measuring and managing time. But it is one thing to be able to keep track of time, and quite another to actually do it.

By modern standards, classical attitudes toward time were casual to the point of negligence. Take, for example, the hours that regiment our days. The Athenians saw no need for them; and though the Romans used hours, they used them eccentrically, dividing both day and night into twelve equal parts that expanded and contracted with the seasons. In midsummer, each daylight hour was about seventy-five minutes long; in midwinter, only forty-five.

Clocks, where they existed, were unreliable. The most common type was the sundial, which appeared in Greece during the sixth century BCE and reached Rome in the third. Early sundials consisted of a staff or pillar whose oscillating shadow gave a rough idea of the time. From the Hellenistic period onward, more sophisticated models with hour lines were developed.* At night and on cloudy days, clepsydras (water clocks) were the only available timepieces. Some were intricate

---

* The grandest of all sundials, constructed by the emperor Augustus in Rome, was a seventy-foot Egyptian obelisk in a plaza with a gilt meridian line. (Thanks to a combination of earthquakes and settling, it soon became inaccurate, and the meridian line had to be re-laid.) On the other end of the scale were the portable sundials carried by the most harried Greeks and Romans.

machines capable of sounding trumpets, ejecting stones, or moving figurines to mark the hour. Most, however, were uncomplicated, like the
perforated vessel used to time Athenian court speeches. Outside court-
rooms and military camps (where they marked the hours of the watch),
water clocks were rare. When they were used, they tended to contradict
every other timepiece in the vicinity.* "Philosophers," quipped Seneca,
"will agree before clocks will."[1]

Keeping track of the days was comparatively straightforward,
though dating conventions differed. In Athens, days were numbered up
to the twentieth day of the month, then counted down to the beginning of the next month. The Romans counted the days to the next
Kalends (the first day of the month), Nones (the fifth or seventh day),
or Ides (the thirteenth or fifteenth). The Macedonian calendar, used
widely in the Hellenistic world, numbered the days serially, as we do.
In most places, the months were, at least theoretically, based on cycles
of the moon, and thus about thirty days long. Beyond this, variety was
the rule. Months in the Greek world were typically named after local
religious festivals. The Roman months—which we still use—reflected
an eclectic mix of gods (March was the month of Mars), numbers (September is "seventh month"; December is "tenth month"), and emperors
(July for Julius Caesar; August for Augustus).[†2]

Since the months—whatever their names—were lunar, and since
the lunar year (twelve cycles of the moon) is eleven days shorter than
the 365-day solar year, periodic adjustments were needed to keep the
months aligned with the seasons. Both the Athenians and the Romans
adopted the expedient of adding an extra month every other year or so.
The Athenians eventually developed a sophisticated scheme for keeping their calendar close to the solar year. From some combination of
carelessness and corruption, however, the Roman officials responsible
for adjusting the calendar regularly failed to do so, causing the date to

---

* Such technical difficulties discouraged more exact timekeeping. Although there were
various schemes for subdividing the hour—ranging from "points" (equivalent to fifteen minutes) to "ounces" (about eight seconds)—these were not used on a daily basis. Minutes and
seconds as we know them are a late medieval innovation.

† We could have ended up with many more imperial months. Nero, for example, named
April after himself (and tried to dub Rome "Neropolis" while he was at it). Domitian
rebranded September and October "Germanicus" (after his victories in Germany) and "Domitian." Commodus, not to be outdone, named every month after himself and his titles, which
included "Amazon," "Hercules," and "Exsuperatorius" (nonpareil). All these months perished
with the tyrants who inspired them.

swing as much as three months out of sync with the seasons. The chaos this caused was finally ended when Julius Caesar announced that the following year—our 46 BCE—would be lengthened to 445 days, and every year thereafter would consist of 365 days, with a leap day added to every fourth year. With a few adjustments,* this is the scheme we use today.[3]

Almost every city had its own way of dating the year. The most common method was to reference the name of an important official. In Athens, for example, the eponymous archon gave his name to the year. The Romans likewise dated by the names of the two consuls.[†] From the late third century CE onward, it also became customary to date by the fifteen-year tax cycles called indictions. An alternative strategy for keeping track of the years was to count from a significant historical event. Some Roman cities, for example, had eras that began with their inclusion in the empire, the formation of the province in which they were located, or the visit of an emperor. For more than a millennium, many cities in Syria employed the Seleucid Era, whose starting point—our 312 BCE—marked the day that one of Alexander the Great's generals seized Babylon.

Historians attempted to create universal chronologies. Greek scholars sometimes dated events with reference to the Olympic Games, which had (reportedly) been held every four years since 776 BCE.[‡] Roman historians preferred to date from the foundation of Rome, which was eventually assigned to 753 BCE. These, however, were only scholarly conventions. In daily life, years continued to be reckoned in terms of archons, consuls, and kings.[4]

---

* Caesar and his contemporaries assumed that the solar year was 365¼ days long. Since the actual length is about eleven minutes shorter, however, the year gradually fell out of sync with the sun. By the sixteenth century, it was a full ten days behind. In 1582, Pope Gregory XIII promulgated a reformed calendar, which minimized the difference between the solar and the calendar year by omitting a few leap days. Though swiftly adopted by Catholic countries, the new scheme took centuries to catch on elsewhere. Caesar's original calendar was used in Greece and Romania until 1924, and it is still dusted off to calculate the date of Easter in Orthodox churches.

† Consular dating persisted into late antiquity. The last western consul held office in 534, and the last eastern consul seven years later. Although it had long been customary for coins and building inscriptions to reference the year of the emperor's reign, Byzantine emperors only began dating by regnal years in the late sixth century.

‡ There was little agreement about dates before the first Olympics. The end of the Trojan War, for example, was placed anywhere from 1334 to 1135 BCE, with a consensus eventually settling around 1183.

The rise of Christianity created new means and motives for calculating a universal chronology. At first, Christians focused on determining the date of the Creation—a matter of practical interest, since many were convinced that the world would end six thousand years after it had been made. After much effusion of ink and ecclesiastic bile, Greek scholars settled on 5509 BCE as the beginning of time and dated their chronicles accordingly.* Egyptian Christians preferred (and still prefer) to use the "Era of the Martyrs," which began in 284 CE with the accession of the persecuting emperor Diocletian. The most important Christian contribution to chronology, however, occurred in the early sixth century, when the AD (anno Domini) system appeared. Its inventor was Dionysius Exiguus, an unassuming Roman monk noted for his mathematical ability. While calculating the dates on which Easter would fall in future years, Dionysius devised a scheme for counting years from the birth of Jesus. He never intended to create a universal dating system. Yet this, slowly and accidentally, AD became.†

We have surveyed how the Greeks and Romans counted the hours, passed the days, and numbered the years. But a pressing question remains: did they have weekends?

They always had holidays, in the form of the annual religious festivals that defined the year. Not all of these could be observed—by the second century CE, more than a third of the Roman year was officially some sort of celebration—but the more important ones certainly were.‡ The recurring holiday of the weekend, however, was slow to develop.

---

* From the early Middle Ages onward, scholars in Western Europe tended to prefer a date around 4000 BCE—an estimate given its final refinements in the seventeenth century by Archbishop Ussher, who calculated that the Creation had occurred on October 23, 4004 BCE.

† The AD system caught on first in Anglo-Saxon England, thanks partly to the eighth-century scholar Bede, who employed it in some of his widely disseminated works on chronology and history. It was widespread in France and western Germany by the late ninth century, and common throughout Italy by the end of the tenth. The Spanish kingdoms, however, had an era of their own and resisted AD until the thirteenth and fourteenth centuries. Even once the system had been generally adopted, AD dates were used almost exclusively in ecclesiastical and scholarly contexts until the early modern period. Remarkably, BC only became common in the late eighteenth century.

‡ By the reign of Marcus Aurelius, 135 days were officially set aside for festivals and games. Although it is impossible to say how many of these actually were observed, the fact that apprentices in Roman Egypt were given between eighteen and thirty-six days off per year suggests that tradesmen worked through all but the most important celebrations.

Although some Greek cities divided their months into nine- or ten-day periods keyed to phases of the moon, these did not significantly affect daily life. The closest Roman equivalents to weekends were the *nundinae*, market days that took place every eighth day. In rural areas, *nundinae* were occasions for local farmers to visit town and sell their produce. But in the city of Rome, *nundinae* functioned as holidays, during which children were excused from school and families visited friends and relatives.

The seven-day week seems to have evolved in the Egyptian metropolis of Alexandria. From the beginning, it was a product of astrology. The Greeks and Romans knew seven planets, which were assumed to circle the Earth in fixed orbits: the moon, Mercury, Venus, the sun, Mars, Jupiter, and Saturn.* Astrologers claimed that every day was governed by a planet and that this celestial influence operated on a regular cycle, with one planet succeeding the next in the order we still assign to the days: Saturn (Saturday), the sun (Sunday), the moon (Monday), Mars (Tuesday), Mercury (Wednesday), Jupiter (Thursday), and Venus (Friday).† By the first century CE, in tandem with a massive surge of interest in astrology, the seven-day week had spread across the Roman Empire.[5]

The much older Jewish week—which happened to also have seven days—was gradually assimilated to the planetary week, with the Jewish Sabbath falling on Saturday. The Romans always had dismissed the Jews' refusal to work on the Sabbath as a sign of laziness. But since Saturday, astrologically speaking, was the least auspicious day of the week (and thus a bad time to conduct business), the Jewish custom began to seem more reasonable. The fact that one first-century Greek scholar

---

* The Greeks seem to have borrowed the practice of naming the planets after the gods from the Babylonians. The Romans, as so often, simply followed suit. Although some interpreters claimed that the gods lived on their namesake planets or even that the gods were the planets, it was usually assumed that the planets and gods were associated in a more general way.

† The English names for the days of the week were devised by the Germanic peoples who settled in the territory of the Roman Empire and borrowed its timekeeping schemes. Since they had no god equivalent to Saturn, Saturn's day was adopted wholesale. Sun's day and moon's day were straightforward. For Mars, however, they substituted their own war god Tiw (Tiw's day = Tuesday); Woden stood in for Mercury (Woden's day = Wednesday), Thor for Jupiter (Thor's day = Thursday), and Frigg for Venus (Frigg's day = Friday). Italian, French, and Spanish preserve the Latin names for the days of the week more or less intact, though they substitute the Lord's day (*domenica, dimanche, domingo*) for the pagan sun's day. In the Byzantine Empire, by contrast, the days of the week were completely Christianized; even now, Greeks name only the Sabbath and the Lord's day and number the weekdays. Portuguese employs a similar scheme.

lectured only on Saturdays—presumably because he could draw larger crowds then—suggests that Saturday had become a de facto holiday for a substantial number of non-Jews.[6]

It was Sunday, however, that was destined to become the late Roman Empire's (and medieval Europe's) day of rest. Christians had venerated Sunday almost from the beginning, and once the emperors converted to Christianity, the idea that Sunday should be devoted to worship quickly became official. Constantine declared Sunday a day of religious observance and prohibited all work besides agricultural labor. At the end of the fourth century, another emperor extended the ban to farmworkers as well. One of his successors delivered the coup de grâce by prohibiting Sunday chariot races, beast fights, and theatrical performances. A weekend of sorts had finally developed—but if the emperors had anything to say about it, it wouldn't be much fun.[7]

The inhabitants of the later Roman Empire used the same year, the same months, and the same week that we do. By the end of antiquity, they even had begun to employ the same dating system. We should not assume, however, that they thought about time in the same way. If you stopped a random passerby on the streets of late antique Rome or Constantinople, he or she probably wouldn't be able to tell you the hour—and might not know the year. Historians of the classical world do well to remember what every procrastinator knows: time only matters when you think it does.

II

SOCIETY

· 9 ·

How Long Did They Live?

$\mathcal{A}$t the age of seventy-three, the philosopher Chrysippus laughed himself to death. Cato the Elder, a Roman politician, was eighty when his youngest son was born. Antigonus the One-eyed, a Hellenistic king, was eighty-one when he fell in battle. Sophocles is said to have died of happiness and/or choking on a grape at the age of ninety. The historian Hieronymus lived to 104, still—we are assured—a vigorous lover. And just as he was accepting an award for his final play, in a scene he might have scripted himself, the tragic poet Alexis collapsed onstage at the age of 106. Clearly, some Greeks and Romans lived to a ripe old age. Just as clearly, these people were few and far between.[1]

Most Greeks and Romans died young. About half of all children died before adolescence. Those who survived to the age of thirty had a reasonable chance of reaching fifty or sixty. The truly elderly, however, were rare.* Because so many died in childhood, life expectancy at birth was probably between twenty and thirty years.† There is no indication

---

* Ulpian's "life table," a Roman document that outlined (for tax purposes) how much longer a person of a given age might be expected to survive, provides an interesting glimpse into the age structure of the ancient population. By the table's projections, people in their early twenties would live an average of twenty-eight more years. Those in their late thirties were assumed to have approximately twenty years left; those older than sixty, only five. By collating the life table with modern demographic models, one scholar has worked out the grim implications of its estimates: half of all those born would be dead by the age of five, two-thirds by age thirty, 80 percent by age fifty, and 90 percent by age sixty.

† Census returns from Roman Egypt suggest a life expectancy at birth of twenty-two years for women and about twenty-five for men. Unlike their modern counterparts, ancient women tended to have slightly shorter life expectancies than men, largely because childbirth was so dangerous. As many as 1 to 2 percent of births may have been fatal to the mother—and since most women gave birth at least five or six times, those odds stacked up.

44

An elderly Roman. *First-century portrait bust now in the Metropolitan Museum of Art. Public domain*

that this changed over time, since the basic causes of death were constant: poor sanitation, malnutrition, and disease.[2]

Ancient doctors speculated that diseases were caused by some combination of changes in the weather, vapors rising from swamps, imbalances in bodily humors, and divine retribution. Yet despite an awareness that some diseases were contagious and vague suspicions that microscopic disease-carrying creatures lived in foul air, they never developed any equivalent of germ theory. They were correspondingly ill equipped to prevent or treat illnesses.

The Classical Greeks were afflicted by (among other diseases) mumps, malaria, diphtheria, dysentery, polio, hepatitis, tuberculosis, and typhoid fever. In addition to these, the Romans had to cope with leprosy, which arrived from Egypt during the era of Augustus; bubonic plague, which began to spread through the eastern provinces about the same time;* and smallpox, which made its devastating debut in the reign of Marcus Aurelius. A century later, the mysterious Plague of Cyprian—which may have been a form of Ebola—appeared suddenly, killed tens of thousands, and vanished. Under normal circumstances, the most prolific killers of adult Greeks and Romans were probably typhoid fever, tuberculosis, and (in low-lying areas) malaria. Among children, dysentery and other gastrointestinal diseases were even deadlier.[3]

Cities—especially large cities—were cesspits of infection. The overcrowded and malaria-ravaged metropolis of Rome was probably the unhealthiest place in the entire empire, and required a constant infusion of immigrants to maintain its population.† The countryside was comparatively safe, especially in areas high above the malarial swamps. In his letters, one Roman senator noted the exceptional longevity of the people who lived in the hills around his villa—though he assumed that the pleasant mountain breezes were responsible.[4]

Despite the ravages of disease, the population of the Mediterranean world seems to have increased slowly but steadily from about the tenth century BCE to the second century CE. Such growth was only possible because of consistently high fertility rates: throughout Greek and Roman history, women must have borne an average of five or six children (of whom two or three survived to adulthood). During periods of war or famine, of course, regional populations shrank, but the general trend was upward.

---

* This strain of plague did not, however, spread widely, probably because the black rat was just beginning to colonize Europe. Five centuries later, when rats were everywhere, a new outbreak of plague brought the empire to its knees.

† In 1876, workers laying the foundations for a new apartment building accidentally uncovered a colossal burial pit just outside one of Rome's ancient gates. The excavator estimated that at least twenty-four thousand bodies had been thrown into the pit, probably during an epidemic. The dozens of other pits he found nearby, however, suggest that so many people died of sickness in Rome that wagonloads of corpses were routinely dumped outside the city.

Like life expectancy, the actual size of the population at any given place and time can be only approximated. The territory of Classical Athens (an area roughly the size of Rhode Island or Luxembourg) likely had a population of about three hundred thousand. The Mediterranean-spanning Roman Empire is thought to have had some fifty million inhabitants during the reign of Augustus. The number of imperial subjects grew substantially over the next century and a half, probably peaking in the mid-second century CE at around sixty million—perhaps a fifth of humanity.

Then smallpox arrived. The initial outbreak is estimated to have killed 10 percent of the empire's population, and the disease may have settled permanently in the major cities.[5] An even greater demographic shock occurred in the early sixth century, when a virulent strain of bubonic plague scythed through the Eastern Roman Empire, killing millions. In the wake of this pandemic and its successors, the population of the Mediterranean world probably fell to less than half of what it had been in the second century.

Between the great epidemics, however, the basic demographic regime did not change: about half of all children died before adolescence and life expectancy at birth remained in the twenties. Only about one in ten managed to reach the age of sixty, and only one in one hundred lived to celebrate his or her eightieth birthday.

Despite these brutal realities, the Greeks and Romans still hoped for long lives. Beyond simple good luck, reaching old age was thought to be partly a matter of living in a salubrious climate and partly a matter of personal health. The importance of a moderate diet was understood: one Greek orator ascribed his longevity to the fact that he never indulged in rich foods or heavy drinking.* The benefits of regular exercise were also recognized. Many Greek cities, in fact, had a gymnasium set aside in whole or part for older men.† Classical Athens even held an annual "beauty contest" to select physically fit old men for a religious

---

* The long lives ascribed to distant peoples were thought to reflect the foods they ate. The people of Sri Lanka supposedly survived to a grand old age on a diet of tree snakes. The Ethiopians reportedly lived to 120 because they ate only boiled meat and drank only milk. The Chinese were said to live three hundred years because they never drank wine. This rumor was contradicted, however, by the hundred-year-old Italian man who told Augustus that the secret to a long life was (to paraphrase) "oil on the skin and wine in the blood."

† One wonders whether the Greek habit of exercising naked is part of the reason the elderly had their own gymnasia. As Plato observes, old men jogging nude were "not pleasant to watch."

procession. Brisk walks and ball games were thought to keep aging bodies supple, especially if complemented by a vigorous massage. One septuagenarian Roman senator insisted on taking a stroll in the nude every afternoon.[6]

The Greeks and Romans had their share of stereotypes about the elderly. Old men, for example, were said to be slow-moving, suspicious, prone to reminisce, and just plain ornery. Such criticism, however, was balanced by a general sense that age conferred wisdom and that the elderly were worthy of respect.* In some places, old men had real political clout. Sparta, for example, had a Council of Elders whose members—all older than sixty—played a critical role in the government. In the Roman Senate, likewise, it was customary for the oldest members to speak first. The Romans also gave old men a great deal of social power: at least in theory, a man retained absolute legal authority over his children and grandchildren until his death.[7]

Members of the elite might enjoy something like modern retirement. After resigning his imperial title, for example, the elderly ex-emperor Diocletian moved into a massive fortified villa and took up gardening. But most people stopped working only when they were physically unable to continue. This might happen at a relatively young age: to judge from skeletal evidence, many men in their thirties were already wracked with arthritis. Those unable to support themselves had to rely on the goodwill of their relatives. The only alternative was begging—or starvation.

For most Greeks and Romans, life was short. Yet as we have seen, there were a few who beat the demographic odds. A modest Roman-era tombstone from what is now Lebanon commemorates "Rufilla, a kind and cheerful woman" who lived one hundred years. Perhaps Rufilla really did live one hundred years (ancient epitaphs tend to round up), and we may hope that she truly was kind and cheerful. Over her century or so of life, however, she probably watched her husband(s), all of her children, almost all of her grandchildren, and half or more of her great-grandchildren die. Old age in the classical world must have been terribly lonely.[8]

---

* There were exceptions to the general rule of respect for the elderly. A popular Roman saying was "toss the old men off the bridge." Other cultures were rumored to be even less reverential. Sardinians reportedly dug their parents' graves while they were still alive, knocked them over the heads, and rolled them in.

· 10 ·

How Tall Were They?

𝒯or a few years in the third century, the Roman Empire was ruled by a giant named Maximinus. His hands were so large that he could wear a woman's bracelet as a ring, and his feet so gargantuan that one of his boots became a tourist attraction. He could defeat any seven men in a wrestling match, crush rocks in his fist, and knock a horse down with a slap. If we can believe the testimony of his awed contemporaries, he was more than eight feet tall.*[1]

Some Greeks and Romans loomed even larger. A nine-foot Arab starred in several Roman processions, and the bodies of still loftier giants were preserved in the gardens of the emperors. The Romans also marveled at a man with a booming voice who happened to be less than two feet tall and gossiped about an equally diminutive courtier who married an imperial freedwoman. Our sources say almost nothing, however, about the heights of less exceptional figures. We do know that the emperor Augustus was just under five feet seven (but wore platform shoes to make himself look taller). We are told that, during some periods, recruits for the most prestigious units of the legions were supposed to be at least five feet eight but ideally would be five feet ten or taller.†

---

* The only source to give his height claims that he was eight and a half feet tall. Since the Roman foot was slightly shorter than its modern equivalent, this would make Maximinus about eight feet three inches. Although we have no way of knowing how tall he actually was, the overgrown facial bones visible in some of his coin portraits suggest that he may have suffered from acromegaly, a disorder frequently associated with gigantism.

† In late antiquity, when the state became increasingly desperate for soldiers, the height requirement was lowered to a little less than five feet five inches. Some standards, however, were maintained: to the bitter end, recruits were still required to have at least one testicle.

Maximinus as emperor. *Portrait bust now in the Capitoline Museums. Photo by Marie-Lan Nguyen, Wikimedia Commons*

But to gain a sense of how tall most Greeks and Romans were, we need to interrogate their corpses.[2]

Skeletons carry the story of a lifetime. Teeth record childhood nutrition and illnesses. The bones of the hands bear the stresses and scars of labor. And long bones (especially femurs) chart height. The skeletons discovered in the ship sheds of Herculaneum—probably the classical world's most famous human remains—reveal how much bones can tell us.

Like the neighboring city of Pompeii, Herculaneum was destroyed by Vesuvius in 79 CE. Most of the inhabitants fled within the first few hours of the eruption. But hundreds remained, sheltering in a row of stone boat sheds by the harbor. Death found them there in the middle of the night, when a wave of superheated gas roared over the city. Buried by sixty feet of volcanic debris and undisturbed until a few decades ago, the refugees' bodies provide a unique cross-section of Roman life.

A few of the Herculaneans in the boat sheds were wealthy; one set of bones, belonging to a man in his mid-forties, had hands unmarked by the stresses of manual labor, but arms and shoulders sculpted by regular exercise in the baths. Other victims were obviously poor, like the so-called Helmsman, whose bones were stunted by childhood malnutrition and warped by a lifetime of constant hard work. A respectable Roman matron with perfect teeth—nicknamed the Ring Lady because of the jewelry she wore—was found near two women (one still haloed by wisps of blond hair) whom the excavators identified as prostitutes. There was even a Roman soldier, whose bones bore the traces of powerful muscles and combat scars.[3]

The soldier, at nearly five feet nine, was among the tallest men in the sheds. The Helmsman, at five feet four, was one of the shortest. The Ring Lady was not quite five feet two; the two women found beside her were five feet one and five feet four. The average height of the men in the sheds was five feet six and a half inches. The female mean was five feet one. These figures correlate well with those from neighboring Pompeii, where the recovered bones suggest male and female averages of five feet five and a half inches and five feet one. Although many other inhabitants of Roman Italy were shorter,* the Classical Greeks seem to have been about the same height; a recent survey of the skeletal evidence suggests a male average of just under five feet seven and a female average of five feet one and a half.[4]

The northern barbarians were significantly taller. When, for example, Julius Caesar's troops began to roll a siege tower toward one Gallic town, the inhabitants stood on the walls and mockingly congratulated them for moving such a big engine despite being such little men.† The difference in height between the average Roman legionary and the average northerner was probably around two or three inches—not dramatic, but real. Though partly a matter of genetics, it stemmed largely from diet. Northerners—especially elite northerners—regularly consumed dairy products and red meat. Most Greeks and Romans did not; when it comes to height, you are what you don't eat.[5]

---

* The male average in Roman central Italy has been estimated at five feet four and a half inches. This is significantly shorter than the pre- and post-Roman averages, probably because population pressures and epidemic diseases were at their worst during the Roman imperial era. The poor inhabitants of the overcrowded and disease-ridden city of Rome itself may have been the shortest population in the entire empire. The residents of Pompeii and Herculaneum likely owed their relatively imposing stature to the fact that both towns were located on the sea and thus had access to ample protein in the form of fresh fish.

† The Romans were especially impressed by Gallic women, who were nearly as tall as their husbands and much tougher; one Roman author compared the punches and kicks of Gallic women to missiles shot by a catapult.

How Much Money Did They Make?

*E*conomics had yet to be invented. Brute force, however, was an old friend. So when the Roman emperor Diocletian and his colleagues decided to end decades of runaway inflation, their solution was straightforward: price controls and wage ceilings, on pain of death. Farm laborers and mule drivers, it was decreed, could receive a maximum of twenty-five denarii (plus meals) daily. A carpenter or baker might earn fifty. A painter of walls was entitled to seventy-five, and a skilled artist to twice that. A barber or a bath attendant could charge only two denarii per clip or dip. A lawyer, however, might wheedle his way to a thousand for pleading a case. Although these numbers had only a tenuous relationship with economic reality, they reflect a clear hierarchy of professions, and the grim dynamics of a world in which few people earned much more than they needed to survive.

The ancient economy was never fully monetized. Coins were most common in cities and military camps, and more prevalent during the Roman imperial era than before or after. They were always used, however, alongside barter and credit.* During the Classical period, the most widespread of the many Greek currencies was the silver Athenian drachma. The larger tetradrachm (four-drachma piece) was standard in commercial transactions. But for everyday purchases, Athenians typically used obols, small silver coins worth one-sixth of a drachma.† During the

---

* Even during the Roman imperial era, some provinces paid some or all of their taxes in wheat.

† "Obol" is derived from the word for "skewer," apparently because iron skewers were used as currency before the advent of coins. "Drachma" likewise meant "handful," in the sense of "a handful of skewers." The Spartans continued to use clattering heaps of skewers as currency through the Classical period.

early imperial era, the most valuable Roman coin was the golden aureus, used primarily to pay special bonuses to soldiers. Each aureus was worth twenty-five silver denarii, which were the real basis of the currency. Each denarius, finally, was equivalent to four sesterces, large brass coins that served as the standard unit of account for prices and wages.

In fourth-century BCE Athens, a citizen and his family were thought to need a daily income of three obols (half a drachma) to live comfortably—roughly 180 drachmas per year.[1] On the basis of known prices, a family of four in second-century CE Rome probably required about twelve hundred sesterces to achieve the same standard.[*2] Although it would not be completely misleading to equate these numbers with a modern middle-class wage, it is more instructive to compare them with the earnings described in our sources.

At the bottom of the classical income hierarchy, just above slaves, were unskilled day laborers. In the countryside, these men were typically hired to provide help with the harvest. In cities (and especially in imperial Rome), they were most visible in large construction projects. Nowhere were they well paid. They usually earned about a drachma each day in Classical Athens—when work was available. Laborers' wages in the Roman world seem to have been close to subsistence level: workers in Pompeii received between one and four sesterces (plus food) daily. Those who knew a trade could count on making more. During work on a sanctuary just outside Athens, for example, skilled workers earned up to two and a half drachmas a day—a drachma more than their unskilled counterparts. In the Roman world, likewise, craftsmen earned substantially more than laborers.[†] Diocletian's price edict, as we have seen, assumed that a baker would make twice as much as a farm worker, a wall painter three times as much, and an artist six times as much.[3]

In the fifth century BCE, both Athenian hoplites and the rowers of the Athenian navy earned one drachma a day, the same as an unskilled laborer.[4] From the late first to late second centuries CE, Roman legionaries earned twelve hundred sesterces each year.[‡] Particu-

---

* Much less than twelve hundred sesterces would have sufficed in other parts of the empire. Although bread (thanks to imperial subsidies) was relatively cheap in Rome, rents were high.

† Trade associations for catapult makers, ladder crafters, taste testers, and more than one hundred other occupations are attested in imperial Rome.

‡ They actually received less than this, since a considerable portion of their pay was deducted for food and equipment. These losses were only partly balanced by the bonuses they received upon the accession of a new emperor and other special occasions.

larly when combined with their massive discharge bonus (twelve thousand sesterces), this put ordinary soldiers on the approximate income level of skilled craftsmen. Officers were paid much better. A regular centurion earned eighteen thousand sesterces a year; the chief centurion of the legion, seventy-two thousand; and the commanding general an eyebrow-raising two hundred thousand sesterces annually—as much as 167 legionaries.[5]

The earnings of ancient lawyers, like those of their modern brethren, ranged from the pitiful to the obscene. Although Athenians were expected to represent themselves in court, they often paid skilled orators to write their speeches. At least a few legal speechwriters were handsomely compensated; one defendant promised eighteen thousand drachmas—enough to support one hundred families for a year—to those who supported him during his trial. Roman lawyers were forbidden to charge for their services until the imperial era, and even when the ban was lifted, their fees were capped at ten thousand sesterces (about eight times a legionary's annual wage). It seems to have always been customary, however, to reward lawyers with expensive "gifts." Cicero, for example, received a "loan" of two million sesterces from one of his clients, which he never felt moved to repay.*[6]

In Classical Greece, doctors were respected and apparently well paid. One doctor could afford to donate six thousand drachmas to the city of Athens, and another was said to earn twelve thousand drachmas every year (an Athenian family, you'll recall, could live for a year on 180 drachmas). Although many Roman doctors were low-status freedmen, a few became extremely wealthy. The personal physician of the emperors Caligula and Claudius received an annual salary of five hundred thousand sesterces (as much as 416 legionaries)—and even this, as he liked to remind his employers, was less than he could have earned in private practice. He was telling the truth: Another Roman celebrity doctor, famous for advocating ice-cold baths, charged a single patient two hundred thousand sesterces for a cure.[7]

Most teachers, then as now, were wretchedly paid. As in law and medicine, however, the select few who catered to the rich and famous made enormous amounts of money. Leading Athenian orators charged pupils between one thousand and ten thousand drachmas for courses in public speaking at a time when most men made one or two drachmas

---

* Less prosperous Romans might reward their lawyers with sacks of beans or barley.

a day. Professors of rhetoric in the Roman world were even better at fleecing aristocratic parents; one reportedly earned four hundred thousand sesterces a year—as much as 333 legionaries.* In Rome, Athens, and other large cities, a few of the most distinguished teachers filled endowed chairs of rhetoric and philosophy—the closest ancient equivalent to a tenured professorship—and so received additional salaries of up to one hundred thousand sesterces.[8]

Entertainers in Classical Athens were not well paid, largely because most of them were slaves.† A few of their Roman counterparts, however, became as rich as any celebrity doctor or professor. One famous mime made two hundred thousand sesterces a year, and the great comic actor Roscius earned still more. Although Roman playwrights seldom became rich from their scripts, the emperor Augustus bestowed one million sesterces on the lucky author of a well-received tragedy. Another emperor gave two hundred thousand each to a pair of particularly lyrical lyre players. Famous retired gladiators might be paid nearly as much for an exhibition performance in the arena. The wealthiest of all Roman entertainers, however, were the charioteers of the Circus Maximus. Over the course of a long and very busy career, one driver managed to win 1,462 races and almost thirty-six million sesterces. This man's prize money, enough to pay the annual salaries of nearly thirty thousand legionaries, made him the equivalent of a modern billionaire.[9]

The richest Greeks and Romans were self-employed. In both Athens and Rome, the elite ideal was a life of public service and cultivated leisure discreetly supported by the revenues of large estates. Though not especially profitable—6 percent was thought to be the average annual return—agricultural land was the classical world's safest and stateliest investment. Few aristocrats, however, were content to live entirely on crop sales. Roman magnates often invested in urban real estate. The fabulously wealthy senator Crassus owned teams of slaves trained as firemen and builders. Whenever a fire broke out in Rome, he would rush to the scene, purchase the burning structures at a knockdown price, and then send in his slaves to extinguish

---

* Most Roman professors of rhetoric probably had annual earnings in the range of two thousand sesterces. Only a few superstars could get away with such exorbitant rates.

† Courtesans were a partial exception to this rule. One reportedly charged ten thousand drachmas for a single night.

the blaze and reconstruct the buildings as rental properties. Slave-worked enterprises were another favorite elite investment: Crassus, for example, trained some of his slaves to be scribes, silversmiths, and table servers for hire. Although direct involvement in commerce was taboo, aristocrats could and did participate through proxies and subordinates. Finally, interest from loans was an important source of income, particularly for the Roman elite. Large sums were lent out at variable rates: as low as 4 percent for friends and up to 60 percent for high-risk ventures.*[10]

So how rich were the Athenian and Roman 1 percent? At any given point during the Classical period, a few hundred Athenians possessed three talents (eighteen thousand drachmas) or more. The largest known Athenian fortune was two hundred talents (1.2 million drachmas)—enough to support more than 6,600 families for a year. Even this gargantuan sum paled beside the wealth of the Roman elite. During the imperial era, senators were required to have personal fortunes of at least one million sesterces (equal to the salaries of 833 legionaries), and most were considerably wealthier. Cicero, with properties worth about thirteen million sesterces, was probably in the middle rank of senatorial wealth. Our fire-fighting friend Crassus, among the wealthiest senators, was worth two hundred million. In the first century CE, we know of two Romans worth four hundred million, enough to pay the annual salaries of 330,000 legionaries. The great generals of the late Republic were even richer; after one of his triumphs, Pompey distributed 384 million sesterces among his soldiers and officers and then gave an additional two hundred million to the state.[11]

The wealthiest of all, of course, were the Roman emperors. Even if we imagine a meaningful separation between the emperors' possessions and the public treasury, the fact that the emperors personally owned Egypt (along with hundreds of massive estates throughout Italy and the provinces) suggests the mind-boggling scale of their fortunes. Some emperors were less subtle about their wealth than others. Caligula liked to recline on heaps of gold coins, and Nero once had ten million sesterces piled up just to see what it looked like. Over the course of his thirteen-year reign, Nero reportedly spent an incredible 2.2 billion

---

* The philosopher Seneca (who happened also to be a fabulously wealthy businessman) helped to bring about the conquest of Britain by calling in the forty million sesterces he had loaned to some British chieftains.

sesterces on gifts alone—equivalent to the annual salaries of more than 1,833,000 mid-imperial legionaries.*[12]

Like the ultrarich of every place and time, the wealthiest Greeks and Romans found creative ways to spend their money. The Roman elite poured enormous sums into furniture: Cicero dished out five hundred thousand sesterces for a citrus wood sideboard, and one of his friends spent twice as much for a table. Choice antiques commanded equally exorbitant prices; one discriminating Roman paid a cool million sesterces for a statuette by a Greek master.† Still greater amounts were paid for villas and townhouses. Cicero shelled out 3.5 million sesterces for a house overlooking the Forum, and one of his contemporaries parted with 15 million for a neighboring mansion.‡ Caligula's wife trumped all of these conspicuous consumers by appearing at a banquet in emeralds and pearls worth 40 million sesterces. The most impressive purchase in classical history, however, took place a century and a half later, when a bribe of 250 million sesterces bought the throne of the Roman Empire. Since the purchaser was assassinated two months later, however, this has to be regarded as a poor investment.[13]

---

* By way of comparison, the annual budget of the Roman military in Nero's reign has been estimated as 500 million sesterces, paid out of a total annual revenue of about 670 million sesterces.

† New statues were much more affordable. A life-size marble or bronze portrait usually seems to have cost between three thousand and six thousand sesterces in the provinces, though some in the city of Rome ran to thirty thousand or more.

‡ An Athenian magnate might pay five talents (thirty thousand drachmas) for an estate. An average Greek house probably cost between fifteen hundred and three thousand drachmas.

How Dangerous Were Their Cities?

*C*lassical cities had many ways of killing and otherwise inconveniencing their residents. The menace of fire crouched on each tinder-dry roof; in every dank sewer lurked the threat of disease. Every passerby was a potential thief; each crowd was a mob in waiting. Streets were spattered with excrement, markets seethed with parasites, buildings teetered at angles of repose. Danger, in short, was everywhere. But threats to life, limb, and intestinal well-being were especially prolific in Rome, the ancient world's biggest and best-documented city.

The wealthiest Romans held court in mansions with whispering fountains and cool marble floors. Everybody else lived in apartments that ran the gamut from well-appointed to squalid. Roman apartment buildings—called *insulae* ("islands")—were typically three or four stories tall.* The ground floor was given over to shops. The best apartments were just above, where relative proximity to the street minimized the number of access steps and made primitive plumbing a possibility. Smaller and cheaper units crowded the upper floors, which were often jerry-built additions.† These penthouses sometimes collapsed onto the street. So did whole *insulae*.[1]

Outside their foundering apartments, Romans had to be wary of thieves. Every morning, cutpurses worked the forums and streets,

---

* Although the height of *insulae* was legally restricted to seventy feet—and later, for good measure, to sixty—a few buildings seem to have shot past this limit. One in particular, the Insula of Felicles, was so tall that it became a tourist attraction.

† In the cheapest rooms, often rented to migrant workers from the countryside, rent was charged daily or weekly. Most apartments, however, had one-year leases. July 1—rent day— was dreaded by the poor, since those unable to pay would join the homeless huddled beneath Rome's bridges and porticoes.

preying on the careless and the distracted. Every afternoon, light-fingered men sauntered through the locker rooms of the baths, discreetly searching for valuables. And every night, expert burglars—some wearing shoes spiked for climbing walls—crept over roofs and into windows. During major festivals, when many neighborhoods were virtually deserted, thefts were so rampant that the emperors sent armed patrols into the streets.[2]

Anyone walking at night was liable to be robbed, beaten, or worse. Even in broad daylight, injury was always a possibility: one author mentions a deranged aristocrat who slapped the face of every person he passed. Street violence was common,* especially during the turbulent last decades of the Republic, when gangs battled in the streets and criminals grew bold enough to organize themselves into guilds.[3]

The Roman government took only limited action to protect its citizens. A few crimes—notably treason and patricide—were aggressively prosecuted on the grounds that they imperiled the stability of the state or the goodwill of the gods. Victims of theft or assault, however, were on their own. They were encouraged to track down the criminal(s) who had wronged them; if they managed to do so, they could bring the matter to court. Alternatively, they were free to avenge the crime vigilante style.

Like virtually all cities before the nineteenth century, Rome had no professional police. In the imperial era, however, the firemen known as the *vigiles* patrolled the streets at night and arrested anyone brazen or sluggish enough to be caught in the act of committing a crime. During the day, likewise, the urban cohorts—legionaries stationed in Rome—were expected to apprehend lawbreakers. Ambitious officials occasionally ordered them to crack down on crime. On a regular basis, however, these soldiers appear to have been much more interested in soliciting bribes than in bringing criminals to justice.[4]

Unable to rely on civil authorities, the people of Rome fended for themselves. Doors were chained, windows barred, and club-carrying watchmen stationed in vestibules. Those who ventured out at night often brought armed backup.† For additional protection, Romans

---

* Senators were routinely searched for daggers before meetings of the Senate. This did nothing to prevent them from being murderous in their free time. Even in the generally stable first century, we hear about senators pushing their wives out of windows and dispatching lovers in fits of passion.

† Wealthy Romans frequently hired gladiators as bodyguards.

appealed to the minor gods who guarded their hinges and doors and ordered anti-theft curses from street magicians.[5]

But no spell could ward off the civil unrest to which Rome was perennially prone. Most riots were sparked by high grain prices or unpopular laws. Others were extensions of larger conflicts: in the fourth century, for example, a disputed papal election left hundreds dead.* If the urban cohorts failed to restore order, the emperors sent in the Praetorian Guard. Even under normal circumstances, the praetorians were notorious for their brutality; one emperor had to explicitly forbid them from beating innocent civilians. They were not known for being gentle about crowd control. Once, after praetorian cavalry butchered hundreds of protesters, the urban cohorts actually joined the rioters in attacking them. On another occasion, the praetorians battled a mob of outraged citizens and freed gladiators for three consecutive days, burning an entire neighborhood in the process.[6]

Even when the praetorians were safely in their camp, fire was a constant threat. Although the exterior walls of most *insulae* were brick-faced concrete, their penthouses, partitions, furniture, and floors were wooden. So were the balconies that overhung the streets, the rafters of the temples, and the upper tiers of seating in Colosseum.† During Rome's long, hot summers, all this wood was tinder-dry—and sparks were everywhere. Many Romans kept a tub of water or jars of vinegar in case a lamp fell or a brazier spilled. But once flames leapt up, they could only grab their valuables, run downstairs, and hope the *vigiles* were on the way.[7]

The *vigiles*, Rome's firefighters, were based in stations throughout the city. Every night, they walked the darkened streets, carrying axes and buckets. When they smelled smoke or saw signs of fire, they rushed to the threatened building, broke down its doors, and formed a bucket chain to the nearest fountain. If this failed to contain the blaze, runners were sent to the station for backup and heavy equipment. When these arrived, the *vigiles* turned to what they did best: demolition. In

---

* Plenty of riots, of course, were sparked by frivolous incidents. A riot in Alexandria began after a slave and a soldier argued over whose shoes were better, and the people of Ephesus reportedly once rose up because the water in their baths was too cold.

† In the early third century, a lightning strike ignited the Colosseum's upper deck. Despite herculean efforts to extinguish it—we are told that the firefighters "drained all the aqueducts"—the blaze gutted the entire building. Years of repairs were required before it could be used again.

A large public latrine in Ostia, Rome's port. *Author's photo*

the absence of pressurized water mains or hoses, the only way to keep a fire from spreading was to starve it of fuel, and the only sure way to starve a fire of fuel was to level every neighboring building. The work of destruction was done with picks, grappling hooks, and small catapults. Vinegar-soaked blankets were spread over the rubble. Once the fire had been contained, the medics attached to each squad of *vigiles* treated wounded civilians. The person whose negligence had started the fire was publicly beaten. And then the firemen returned to their rounds, leaving landlords (and their insurers) to deal with the smoldering ruins.[8]

On dry and windy nights, when flames leapt from roof to roof faster than the *vigiles* could contain them, the emperor might deputize slaves or call for civilian volunteers to help battle the inferno. Sometimes, however, there was little anyone could do. The fire of 64 CE, the worst in Rome's history, raged for six days and nights, and was contained only after hundreds of buildings were demolished to create a huge firebreak. Nero attempted to fireproof the city with broad streets and all-stone structures. One of his successors dedicated fourteen

"Altars of the Neronian Fire" to Neptune—the god responsible for aquatic matters and a good ally for fighting fires.* Not even Neptune, however, could keep Rome from burning.[9]

Neptune was equally irresponsible in his management of the Tiber River. After heavy winter rains, the Tiber could rise fifty feet, submerging the entire city center for up to a week. Various schemes were proposed for ending the floods: Julius Caesar considered digging a new river channel below the city, and a senatorial commission suggested rerouting some of the Tiber's tributaries. But nothing substantial was done, and floods continued to subvert buildings, speckle walls with mold, and spoil grain supplies.[10]

Rome's grain supply was a frequent source of trouble. Bread made up the bulk of most Romans' diets, and something like two hundred thousand tons of wheat were needed to feed the city every year. Perhaps a third of this was distributed via the famous grain dole.† The rest was sold on the free market, but at prices regulated by the government. Free or subsidized, Rome's grain was imported from the fertile fields of Sicily, Tunisia, and—above all—Egypt. Every summer, hundreds of grain ships sailed into the vast harbor complex at the mouth of the Tiber. Their cargo was brought upstream to Rome in barges towed by teams of men or oxen and stored in colossal warehouses. When the system worked, there was a comfortable surplus of grain in and around the city. But when bad weather, floods, or unrest caused supply problems, Rome felt the pinch. Although actual starvation was rare, food shortages and price hikes were not.

Thanks to eleven aqueducts capable of carrying hundreds of millions of gallons every day, water supplies were more reliable. Contrary to semipopular belief, the Romans were not poisoned by their lead water pipes. They knew that lead was poisonous and made most of their pipes from terra-cotta. Moreover, since the water carried by Rome's

---

* The divinity responsible for actually preventing fires was the minor goddess Stata Mater ("Fire-stopping Mother").

† During the late Republic, the Roman government began to provide free grain to male Roman citizens. In the early imperial era, the number of recipients was limited to about two hundred thousand, each of whom received enough to feed himself and a single dependent for a month. To collect his sack of grain, a Roman went to the distribution center—a large portico—and presented a token. Over the ensuing month, he would take portions of this grain to a neighborhood baker to have it milled and baked. Eventually, the emperors cut out the middlemen and began distributing baked bread.

aqueducts had a high calcium content, lime quickly coated the few pipes that were made of lead, preventing metal from leaching into the water. Rome's water, in short, was reasonably salubrious. The same could not be said of the city's rudimentary sewage system.[11]

The population of Rome produced an estimated one hundred thousand pounds of excrement each day. Some of this was funneled through the city's public latrines. These structures—frequently decorated, occasionally heated—were located beside busy thoroughfares and in discreet corners of baths. They often had a dozen or more seats— sometimes as many as sixty-four—side by side, without partitions or any apparent concern for privacy. The atmosphere in public latrines, in fact, could be downright convivial; one Roman poet describes a man trying to wheedle a dinner invitation from his latrine mates. Since aqueduct overflow flushed the trough beneath the seats, the facilities were relatively sanitary—unlike the communal sponges used in place of toilet paper.* A more urgent health hazard was the methane gas that built up in the poorly ventilated sewage channels, which occasionally ignited, sending fireballs through the seats.[†12]

Few private bathrooms were connected to sewers. Since ancient plumbing lacked traps, direct connection to a sewage line opened one's home to noxious gases and pests ranging from rats to octopi.[‡] Most Romans understandably preferred cesspit latrines, often in or near the kitchen so that food waste could be tossed down the hole. A few apartment buildings featured a communal cesspit connected to multiple units by terracotta pipes. The great majority of Romans, however, had only chamber pots in their apartments. The courteous emptied their pots into a sewer or latrine. The rest hurled their waste onto the street, where it mingled with manure, refuse, and dead animals. In theory, the streets were cleaned by overflow from nearby fountains, which ran along

---

* It has been suggested that small jugs filled with water—the classical equivalent of the modern *lota* or bidet—were sometimes used for anal hygiene.

† Despite their unsavory aspects, latrines did put at least a dent in public defecation rates; many Roman homeowners found it necessary to paint the warning *cacator cave malum* ("crap and you're cursed") on their streetside walls. Public urination, on the other hand, was actively encouraged by the city's fullers, who set out jars on street corners to collect the urine they used to clean clothes.

‡ According to one Roman author, a large octopus broke into a warehouse by squeezing through the sewage pipes. The owners finally caught it as it emerged from the toilet and subdued it after a dubious battle of hatchets and tentacles.

the gutters and into the sewers. In reality, this water probably did little more than moisten the filth. The manure and human waste, at least, may have been periodically cleared by fertilizer collectors. The rest rotted and reeked until a heavy rain washed it away.[13]

Since Rome's filthy streets were breeding grounds for disease, the average Roman was crawling with internal parasites, wracked by bouts of gastroenteritis-induced diarrhea, and visited each year by the fever and chills of malaria. It was sewer-spawned mosquitos and invisible pathogens, not fires or thieves, that most often made living in Rome a brief and unpleasant prelude to dying there.

· 13 ·

How Often Were Slaves Freed?

$\mathcal{I}$n Classical Athens and late republican Rome, every third person was a slave.* Slaves walked, worked, and lived alongside the freeborn, speaking the same language and wearing the same clothes. But unlike even the lowliest of their free neighbors, they could be sold without warning, punished without mercy, and killed without fear of reprisal. In the eyes of the law, a slave was not a person; a slave was a tool or beast of burden—in Greek, an *andropodon*, a thing on human feet. Beyond this basic fact, however, the lives of slaves varied immensely.

Many slaves lived and worked in the countryside, often on large estates owned by members of the elite. Others manned workshops in the cities, making everything from shields to shoes. A few lived independently, running storefronts "rented" from their masters with a portion of their earnings. The slaves most visible in our sources, however, are the relatively privileged minority that ran the houses of the rich.†
These slaves feted and waited on their master, massaged his limbs and finances, followed him into battle and the baths, and (in the case of at least one decrepit senator) brushed his teeth. They were trained to

---

* Though always present, slaves were less numerous in most other classical places and periods. On the basis of evidence from Egyptian papyri, it is sometimes estimated that about 10 percent of the Roman Empire's population was enslaved in the early imperial era.

† Aristocratic Roman households often had hundreds of hyperspecialized slaves. Jobs included mirror holder, silver polisher, manager of paintings, and master of perfumed oils. Tiberius had a slave who specialized in doing humorous impressions of prominent Romans.

answer every whim.* One rich but uneducated social climber purchased nine intelligent slaves, instructed them to memorize a series of literary classics, and then brought them along to dinner parties so that they could feed him clever quotations. A less pretentious old lady cherished her troupe of male dancers, whom she liked to watch between games of checkers.[1]

Besides managing the mansions of the wealthy, slaves helped run cities and nations. In Classical Athens, slaves maintained order at public assemblies and did the dirty work of executing prisoners and filing legal documents. In Rome, likewise, slaves kept the aqueducts flowing and (once freed) manned the fire brigades. The slaves of the imperial household comprised a special and highly prestigious group that was responsible for running the palace, overseeing the gargantuan network of imperial estates, and helping to administer the finances of the Roman Empire.

Slaves who worked closely with their masters sometimes became their confidants. Cicero, for example, trusted his slave secretary Tiro to manage his financial affairs, described him as a friend, and arranged for the best available medical treatment when he got sick. Another Roman senator paid for one of his freed slaves—his favorite reader of Greek comedies—to travel to Egypt for his health. Few slaves, however, were so fortunate. Those who lacked the master's favor typically received only basic food, slept in cramped cells, and were denied anything like a normal family life.† Life was hard for the legions of slaves who labored in the fields, and hellish for the tens of thousands condemned to the mines. These men and women, chained in suffocating darkness, experienced the inhumanity of slavery in its most brutal form.[2]

Even in more benign settings, slaves always were subject to casual humiliation and brutality. Augustus, for example, once had a slave's legs shattered as a punishment and casually crucified one of his freedmen for

---

* Particularly in the Roman world, wealthy owners paid astronomical prices for slaves with special talents. At a time when most slaves cost between one thousand and three thousand sesterces, wealthy Romans are known to have paid one hundred thousand sesterces for handsome young cupbearers, two hundred thousand for (fake) identical twins, and seven hundred thousand for a famous scholar.

† Few Greek slaves were allowed to form permanent relationships. Roman slaves, likewise, were not permitted to marry, though informal unions seem to have been fairly common. Some masters may have encouraged slaves to have children, but those who did so had to live with the terrible possibility that their families would be broken up by sale—a practice legal until the reign of Constantine.

eating a prize fighting quail.* Later emperors passed laws forbidding owners to castrate their slaves or sell them (without cause) as prostitutes or gladiators. Slaves who conspired against their masters, however, could be burned alive quite legally. On a daily basis, there were no real restrictions, legal or social, on a master's treatment of his slaves. An abused slave's only recourse was to flee to a temple (or, in the Roman world, a statue of the emperor) and ask to be sold to someone else.[3]

Although the Greeks and Romans eventually developed scruples about enslaving their fellow citizens, they never questioned the institution of slavery itself. Aristotle claimed that those who lacked the capacity to master themselves (in other words, barbarians) were natural slaves. Plato objected only to the slavery of Greeks, and particularly to the enslavement of Plato (he had once been sold into captivity by an irritable tyrant). Even the Stoics, who asserted that all men were naturally equal, regarded physical slavery as less harmful than spiritual slavery to ambition and greed, and went no further than urging masters to be humane. The early Christians sharply criticized the sexual abuse of slaves. Yet despite the expectation that believers who embraced an ascetic lifestyle would free their slaves—one pious and very wealthy lady liberated no fewer than eight thousand of hers—few bishops raised objections to slavery itself, and the growth of the church does not seem to have significantly reduced slave numbers.[4]

Since there were no social pressures on Greek and Roman masters to free their slaves, emancipation was largely a matter of luck. During crises, large numbers of slaves might be liberated to become soldiers. Unrest also created the conditions for antiquity's few large-scale slave revolts; the most famous of these, led by the gladiator Spartacus, involved seventy thousand slaves and destroyed two Roman legions before it was suppressed. On a more regular basis, individual slaves slipped away.† One of Cicero's slave librarians, for example, fled to the mountains of Croatia and was never heard from again. Escape attempts, however, were relatively rare. Captured fugitives were savagely punished and were likely to find themselves outcasts even if they managed to evade the slave catchers.[5]

---

* Romans squeamish about punishing their own slaves could rent out the public torturer for a flat fee.

† At least once, slave owners were able to purchase runaway insurance. One of Alexander the Great's officials, in need of bearers for his baggage train, allowed any owner willing to lend him labor to register the value of his slaves and buy full coverage for a few drachmas.

For most slaves, manumission (a grant of freedom) was the only viable path out of bondage. A slave's chances of being freed depended on his or her relationship with the master. Slaves on rural estates had little hope of establishing a useful rapport. Favored house slaves, on the other hand, had a reasonable chance. Masters often freed their lovers, sometimes—at least in the Roman world—for the purpose of marrying them.* Some also liberated young slaves (usually their biological children) and adopted them as heirs. Slaves who served as personal secretaries and research assistants could expect freedom, as could those with key roles in their masters' commercial enterprises. Slaves set up as independent craftsmen were often able to buy their liberty.

Manumission ceremonies varied. In the Greek world, an owner might formally "sell" the slave to a god, declare the slave free at a festival, or even stage a trial in which he sued the slave and lost. Roman slaves could be formally enrolled as citizens, declared free before an official (even if the official was just walking by), or simply liberated in the presence of witnesses. Both Greek and Roman owners freed slaves in their wills.†6

In Athens and other Greek cities, freedmen were noncitizens, unable to participate in politics or own real estate. Roman freedmen, by contrast, became full citizens (though they were disqualified from major public offices). Freed slaves in both societies had continuing obligations to their erstwhile masters, which sometimes included part-time unpaid labor and always entailed public deference. Although some former slaves struggled to adapt to freedom, many prospered, typically in trades they had learned while still enslaved. The most famous freedmen in classical Athens, for example, were the wealthy bankers Pasion and Phormion, both of whom had begun as slave clerks. Some Roman freedmen amassed huge fortunes through commercial ventures or government service, and a few became eminent enough to marry high-status freeborn women. One freedman accumulated no fewer than 4,116 slaves of his own.7

---

* After the deaths of their wives, the emperors Vespasian, Antoninus Pius, and Marcus Aurelius all lived with freed mistresses (who could not produce legitimate children and thus would not create a succession crisis). One eminent orator was said to have a whole network of freed lovers scattered around Athens.

† Uneasy about the social and economic ramifications of freeing hundreds—or even thousands—of slaves at once, the Romans limited the number that could be manumitted by will to one hundred.

Particularly in the Roman world, freed slaves and their descendants rose to distinction in many fields. The playwright Terrence was a former slave, and the poet Horace was a freedman's son. The Stoic philosopher Epictetus was another freedman, crippled by an injury suffered at his master's hands. Pope Callixtus I was a former slave; Emperor Diocletian, the great persecutor of the Christians, may have been a freedman's son. The most impressive resume of all, however, belonged to the Roman slave girl Musa, who managed to become Queen Mother of the Parthian Empire. Ancient slavery, in short, could be something less than a life sentence—but only for a talented and fortunate few.[8]

Was Divorce Common?

$\mathcal{E}$veryone who knew the couple saw the split coming. He was impulsive and tactless, with a mean streak and a terrible temper. She was suspicious, domineering, and as hot-tempered as her husband. They sniped, they squabbled, they screamed at each other in front of squirming guests. Finally, after years of steadily mounting misery, the inevitable happened: she moved out, and he moved on. We all know similar stories. This particular couple, however, was Quintus and Pomponia, and this particular marriage failed in 45 BCE.[1]

A few philosophers regarded marriage as a distraction. A few rich men accounted it a bad investment. A few cults condemned it as a sin. Almost everyone else in the classical world, however, saw marriage as a necessity. Only through marriage could a couple produce legitimate children. Only through marriage could most men and women achieve some measure of social and economic stability. Only through marriage could the power elite remain elite and powerful.

Marriage, in short, was indispensable. It was also far too important a matter to be unduly influenced by emotion. Almost all marriages were arranged between the suitor and the family of the prospective bride. The bride herself had little say in the matter, in part because she was usually very young. Most Greek and Roman women married in their mid-teens. Aristocratic brides were often barely past puberty; the minimum age allowed by Roman law was twelve. Most men, by contrast, married in their late twenties or early thirties. The ten- or fifteen-year age gap between husband and wife reflected ancient ideas about the purpose of marriage: the man was established enough to provide for a family, and the woman stood at the threshold of her childbearing years. It was not thought to be necessary—or even very desirable—that the couple begin their relationship with romantic feelings toward one another.[2]

Despite the businesslike considerations that surrounded the beginnings of a marriage, the ideal was always a harmonious and lifelong relationship. Particularly among wealthier urban families, spouses were assumed to have complementary spheres of responsibility, the husband earning income in the wider world, the wife raising their children at home. Although a husband was always expected to take the leading role, he also was supposed to respect his wife. This ideal, however, was undermined by the double standard for sexual propriety. Since the paternity of a man's children and his own masculinity could never be in doubt, female adultery was condemned in the strongest possible terms. Married men, however, generally were free to sleep with prostitutes, slaves, and (in Classical Greece) citizen boys,* and they faced legal penalties only if they seduced a citizen woman.

Although many Greek and Roman women had excellent reasons to leave their husbands, most divorces were initiated by men. Consequently, the most common grounds for divorce was female adultery. Both Roman and Athenian citizens were required by law to divorce unfaithful wives. A woman caught in flagrante was sent back to her parents' home in disgrace. Her partner—if not murdered on the spot by the outraged husband—was likely to be publicly humiliated, sometimes by having a fist-sized radish or spiny fish jammed into his anus. Divorce could also be motivated by infertility. One impotent Athenian took the ostensibly gallant step of divorcing his wife so that she could have a family, and a king of Sparta managed to avoid leaving his beloved but barren better half only by the expedient of taking an additional wife.[†] According to later tradition, likewise, the first divorce in Roman history involved a woman who was incapable of bearing

---

* In some places and periods, however, philandering was hobbled by social expectations. Marriage contracts in Hellenistic and Roman Egypt sometimes made affairs (with women or boys) grounds for divorce. And, to judge from the advice of popular philosophers and doctors, there seems to have been a widespread sense by the Roman imperial era that husbands should confine their amorous impulses to the marital bed.

† Although monogamy was always the rule in the classical world, there were a few exceptions. In Sparta, an elderly or impotent husband could invite a more vigorous acquaintance to sire children with his wife, and any woman could (with her husband's permission) share another Spartan citizen's bed. The Athenians experimented with bigamy during the Peloponnesian War, apparently as a means of supporting war widows. Not all unorthodox living arrangements, of course, were sanctioned by the state; the epitaph of one Roman freedwoman unblushingly describes a ménage à trois.

children. Sometimes, finally, a couple simply drifted apart. The Athenian statesman Pericles, for example, separated amicably from his wife and helped to arrange her second marriage. Incompatibility seems to have been the usual cause of the middle-class divorces described in papyri from Roman Egypt.[3]

By modern standards, divorce was strikingly informal. There were no ceremonies, no formal proceedings, and—strangest and most wonderful of all—no lawyers. In Classical Athens, a divorce could be initiated by the husband, by the wife's father, or (with more difficulty) by the wife.* In each case, the woman returned to her family. The man's only legal obligation was to return her dowry; if he failed to do so, he could be sued in court. Although divorce was equally straightforward in Rome—a couple was legally divorced as soon as they ceased to consider themselves married—it was customary among the elite for the divorcing party to notify their spouse with a short message carried by a freedman. The split might be formally marked by a woman handing the house keys to her former husband, who responded with the ritual phrase, "take your things and go!" Like his Athenian counterpart, a Roman man was responsible for returning his wife's dowry. As in Athens, however, he normally kept sole custody of any children produced by the marriage.

The frequency of divorce in the classical world is difficult to gauge. In the last days of the Republic, ambitious Roman politicians matched their wives to their political allegiances and changed them almost as frequently. Julius Caesar, for example, married four times, and both his rival Pompey and his protégé Mark Antony were five-time grooms.† Although the emperor Augustus was himself a two-time divorcee, the marriage laws he sponsored (and the lower stakes of political maneuvering under the empire) seem to have reduced the divorce rate of the Roman elite.

We know much less about the frequency of divorce among other classical populations. To judge from papyri, divorce was familiar but not especially frequent in Roman Egypt. There is no reason to assume

---

* If the wife's father died and she was the sole heir, she was legally required to leave her husband and marry one of her uncles or cousins to keep the family wealth intact.

† Not all late republican divorces, of course, were political. Cicero left his wife of thirty years to marry a much younger woman (probably for her dowry), whom he then rather promptly divorced. Cato the Younger divorced his wife to allow her to marry a childless friend, and re-married her after his friend's death.

that marriages were more fragile elsewhere. Both economic and social pressures discouraged divorce. For a man, divorce meant the loss of his wife's dowry. For a woman, it meant an end to respectability, a return to an often-hostile family, and the effective loss of her children. We have no statistics, but there can be little doubt that most Greeks and Romans remained married, for better or for worse, until death did them part.

· *15* ·

Were Relationships between Men and Boys Controversial?

*I*n 130 CE, the Roman Empire acquired a new god. Of itself, this was not remarkable; the Roman pantheon always had room for a late-blooming deity. Until his recent death, however, this particular god had been Antinous, Hadrian's adolescent lover. After he drowned in the Nile, the grieving emperor had decided—and the rest of the empire had diplomatically agreed—that Antinous was now one of the immortals. A previously unremarkable star was discovered to be the soul of the ascended youth, and loyal cities found reasons to commission a statue or two of his comely divinity. Cults and oracles of Antinous sprang up throughout the provinces. And on the banks of the Nile, Hadrian founded Antinoopolis, a city graced with grand avenues, a colossal temple of Antinous-Osiris, and sad-eyed portraits of the drowned boy.[1]

Greek and Roman men who had sexual relationships with boys were not considered perverts or child molesters. It was assumed that men were naturally attracted to both women and boys. As long as they confined their attentions to the right boys and conducted their relationships with them in the proper manner, their actions were neither punished nor criticized. Nor were boy-lovers considered homosexuals. In the classical world, a man's sexual identity was not defined by the objects of his desire, but by the role he took in sexual relations. Freeborn men were always supposed to assume an active, penetrative role in sex.*

---

* Ancient notions of masculinity were inseparable from sexual assertiveness: one ancient fable claimed that men who enjoyed being penetrated were created when Prometheus, in the process of molding mankind from clay, got drunk and mistakenly stuck male genitals on a batch of female bodies.

75

Figure 15.1. The deified Antinous, represented with attributes of Dionysus and Osiris. *Colossal statue now in the Vatican Museums. Author's photo*

Whether their partners were women or boys was comparatively unimportant, since both were socially inferior.[2]

Relations between men and boys were most visible in Classical Greece, where the practice of pederasty (literally, "boy loving") was open and widespread. Pederasty involved a mature male citizen—often in his twenties, sometimes older—and a citizen boy in his early to middle teens.* Though nominally, and to some degree actually, a means of mentoring youths and inducting them into adult society, pederasty was always founded on physical attraction, and on what we would call statutory rape.

The origins of pederasty are mysterious. Ancient authors speculated that it began as a population control measure, or possibly after the father of Oedipus took a fancy to the son of another mythical prince. Modern scholars have cited other factors, such as the exclusion of Greek women from the public sphere, traditions of male initiation rituals, and a desire to advertise aristocratic solidarity. Whatever the reasons for its rise, pederasty was practiced throughout Greece by the sixth century BCE. Customs varied from region to region. Relations between young men and boys were integrated into Sparta's famously ferocious military education.† The city of Thebes developed the Sacred Band, a highly respected regiment consisting of 150 pairs of lovers. We know most, however, about Athens, where pederasty was a hallmark of upper-class society.[3]

Athenian pederasty always flourished most amid the tight-knit clans and wine-soaked symposia of the aristocracy. Since the men and boys involved belonged to the city's best families, pederastic relationships were hedged about by conventions designed to protect both parties from dishonor. As we have seen, it was taken for granted that men were attracted to adolescent boys. It was also assumed that boys had only a mild sexual interest in adult men. Boys, in other words, had to be courted. They could not simply be given money, since this would imply that they were prostitutes. They had, instead, to be offered gifts that symbolized the man's affection, such as hares or fighting cocks. At least in theory, a boy was free to reject such advances.

---

* The usual age range seems to have been about twelve to eighteen—roughly from the beginning of puberty to its end. Boys were thought to be most attractive around the age of fourteen, when the first stubble sprouted on their cheeks.

† The Spartan addiction to buggery was a running joke in Athens, where anal sex was sometimes called "Spartan style."

A boy who chose to become his suitor's beloved would accompany him to social gatherings, be introduced to his network of friends and allies, and gain a first foothold in the world of civic politics. He would also, however, be expected to gratify the man sexually. If we can trust the evidence of vase paintings, a respectful lover would restrict himself to thrusting his penis between the boy's thighs, and thus avoid subjecting him to the disgrace of penetration. Most men, however, were probably less than respectful. Such relations continued until the boy reached maturity. Past that point, sex was shameful, since the man was now debasing a fellow citizen, and the boy refusing to assume his proper role as an independent and dominant adult.

Sexual relationships between citizen men and citizen boys were unthinkable in Roman society. Roman men were perfectly free, however, to sleep with slave boys. The practice was widespread among the elite, who paid enormous sums for handsome youths.* At banquets, these favorites were often the master's cupbearers; like Hadrian's Antinous, they accompanied him on journeys, sometimes wearing silk masks to protect their complexions.† Although later emperors outlawed the prostitution of slave boys, masters continued to sleep openly with young favorites well into late antiquity. Only after the Roman world became Christian were such relationships made illegal.[4]

A thousand years of boy-loving produced little direct criticism from contemporaries. Though mocked in comedies and condemned by a late work of Plato, pederasty seems to have been relatively uncontroversial in Classical Athens. Later, especially in intellectual circles influenced by the Stoics, moral condemnation was more widespread, though never to the point of significantly discouraging the practice. Greek authors of the Roman imperial era produced stylized debates contrasting the virtues of women and boys. In the longest of these, women came out on top, but only after a great deal of unrepentant rhapsodizing about the love of boys. Philosophically inclined Roman authors tended to be more dismissive, describing pederasty as unnatural or, at best, frivolous.

---

* Knowing that boys on the cusp of adolescence fetched the highest prices, slave traders smeared the faces of handsome youths with lamb testicle blood, which was thought to inhibit beard growth.

† As always, we hear most about the crimes of the emperors. Tiberius was rumored to have a whole troupe of slave boys trained to nibble him like minnows as he swam. Nero reportedly castrated an adolescent boy to make him resemble his dead wife.

Marcus Aurelius was grateful that he had the restraint to resist the charms of slave boys.[5]

Roman slaves, of course, had no choice but to submit to their masters. Greek boys, who had at least some agency, were assumed to enjoy and even to be honored by their lovers' attentions. Some youths really may have seen the men who courted them as role models or surrogate fathers: an Athenian graffito, apparently written by a boy, praises his lover's courage. We also hear, however, about boys resisting the advances of men. One handsome youth reportedly leapt into a cauldron of boiling water to escape a tyrant who wanted to sleep with him. And in at least one gymnasium, there was a formal ban on drunkards, madmen, and boy-lovers.[6]

Why Are So Many of
Their Statues Naked?

*W*e don't know his name. All we know is that he had a hammer, a chisel, and a mission: to obliterate every stone penis in sight. For centuries, the Greek city of Aphrodisias had been studded with nude statues and reliefs. Now, however, the Roman Empire was Christian, artistic nudity had become taboo, and the good people of Aphrodisias had resolved to sanitize their statuary. The workman they hired for the task paused to pulverize the perkier nipples among the female nudes. But it was penises he had come for. Some gods and heroes were castrated with a single well-aimed hammer blow. Others were unmanned by careful chisel work. None was spared.[1]

The nervousness about nudity that led the Aphrodisians to neuter their statues was almost unknown until late antiquity. For a millennium, the Greeks and Romans commissioned and displayed naked statues without fig leaves or misgivings. Thanks to imitation of this custom since the Renaissance, many of us share the Greco-Roman assumption that the nude form is an appropriate subject for artists. We tend to forget, however, how culturally specific this assumption is—and how exceptional the nudity of Greco-Roman sculpture really was.

It all started with the Greeks, who appreciated the naked male body like no civilization before or since. In part, this reflected the fact that Greek men spent an unusual amount of time unclothed; whenever they exercised, competed in athletic contests, or simply hung around the gymnasium, they did so in the buff. The reasons behind this custom are obscure. The Greeks seem to have thought that exercise was easier without clothes, and possibly safer.* Loincloths, however, are no real impediment to movement, and the competitors in some Greek sports—such as pankration, a brutal combination of boxing and wrestling that involved a great deal of kicking—would have been better served by protecting their genitals. Ultimately, nudity in the gymnasium and athletic contests may have been about equality. Naked men couldn't advertise wealth or status.[2]

Statues of naked men began to appear around the same time that nudity became standard in Greek athletics. Although the idealized bodies of these statues must have been modeled on gymnasium-toned athletes, they were never meant to be realistic.† Their nudity was intended to communicate something. The nature of the message varied with period, setting, and subject. Since most Classical Greek statues and reliefs either honored the gods or commemorated the dead, it used to be assumed that nudity in Greek art was a way of signaling that someone was (or was similar to) a god or hero. But scholars now think that nudity had a broader range of meanings, and was sometimes little more than a flourish. By the Hellenistic era, if not before, it was an artistic convention, used almost automatically in a variety of contexts.[3]

Since women were excluded from the world of gymnasium and stood outside the nexus of athleticism, politics, and war that dominated both public life and public sculpture, female nudes were a later development. There was a tradition of showing naked women—usually prostitutes—in Greek vase painting. But it was only at the end of the Classical period that the Aphrodite of Knidos, the first life-size female nude, was created. The model for this statue, which showed the goddess of love bathing, was the famous courtesan Phryne, a woman so beautiful that she was said to have once won a court case by exposing her breasts. Whatever the truth of that story, the Aphrodite was an immediate

---

* The custom of competing nude in athletic contests was sometimes said to have begun when a sprinter won the Olympic footrace after losing his loincloth. Another story claimed that a runner somehow tripped over his own loincloth and broke his neck. A third legend explained why trainers at the Olympic Games (who engaged in no physical activity) were unclothed. Supposedly, a widow once disguised herself as a trainer and followed her son to the Olympic Games. When discovered, she was spared the usual penalty—being hurled off the nearest cliff—but it was decreed that all trainers were to be naked henceforth.

†. Sometimes, however, life imitated art. Nikostratos of Argos, an eccentric Greek general, liked to advertise his strength and courage by going into battle dressed as Hercules: nude, with a lion skin over his shoulders.

One of the many Roman copies of the
Aphrodite of Knidos. *Restored second-century
statue, now in the Palazzo Altemps. Photo by
Marie-Lan Nguyen, Wikimedia Commons*

sensation,* firmly establishing female nudes in the repertoire of Greco-Roman sculpture.[4]

Nudity, male or female, had a very limited place in the life and art of the early Roman Republic. Initially, public nakedness of any kind seems to have been taboo: it was thought improper, for example, for a man to be seen unclothed even by his own son. Unsurprisingly, there was no native Roman tradition of nude sculpture. But once generals began to bring Greek masterpieces back from their conquests in the east, many members of the Roman elite became collectors and connoisseurs of Greek nudes. Soon, prominent Romans were commissioning nude statues of themselves.[†5]

Some elite Romans—including, for the first time, a few women—continued to order nude portrait statues under the empire. Most Roman nudes of the imperial era, however, were either copies of Greek masterpieces (which were churned out by the dozen for display in villas and gardens) or portraits of the emperors. These imperial statues evoked Greek representations of heroes and gods and impressively conveyed the emperor's superhuman power. Some were colossal in scale. Yet even the most awe-inspiring were distinguished, like all respectable Greco-Roman nudes, by undersized penises.

We have no reason to think that ancient men were less well-endowed than their modern counterparts.[‡] In classical art, however, only slaves, barbarians, and a scattering of mythological figures were shown with large penises. There were several reasons for such disproportionate disproportioning. First, male nudity in Greek sculpture, as we have seen, was tied to the world of the gymnasium. The artistic ideal was always the adolescent athlete, represented as he would look during or just after hard exercise. A vigorous workout—and especially a vigorous workout

---

* The statue, housed among gardens in a small temple, became a famous tourist attraction. One young man was said to have been so entranced by its beauty that he made illicit love to the statue, leaving a discolored spot that the custodians could never quite scrub away.

† Roman nudes differed from their Greek models, however, in two respects. The heads tended to be realistic, in sometimes jarring contrast to their youthful and idealized bodies. And they often managed to stop just short of full nudity by being depicted with a mantle strategically covered the genitals.

‡ Nor were they shy about their penises. Members of one Athenian street gang called themselves the Ithyphalloi—that is, "the erect penises." A less literal translation might be "the dauntless dicks."

vigorously conducted in the nude—causes the penis and testicles to retract. After a long run or wrestling match, a nude athlete's genitals would be diminished appreciably. This fact doubtless helped to establish the artistic convention.[6]

Undersized genitals, however, were always a stylization of reality, intended to communicate something about the man from whom they so tentatively protruded. Above all, a diminutive and pointedly unpointed penis advertised self-control.* In Greek vase paintings and the occasional sculpture, this message was emphasized by showing men whose members were fitted with a "dog leash"—a string tied to pull the foreskin over the head of the penis and curl back the shaft. Although athletes sometimes may have corralled their genitals in this way while exercising, the "dog leash" was emphasized in art as a message about less literal forms of self-restraint.[†7]

The antitheses of the neatly genitalled gentlemen who populate Greek and Roman art were well-hung barbarians and monsters—men and beasts defined by their lack of self-control. The most spectacular penises in classical art, however, belonged to gods. In Classical Greece, the phallic god par excellence was Dionysus, responsible for wine and vegetation (among other things). In processions honoring Dionysus, this association with fertility was emblematized by enormous wooden phalluses, which were carried on wagons or by teams of men. The largest on record was a whopping 180 feet long.[‡] Later, Dionysus was joined by his massively membered son Priapus. Never an important deity, Priapus was basically an X-rated lawn gnome, whose statuettes were stationed in gardens to frighten birds and baffle thieves.[8]

---

* In sculpture, as in life, a civilized penis was also an uncircumcised penis. Although circumcision was practiced in Egypt and parts of the Middle East through much of classical history, the Greeks and Romans regarded it as a disgusting mutilation of the human form. One Roman doctor went so far as to say that circumcision was permissible only if the foreskin was dropping off due to gangrene. The emperor Hadrian, considering it tantamount to castration, made circumcision a crime punishable by death. The stigma was so strong that Jews who wanted to use the local gymnasium or baths sometimes underwent a reverse circumcision procedure known as epispasm, which was even less pleasant than it sounds.

† The "dog leash" was exclusively Greek. The Romans preferred infibulation, a minor surgery that involved stringing thread (and later a ring) through perforations in the foreskin to conceal the head of the penis. This procedure seems to have been suffered primarily by adolescents (to keep them from masturbating), by singers (to keep their voices higher), and by slaves (to give them a suitably decorous appearance when they attended their masters in the baths).

‡ One wonders how it managed corners.

In keeping with their role as fertility symbols, sculpted or painted phalluses were regarded as good luck charms. Crude statues of Hermes with prominent penises stood on roadsides and beside the doors of many houses in Classical Athens. Roman children wore phallic amulets to ward off evil. And beneath the chariot of every triumphing Roman general swung a sacred phallus, loaned by (of all people) the Vestal Virgins. Whether good luck charms or barometers of temperance, sculpted penises were an integral part of classical cityscapes. Only gradually, as Christianity changed attitudes toward nudity, did all this marbled meat begin to seem unpalatable.

III

BELIEFS

· 17 ·

Did They Believe Their Myths?

According to reputable authors, Zeus had sex with two of his sisters, at least a half dozen of his aunts, 115 mortal women, nymphs uncounted, and Mother Earth herself (who was also his grandmother). He transformed one of his lovers into a cow, accidentally melted another, and quite deliberately ate a third. In the rare moments between affairs, he was a rather absentminded ruler of the universe, prone to squabbling with other gods, smiting hapless mortals, and getting hamstrung by monsters. Did the Greeks and Romans really think that their supreme deity acted this way?

To understand the significance of the myths, we have to begin with the nature of Greco-Roman religion. Virtually all Greeks and Romans accepted that the gods existed and that they were interested in the affairs of mankind. Although philosophically minded members of the elite speculated on the existence of a single supreme god or divine principle, most agreed that there were many gods. Of these, the twelve (or so) "Olympians"—the anarchic heavenly family headed by Zeus/ Jupiter—were generally acknowledged to be the greatest.* But it was assumed that there were countless other divinities, ranging from minor demons to the awesome mother-goddesses Cybele and Isis.[1]

Greek and Roman religious practice was local, traditional, and this-worldly. Although belief in the gods was expected, it was assumed

---

* The Greeks and Romans usually assumed that their gods were worshipped by all peoples, albeit under different names. One myth, for example, claimed that the Egyptian deities were animal-headed because the Greek gods had fled to Egypt and disguised themselves as animals to escape the terrible monster Typhoeus. Some Greeks speculated that the Jewish God was really Dionysus.

The twelve Olympian gods. From left to right: Hestia, Hermes, Aphrodite, Ares, Demeter, Hephaestus, Hera, Poseidon, Athena, Zeus, Artemis, and Apollo. Each of the gods is shown with his or her attributes. Hera, for example, carries a scepter, Poseidon has his trident, and Zeus wields his thunderbolt. *Roman-era relief from Tarentum representing the procession of the Olympians, now in the Walters Art Museum. Public domain*

that what you thought about the gods mattered much less than what you did for them. The gods were not in the habit of reading the minds or scanning the souls of their worshippers. But they demanded honor in return for their gifts; and the most effective way mortals could show them honor was by offering sacrifice.

Individuals sacrificed to the gods on their own behalf, offering anything from humble honey cakes to cows. They also took part in communal sacrifices, at which dozens or even hundreds of animals might be killed for the general welfare. These scrupulously performed rituals were always the heart of classical religion. Neither the Greeks nor the Romans ever developed a canon of sacred texts, caste of priests, or code of moral rules. Neither, in fact, had a truly cohesive religion at all, since every city and village treasured its own traditions of honoring the gods. This teeming variety was balanced by a few commonalities: a shared pantheon centered on the Olympians, some famous sanctuaries and oracles, and the vast and amorphous collection of stories about the gods that we call the myths.

The *Iliad* and *Odyssey*, the first works of Greek literature, were composed in the eighth century BCE. By then, all the familiar figures of Greek myth had appeared: a pantheon of gods headed by Zeus, a nebulous galaxy of lesser divinities, and a gaggle of mortal but super-human heroes. Classical Greek authors speculated that the myths had taken place about a thousand years before their own time—between

1500 and 1200 BCE by our reckoning. It was understood, however, that the mythic past was qualitatively different from the present: men had been taller and stronger, fearsome monsters had roamed the wilderness, and gods had mingled more freely with humanity (in more ways than one).[2]

Culturally, Greek myths had many functions. Some explained natural phenomena. Others described the origins of religious rituals. Still others validated social institutions, advanced territorial claims, or endorsed ethical principles. But few myths had any single purpose. Most were nothing more and nothing less than stories—deeply familiar and almost infinitely elastic, told and retold, interpreted and reinterpreted. Although literary accounts of certain myths became highly prestigious, no version was ever definitive.

So did the Greeks and Romans believe their myths? As might be expected, there is no simple answer. We are almost completely ignorant about what the illiterate majority thought. Members of the elite, at least, tended to assume that the masses took the myths literally. One author, a professional dream interpreter, observed that most people believed the stories about the gods and heroes and so tended to dream about them. Another author claimed that the peasants around his home imagined Agamemnon, the mythical Greek war leader at Troy, to be the current Roman emperor.* If nothing else, the myths certainly shaped how the gods were imagined and may—in their presentation of the gods as familiar and accessible—have had genuine popular appeal.[3]

Elite opinions about the myths are better attested. Most educated Greeks and Romans accepted that the gods existed, endorsed the performance of traditional religious rituals, and were familiar with the canonical tales. But as early as the sixth century BCE, some Greek philosophers and public intellectuals began to criticize the traditional stories. A few of the more radical thinkers of the Classical period theorized that the myths were half-forgotten episodes from ancient history, and that the gods were misremembered human kings. Others speculated that the gods and the myths had been invented in the distant past as a means of political control. Plato thought the myths subversive and unsuitable for children; Aristotle dismissed them as an opiate of the masses. Later philosophers were equally critical. The Epicureans

---

* The epitaph of one Roman centurion laconically notes that he saw "naked nymphs." It is hard to say how mythological these particular nymphs were.

rejected the myths as products of human ignorance and fear. Their Stoic rivals reinterpreted the myths as allegories.*[4]

Early in their history, the Romans had assimilated their gods and myths to those of the Greeks. The Roman elite, however, seem to have regarded knowledge of Greek myth as basically a matter of cultural literacy. Many sympathized with the prevailing philosophical approaches to myth. In his *Meditations*, for example, the Stoic Marcus Aurelius allegorized the gods, identifying Zeus with nature. His contemporary, the satirist Lucian, wrote several treatises poking fun at the myths, including one in which the horrified gods watch an Epicurean philosopher demonstrate their nonexistence.[5]

Whatever their philosophical leanings, educated Greeks and Romans of the imperial era tended to combine a sincere belief in the gods with distaste for the amorality of the myths. An increasingly popular compromise was to blame the myths on demons. Demons, minor spirits that wandered the skies, had long been a feature of popular religion. But they became more prominent under the empire, when Platonic philosophers began to emphasize their importance as intermediaries between humanity and the gods. Many members of the elite came to believe that the gods of myth were actually demons—some evil, some merely mischievous—who had bedeviled mankind in the distant past.[6]

Allegories deepened and demons multiplied in late antique interpretations of myth. Neoplatonism, the era's dominant philosophical school, theorized many levels of demons (including the Olympian gods) between mankind and an ineffable supreme being. On these terms, the myths tended to be understood as elaborate allegories. One philosopher even wrote a sort of pagan catechism, in which he insisted that the traditional myths were divine, because they presented the gods and their gifts to humanity. But they could not, he hastened to add, be taken literally.[7]

Early Christian authors borrowed pagan strategies for attacking the myths. Some developed the argument that the gods of myth were demons, claiming that these spirits had been sent by Satan to lead mankind away from the truth. Other authors revived the rationalizing claim that the gods and myths represented dim memories of ancient human

---

* These allegories were often based on etymology. It was pointed out, for example, that the name of the war god Ares sounded rather like the Greek word for "harm." All sorts of enthusiastic philosophizing ensued.

kings. Still others simply urged fellow Christians to read the myths as literature and focus on their moral lessons.[8]

It might be helpful to close with a related question: did the Greeks and Romans think that the gods actually lived on Mount Olympus?

Olympus—at 9,570 feet, the highest peak in Greece—was closely associated with the gods. But the mountain was always a metaphor—sometimes described as a physical place, sometimes used as a synonym for the sky. This dual conception of Olympus, already present in Homer, persisted throughout Greek (and eventually Latin) literature.[9]

Most members of the educated elite assumed that the gods were everywhere, nowhere, or very far away.* Olympus, however, continued to be regarded as a special place. Around 300 BCE, an altar was established on one of the mountain's lower peaks. Here, for nearly a millennium, worshippers sacrificed to Zeus about a mile from the summit. From that distance, it would have been clear that there were no gilded palaces or sunbathing deities on top. Descriptions of the altar, however, emphasized the otherworldliness of the setting—wind and rain, we are told, never touched it—and suggest that at least some Greeks and Romans continued to imagine a divine presence on the sacred mountain.[10]

Like every other aspect of Greco-Roman myth, the idea that the gods were physically present on Olympus was doubted, disputed, and dutifully referenced in art and literature for centuries. In all probability, few believed that it was literal truth. But many, perhaps most, thought that it shed some light, however faint, on the nature of the divine. The gods, after all, were hard to know, and the myths had so much to say.

---

* Each philosophical sect had its own ideas on the subject. The Stoics claimed that the divine principle was implicit in all things. The Platonists scattered the gods among the stars. The Epicureans assigned them a blissful realm far from the troubled world of mankind or denied their physical existence altogether.

Did They Believe in Ghosts, Monsters, and/or Aliens?

*O*nce upon a time, a philosopher rented a haunted house. He had practical reasons (the rent was quite reasonable). But he also had something to prove. This philosopher, you see, did not believe in ghosts. In his very learned opinion, the dead were dead, and claims to the contrary were utter and unutterable hogwash. A man of wit and discernment (as he surely was) had nothing to fear but fear itself. So one sunny afternoon, he entered his new house, unfolded his writing desk in a dusty room, and began composing a treatise fiendishly subtle enough to keep his mind from inventing any terrors. Soon, as planned, he was absorbed in his work.

Shadows gathered in quiet corners. In dusky groves, the first night birds called. At length the philosopher, finding the desk before him almost invisible, stirred from his reverie to light a lamp. And then, just as he was slipping back into the tranquil sea of thought, he fancied that he heard something in the distance—a rasping sound, like iron on stone. Shaking his head, he returned to work.

The lamp on his desk shone cheerily, and his pen scratched with its familiar sound over the dimpled parchment. What a fool he had been to imagine—Wait! There it was again! The noise, closer. Now it was unmistakable: chains, vast vermiculate coils of chains, hissing and slithering over the floor of the adjacent hall. Hand atremble, pen skittering over the page, he continued to write. For a moment, all was quiet. Then the chains clanked again. This time, they were inside the room.

Slowly, the philosopher set down his pen. Deliberately, he raised his head. And before him, as he had known he would, he saw a ghost. It was an apparition in the shape of an old man, translucent, with

Skeletons in the underworld. *Nineteenth-century reproduction of one of the Boscoreale Cups, now in the Wellcome Collection. Public domain*

phantasmal fetters trailing from its hands and feet. The spirit regarded the philosopher with fathomless eyes. Then, raising a wispy arm, it beckoned and began to withdraw from the room. After a brief hesitation, the philosopher followed.

The ghost glided down the hall, glowing as it crossed puddles of moonlight. At the hall's end, in a courtyard where dead trees clutched at the sky, the phantom stopped. For a moment it stood still, stars shining through its head. Then, without warning, it disappeared.

The next day, the philosopher ordered the courtyard where the ghost had vanished to be taken up. Beneath the flagstones, in a tangle of rusty chains, the workmen discovered a skeleton. The bones were honorably buried, the ghost was never seen again, and the philosopher lived happily ever after in his low-rent apartment. Or so the story goes.[1]

Some philosophers denied the immortality of the soul. Others believed in reincarnation or in the final union of all mortals with their creator. The majority of Greeks and Romans, however, thought that the dead resided in caverns beneath the earth. Although there was no single or simple conception of this underworld, most authors divided it into zones of punishment and reward, gathering the souls of the righteous into blissful Elysium and condemning the wicked to the pit of Tartarus.* As always in matters of myth, however, we have little sense of how much was believed, or by how many.

It is clear, in any case, that the spirits of the departed were not thought to be completely severed from the land of the living. Both the Greeks and Romans assumed that the dead were able to appreciate offerings left at their tombs and that it was prudent to keep them happy. The Greeks believed that some souls possessed the power to bless or blight whole communities and had to be placated with special sacrifices. The Romans focused more on gaining the favor of the departed, leaving them offerings in household shrines and praying for their blessings during personal and national crises.

Not all spirits, however, could be appeased. Some, unable or unwilling to cross over to the afterlife, roamed the earth as malevolent ghosts. The souls of those who died young remained among the living, embittered by their untimely ends. Those who perished violently often lingered to wreak vengeance on their killers.† Executed criminals and suicides lurked at the scenes of their demise. And the shades of the unburied, barred from entering Hades, wandered until they received funeral rites.‡

Some ghosts looked like pale echoes of their living selves. Others were jet black, charred by their funeral pyres. Still others were animated skeletons. Though usually wraithlike, ghosts could be substantial

---

* In the *Odyssey*, which provides our oldest description of the Greek underworld, only a few exceptional souls are rewarded or punished. The idea that every soul was posthumously judged seems to have emerged later, possibly under the influence of Egyptian religion.

†.   Murderers occasionally took the precaution of hacking off victims' limbs to cripple their ghosts.

‡.   If a body could not be recovered—as, for example, when someone died at sea—a cenotaph (empty tomb) was constructed, and the name of the dead was called three times to summon the wandering soul into it.

enough to touch, fight, or—in at least one case—make passionate love to.* They tended to be hostile to the living.† Some merely frightened those they encountered. More malevolent shades induced fits of epilepsy in their victims, beat them up in the middle of the night, whispered to them until they committed suicide, or just tore them to pieces.‡ It was thus wise to avoid places where ghosts were found.[2]

Those who perished violently haunted the places of their deaths, sometimes for an unconscionably long time. One bathhouse was troubled by phantoms for centuries after a young man was murdered there, and Greek and Persian spirits were still clashing nightly at Marathon seven hundred years after the great battle. Ghosts could also be found in cemeteries. One late antique author tells the story of a man who broke into a tomb: just as he finished stripping the valuables, the corpse sat up and clawed out the robber's eyes. The graves of evil men were especially dangerous: venomous snakes, it was said, spawned from the bones of the wicked. On moonless nights, restless spirits converged at crossroads, which were sacred to the dread goddess Hecate. Travelers who heard wails in the distance prayed that they belonged to watchdogs, not to the murderous spirits in Hecate's train.[3]

Despite their hostility, ghosts had their uses. With a bit of magical coaxing, vengeful spirits could be unleashed on enemies and rivals.§ Less malicious ghosts might be summoned to learn the future. It was easiest to call such spirits at the smoking pools and clammy caves that

---

* A young man was staying as a guest in a strange city. Late one night, a beautiful woman he had never seen before appeared in his room, whispered that she needed him, and slipped into his bed. The man didn't ask any questions. The woman came the following night and the night after; each time she appeared, they made love. This went on for some time, until the mistress of the house became aware of their meetings. When she saw a ring and breast band that the mysterious woman had left behind, she began to weep. These tokens, she told the astonished young man, had belonged to her daughter, who had been dead for six months. The next night, the mistress and her husband lay in wait for the ghost, but when they confronted their daughter, she fell to the floor—a rotting corpse.

† Some ghosts were merely indifferent. In the early third century, the ghost of Alexander the Great supposedly appeared on the Roman frontier, proceeded across two provinces, and vanished after performing a mysterious ritual. Throughout, by all accounts, the ghost and its attendants were perfect gentlemen and caused no harm to anyone.

‡ According to one gruesome story, the ghost of Achilles—said to reside on an islet in the Black Sea—once asked a passing merchant to bring a woman with Trojan blood to his island. When the merchant obliged, the ghost thanked him and promptly dismembered the woman.

§ Those who suspected that they were being subjected to spectral attack might resort to a variety of ghostbusting measures: clinking bronze or iron, making protective signs with their hands, uttering exotic charms (those in Egyptian were said to be especially effective), or attempting to trap the troublesome spirit in a clay doll.

served as entrances to the underworld. A few of these portals acquired full-fledged oracles, where suppliants could commune with the dead in their dreams. A more convenient means of contacting the departed involved the ancient equivalent of the Ouija board.*[4]

A few Greeks and Romans were skeptical about specters. The philosopher Democritus, who theorized that all things were composed of the invisible particles he dubbed "atoms," actually moved into a tomb to investigate the material composition of ghosts. Nearly a millennium later, Saint Augustine wrote a shrewd explanation of how people might imagine that they saw the images of departed loved ones, comparing such apparitions to waking dreams. As far as we can tell, however, most had little doubt that the spirits of the dead moved among them.[5]

The Greeks and Romans were also ready to accept the existence of strange and wondrous animals, particularly if these creatures lived in distant places. The historian Herodotus—to use a famous example—claimed that the highlands of northern India were infested with dog-sized ants. As they tunneled, these creatures excavated vast quantities of gold, which they piled in glittering heaps around their nests. During the hottest part of the day, when the ants were underground, men gathered all the gold they could, stuffed it into sacks, and galloped off on fast camels. They had good reason to hurry, since the ants were incredibly swift and more than capable of tearing treasure hunters to shreds.†[6]

There were stranger things than oversized ants in other corners of the Greco-Roman world. Take, for example, the basilisk, a Libyan serpent so venomous that its breath withered trees and split stones.‡ Or consider the catoblepas, a horse-sized creature whose head was almost always turned to the ground—which was fortunate, since anyone who caught its eyes was instantly killed. A single catoblepas, it was said, once decimated an entire troop of Roman soldiers with its malevolent gaze.

---

* The usual setup was a circular metal dish, whose rim was engraved with the letters of the alphabet. A ring suspended from a fine linen thread was held over the dish and made to swing. As it crossed back and forth over the letters on the rim, it would, with the proper incantations and some creative interpretation, spell out words. An ancient scholar claimed to have discovered the native city of Homer (a matter hotly disputed among literati) by this method.

† Herodotus's description of the gold-digging ants was probably inspired by stories of Himalayan marmots, whose deep burrows sometimes turn up gold dust.

‡ One Greek temple purchased (what was marketed as) a basilisk skin, hoping that its poisonous aura would keep birds and spiders away from a valuable mural.

Even the catoblepas paled beside the inimitable Fanged Tyrant, a Brob-
dingnagian beast that reared from Indian rivers to devour elephants
whole.*[7]

Monsters were also fixtures of Greek and Roman folklore. Were-
wolves crop up particularly often. The most famous ancient werewolf
story, which appears in a Roman novel, begins with the narrator walking down a moonlit road with a stranger. The stranger stops suddenly
beside a roadside tomb, removes his clothes, and transforms into a
wolf. The terrified narrator runs to his lover's house, where he learns
that the slaves have just chased off a savage beast, wounding it in the
neck. The next day, he finds the stranger lying in bed, his neck being
bandaged by a doctor. There was even a festival in a remote region
of Greece said to feature the sacrificial transformation of a man into
a wolf (as long as he didn't taste human flesh, he would change back
after nine years).[8]

Vampires made occasional appearances in ancient literature. In
one vivid tale, a student was seduced by a vampire that had taken the
form of a beautiful woman. The creature enchanted its victim, coaxing
him each night into a mansion filled with phantom servants. Finally, on
the day he was to marry the vampire, the student brought his teacher
to meet the bride-to-be. The teacher, sensing the truth, compelled
the vampire to reveal its true nature. It fled with a flash of scales and
teeth. The Greeks and Romans also told stories about the vast serpents
they called dragons. The most notorious of these, encountered by the
Roman general Regulus in North Africa, crushed and devoured many
men, javelins bouncing harmlessly from its armored sides, before finally
being defeated by a catapult barrage. Its skin, sent back to Rome, was
reportedly 120 feet long.[9]

The most prominent Greek and Roman monsters were the creatures of myth. The myths themselves, as we have seen, were always
subject to criticism. But many ancient authors were ready to believe
that mythical beasts had basis in fact. There were several accounts, for
example, of encounters with satyrs, manlike creatures with hooves and
hyperactive libidos. A satyr was reportedly captured alive and brought
before the Roman general Sulla, who attempted to question it through

---

* Tales of the basilisk may have been inspired by the Egyptian cobra. The catoblepas likely
originated in reports of the gnu (wildebeest), which has a heavy, downward-drooping head.
The Fanged Tyrant (which managed to acquire three horns in medieval bestiaries) was probably an embellished saltwater crocodile.

interpreters. Satyrs were also said to inhabit the Canary Islands. Once, we are told, a ship blown ashore there was swarmed by a troop of satyrs, and the sailors were able to escape only through the less-than-gallant gesture of throwing a woman overboard to distract them. More civilized satyrs could be found in the depths of the Egyptian desert. Saint Anthony encountered one in a secluded valley that offered him fruit, spoke passable Greek, and professed itself a Christian.*[10]

Tritons and Nereids (mermen and mermaids) were sighted almost as frequently as satyrs. A Spanish Triton was in the habit of boarding ships at night and lounging on deck, sometimes sinking small vessels with his weight.† Centaurs, likewise, were periodically seen in the wilds of the classical world. One centaur, captured alive in the Arabian mountains, was sent to the Roman governor of Egypt. Unfortunately, and despite being given all the meat it desired, the creature died along the way. The embalmed remains were forwarded to the emperor, and they could be visited for centuries in a palace storehouse.[11]

Fossils were interpreted as the remains of characters and creatures from myth.‡ Some were thought to be human. The Spartans, for example, mistook the bones of a large Ice Age mammal for those of the hero Orestes and gave them a formal burial. In Crete, an enormous skeleton (perhaps of a whale) revealed by an earthquake was identified as the giant Orion. And when another earthquake disclosed the bones of a mammoth in what is now Turkey, the locals—reluctant to disturb what they assumed to be the remains of an ancient hero—sent a single foot-long molar to the Roman emperor. The emperor, intrigued, commissioned a plaster model of a head proportionate to the enormous tooth. Other fossils were recognized as the remains of monsters from famous myths. A Greek temple proudly displayed the tusks of the gargantuan Calydonian Boar. A Roman temple likewise gloried in the bones of a

---

* A few dog-headed men, though cannibalistic and otherwise uncouth, also accepted Christianity. Two served as bodyguards to the Egyptian Saint Mercurius. Another dog-headed convert, Christopher, had a long and illustrious career (sans dog head) as the patron saint of travelers.

† A pickled Triton could be viewed in one Greek temple. It was, we are told, rather scalier than one might expect a merman to be. It was also missing its head, since the locals had reportedly secured their specimen by getting it drunk and decapitating it. The Triton became such a popular tourist attraction that it appeared (with head attached) on local coins.

‡ Sometimes fossils even shaped myths: the skulls of mammoths, with their single eye hole, may lie behind the mythical cyclops.

creature forty feet long, said to be the remains of the sea monster Poseidon sent to devour Andromeda.[12]

Many Greeks and Romans were ready to accept that strange beasts existed on the margins of the unknown. Even Herodotus's gold-digging ants seemed credible: a few of their skins (which looked suspiciously like panther hides) graced Alexander the Great's camp, and a majestic pair of ant antlers could be visited in a Roman temple. Not all reports of fantastic animals, however, were accepted. One author acknowledged that some skeptical readers might be unwilling to believe that a Greek island had been terrorized by a winged pig. Another mocked the credulity of those who thought that a man could transform into a wolf. Some monsters were even attacked on scientific grounds. Galen, for example, pointed out that half-human creatures like centaurs were physically impossible, since the human and animal parts would require different foods and were otherwise ill-suited to cohabitation. It was a pity, another ancient scholar concluded, that real wonders were so often cloaked in lies.[13]

The ancient willingness to give mythical monsters the benefit of the doubt did not extend to extraterrestrials. Modern enthusiasts have occasionally claimed that the Greeks and Romans unwittingly observed UFOs. The Greeks and Romans themselves, however, had no conception of intelligent life among the stars. The realms beyond the moon's orbit were thought to be perfect and changeless, the dwelling places of gods and demons. Some philosophers thought that the stars themselves were gods, and popular belief concurred to the degree that the appearance of a new star could be accepted as the advent of a divinity.* But the star gods never descended to Earth.[14]

The planets were also associated with individual gods who were sometimes said to dwell on them. No ancient author, however, assumed that the gods had mortal company in their cosmic abodes.† Only the

---

* The brilliant comet that appeared shortly after the death of Julius Caesar was taken as a sign that the dictator had become a god. A gilded image of the comet graced the pediment of Caesar's temple in the Roman Forum.

† Some philosophers thought that there were many more planets than the canonical seven (sun, moon, Mercury, Venus, Mars, Jupiter, Saturn). There was, however, no sustained speculation about the inhabitants of these superfluous satellites.

moon, the threshold of eternity, was inhabited by lesser beings; for it was on the moon—some philosophers claimed—that the souls of the newly dead gathered. There they remained for centuries, being purified by the light of the sun. And thence they fell back to Earth, to be reborn—or to linger as ghosts.[15]

Did They Practice Magic?

$\mathcal{T}$he soul refused to cooperate. Wavering, struggling, it flickered at the glade's edge, unwilling to be fleshed. But the witch had no time for the whims of the dead. With a muttered incantation, she dragged the reluctant spirit into the corpse at her feet. At once, the dead man's eyes snapped open. The lips parted. And with a sign of distended tissue, the thing lurched upright. Facing her puppet, the witch commanded the soul within to reveal the outcome of the war ravaging the Roman world. It obeyed, voice catching on rotted vocal cords. When the spirit had uttered its prophecy, the witch motioned the corpse to a waiting pyre. It laid itself down and watched with milky eyes as the wood was kindled. Flames began to lick and bite. The stiffened limbs convulsed. The jaw unhinged in a silent scream, and—the magical bond snapped. A slow fall of ash settled on the quiet glade.[1]

This scene comes from the *Pharsalia*, a Latin epic notable for its rhetorical style and general indifference to good taste.* For all its luridness, the poem reflects widespread anxieties surrounding magicians and magic in the classical world. The Greeks and Romans tended to use "magic" as a blanket term for ritual practices they regarded as illegitimate or dangerous. As a result, classical authors generally found it easier to describe what magic wasn't than to define what it was. They agreed, however, on a few key points. First, magic was secret and secretive, founded on hidden knowledge and clandestine practice. Second, magic was deployed by and for individuals, without the sanction of state

---

* At one point, for example, the author devotes several hundred lines to a gruesome snake attack, during which victims shoot geysers of blood, dissolve into goo, and are impaled by flying serpents.

or society. Finally, magic was at least potentially aggressive and subversive. Magic, in short, had a bad reputation. Yet despite philosophical skepticism—both Plato and Marcus Aurelius thought magicians were frauds—the effectiveness of magical practices was almost universally accepted.[2]

Many Greeks and Romans wore charmed amulets to protect themselves from plague, possession, and other predicaments.* Not until late antiquity, however, could any class of magician be called socially respectable.† Most Greek and Roman magicians operated on the margins of society.‡ The most visible were the street conjurers who worked wonders for appreciative crowds. Some of these men contented themselves with snake charming and shadow puppets. More ambitious performers summoned demons, turned their beards red, and made statues smile.§ Many wonder workers had a lucrative sideline in divination. One method of scrying the future was to summon (conveniently invisible) ghosts. Others involved watching oil spread over water, gazing intently at the flickering flame of an oil lamp, and staring into the depths of a mirror. Since boys were thought to be particularly susceptible to spiritual emanations (and were, one imagines, good at winning tips from a crowd), magicians often employed a young assistant to help interpret the omens.[3]

Other magical practices were aggressive. Unscrupulous magicians were sometimes recruited to prepare poisons. They were more

---

* Some amulets were fashioned from gemstones that were thought to have beneficial properties (amethyst, for example, supposedly delayed the onset of drunkenness). Artisans engraved short messages into the stones to enhance the intended effect; amulets intended to quell heartburn were inscribed "Digest! Digest! Digest!" Other amulets incorporated animal parts (snake heads, crocodile teeth, etc.) or spells written on miniature scrolls. One example contained an entire short story written on silver foil, which described Artemis's defeat of the headache demoness Antaura.

† Late antiquity witnessed the advent of the philosophical magic known as theurgy. The rituals of theurgy were intended to facilitate a mystical union between a philosopher's mind and the supreme deity. Theurgists insisted that—unlike magicians—they were not attempting to bend the gods and the universe to their will; instead, they were allowing the gods and the universe to work through them. In practice, however, theurgists were not above the tricks of street magicians. The arch-theurgist Iamblichus, for example, once summoned demons from the hot springs by which he was lounging.

‡ Although many magicians were male, the stereotypical magic worker in ancient literature was an old woman. The witches of Thessaly, in northern Greece, were said to be powerful enough to draw the moon down from the heavens—or, less ambitiously, to transform passing travelers into animals.

§ The leader of a Roman slave revolt, who had been trained to perform such marvels, liked to astonish his followers by breathing fire.

commonly called upon, however, to produce curse tablets. Most curse tablets were thin sheets of lead, inscribed with spells condemning enemies or competitors to some combination of blindness, broken limbs, impotence, poverty, public humiliation, and gruesome death. Once crafted to sadistic perfection, the lead sheet was rolled up and slipped into a tomb, hot spring, or some other place near and dear to restless spirits. Curse tablets were frequently accompanied by the classical equivalent of voodoo dolls, small figurines (ideally containing the hair or nail clippings of the intended victim) that were twisted, mutilated, and impaled in inventive ways. The threat posed by these implements of black magic was taken very seriously. A Roman prince was thought to have been killed by curse tablets hidden in the walls and floor of his house. Centuries later, an orator beset by blinding headaches was horrified to discover a voodoo doll—made, eccentrically, from a decapitated lizard—hidden in his classroom.[4]

All magic, whatever its purpose, could be conceptualized as sympathetic or demonic. Sympathetic magic drew on the natural affinities and antipathies that were assumed to exist between all substances. Voodoo dolls, for example, "worked" because they resembled the intended victim, and were most effective when the correspondence could be strengthened with hair or nails.* Healing magic, likewise, was often sympathetic. One Roman author claimed that a broken bone could be mended by slowly uniting the halves of a cut reed while speaking a magic charm and then touching the joined pieces to the fracture.

The most spectacular magic, however, was demonic. Demons were spirits of the air, immortal or nearly so, who functioned as intermediaries between the gods and mankind. The lowliest and most accessible demons were ghosts. Others, more exalted and difficult to summon, were primeval spirits. At least in Roman Egypt, a few of these greater demons—Typhon, Abraxas, the Headless One—were closely associated with magic, and frequently invoked in spells. The grandest of all demons were the pagan gods themselves, whom late antique thought

---

* It was sometimes thought that full-sized statues could become the magical doppelgangers of living people. This belief was especially prevalent in early medieval Constantinople, which was awash in antique statuary. One Byzantine emperor attempted to cure his impotence by having shiny new genitals welded onto the bronze boar he regarded as his doppelganger.

identified as servants and agents of an ineffable supreme deity.* All demons, however powerful, were invisible and insubstantial, sustained by the smoke of sacrifices and the breath of mortal creatures. They could assume any shape they wished: a human, a satyr, an enormous dog, even one of the gods. Some demons were good, others morally neutral. But the humbler a demon was, the likelier it was to be mischievous or wicked. Any magician who failed to take the proper precautions (charmed amulets, aromatic herbs, tinkling bells) ran the risk of being possessed or killed. For all their dangers, however, demons were supremely useful. They attacked enemies, seduced lovers, foretold the future, and—if summoned with a binding spell—served as assistants in all matters magical.[5]

With or without demonic assistance, the practice of magic was founded on knowledge. Any magician worth his salt had a healthy stock of spells (memorized or scrawled on papyri) for preventing hail, attacking enemies, and everything between. Though typically declaimed in Greek or Latin, most spells incorporated at least a few unintelligible and mysterious-sounding phrases. Some of these were mangled bits of Egyptian or Hebrew; others—like the famous "abracadabra"—were pure polysyllabic gibberish.† Occasionally, speaking the words was insufficient; one spell stipulated that the magician write a mystical name on the leaf of a certain tree and then lick it off.[6]

Besides sacred words, magicians had to know the properties of magical substances. Herbs and other plants were important, particularly for healing. Various spells called for surprising bits of animals—including, if we may believe one Roman poet, wolf beard and snake teeth—and exotic spices, which both helped to create a suitably evocative atmosphere and masked the stench of the other ingredients. Black magic often required materials linked with death: the blood and hair of murder victims, nails from sunken ships, or bits of used crucifix. Whole corpses were also useful; one spell involved attaching a scroll to the body of a freshly executed criminal.[7]

---

* Adventurous magicians could even summon Cronus from his underworld prison; those who attempted this, however, were advised to wear a protective boar bone amulet, lest they be murdered by that irascible titan.

† Some of the more theatrical sorcerers may (in the company of impressionable clients, at least) have addressed ghosts in the language of the dead, which appears to have consisted of shrieks and groans.

Even if no corpses were involved, casting a spell was often a lengthy and complex process. A spell for winning a lover, for example, entailed going to a gladiatorial arena in the dead of night, invoking the souls of those who had died there, and gathering bloodstained sand to sift over the prospective paramour's threshold. Summoning a demon assistant was even more convoluted. First—according to one of the several spells designated for this purpose—it was necessary to sculpt a small wax figurine of the demon. After presenting the figurine with a series of ritual offerings, one strangled seven birds in front of it, so that the demon could savor their life force. At length, having throttled additional birds (and eaten one of them raw), the traumatized magician uttered three ritual formulas. Then, and only then, would the demon deign to appear. It was comparatively simple to curse one's opponent in a chariot race. All that was required was to inscribe the curse on a lead tablet, naming the rival and solemnly wishing him blindness, agony, and/or death. This done, the text might be garnished with a drawing or two of the cursed individual being strangled by generously fanged serpents. Some enchanted evening, the tablet could be slipped into a tomb known to house a restless ghost or buried beneath the starting gates of the circus in the company of a mutilated rooster.[8]

Perhaps unsurprisingly, many Greeks and Romans objected to the practice of magic. Both early Rome and a scattering of Greek cities banned spells that caused harm to citizens, and Athenian court cases sometimes hinged on accusations of sorcery. Blanket condemnations of magic came later, when some of the more suspicious emperors, always ready to regard sorcery as treasonous, conducted full-scale witch hunts to ferret out magic users among the Roman aristocracy. A legal commentary composed around 300 CE prescribes grim punishments—ranging from slavery in the mines to death by wild beasts—for those proven to be practitioners of the magical arts. The following decades witnessed imperial edicts confirming these penalties and an exceptionally lethal round of witch hunts, both partly inspired by the rise of Christianity.[9]

Unlike their pagan neighbors, early Christians assumed that all magic was demonic and that demons were servants of a supreme devil. Magic was thus categorically condemned both by the church and—after Constantine—by the state. Although these measures drove the more exhibitionist forms of magic underground, spells continued to be cast, sometimes citing passages from scripture and evoking saints and angels. Amulets were still worn at all levels of society. And the inertia of tradition ensured that a basically classical conception of magic, with its demons and exotic spells, would survive into the Middle Ages and beyond.[10]

· *20* ·

Did They Practice Human Sacrifice?

The maiden lay, eyes empty, in the circle of torches. The priest had caught her and run her through. She had died instantly. The other maidens clustered around the body, whispering. Every year they ran in the Festival of Dionysus, as their mothers and grandmothers had run before them. And every year the old priest pursued, rusty sword drawn, through the torchlit woods. The ritual had always been strange, but more exciting than frightening. Nobody could remember a maiden dying. Until now. The dead girl's friends were beginning to weep. The priest, looking stunned, had fallen to his knees. The same thought crept through every mind: did Dionysus really demand human blood?[1]

As far as we know, this was the final time he did. The maiden who died on the priest's sword that night was the last known victim of human sacrifice in Greece. By the time of her murder—around the end of the first century CE—virtually all Greeks and Romans regarded human sacrifice with disgust. They acknowledged, however, that their own ancestors had practiced it. And, occasionally, they indulged in it themselves.

Sacrifice was always the supreme act of Greco-Roman piety. Some thought that the gods were nourished by sacrificial smoke. Others speculated that they liked the smell or simply appreciated the gesture. Whatever the reason, it was agreed that sacrifice was the single most effective means of restraining the gods' wrath and winning their favor. In the Greek world, most sacrifices followed a standard pattern. The sacrificial animal was led to the altar.* Droplets of water were flicked

---

* The main altar of most Greek sanctuaries was situated in front of the temple door, so that the god's cult statue could "watch" the act of sacrifice.

into its face to make it nod, as though assenting to the sacrifice. This formality concluded, a fire was kindled on the altar, and a few of the victim's hairs were dropped into it. The presiding priest intoned a prayer; then, as women around the altar wailed, the animal's throat was slit. The carcass was butchered, and the entrails roasted on spits. As the thighbones, wrapped in fat, smoked and sizzled on the altar fire, the rest of the meat was boiled or roasted and shared among the participants. The Romans sacrificed in much the same way, though they added an inspection of the victim's entrails after the sacrifice. If the organs were normal, the gods were assumed to approve of the offering; if they were not, the sacrifice had to be repeated.[2]

Honeyed cakes, incense, bowls of wine, and a whole host of other bloodless offerings could be and were made to the gods. Animals, however, were always the sacrificial default. The most affordable victims were piglets and chickens. More common, though also more expensive, were sheep, goats, and pigs. The costliest and most prestigious were oxen, which often had their horns gilded for the occasion.* Although almost any animal could be offered to almost any god, each deity had his or her preferred victims. Demeter was fond of piglets; Aphrodite liked doves; Hecate insisted on dogs. Sacrificial customs, moreover, were deeply conservative and varied from city to city. Every October, for example, the Romans sacrificed a single horse to Mars, after which the residents of two neighborhoods battled for possession of the head. The residents of Lampsacus, a city in what is now western Turkey, offered braying donkeys to the phallic god Priapus. And during an annual festival of Artemis at the Greek city of Patrae, worshippers herded live boars, deer, wolves, and the occasional bear into an immense sacrificial bonfire.[3]

Human sacrifice, the Greeks and Romans agreed, was barbaric. The most notorious offenders were the Carthaginians, who offered young children to the god Baal. Their custom—if we can trust the sensationalist account of one Greek author—was to lay infants in the sloping bronze palms of an idol, from which they slid into a gaping pit of fire. The Gauls were said to build colossal wicker men, pack them with

---

* In Classical Athens, where the average daily wage was around one drachma, piglets usually cost about three drachmas; a sheep or goat, roughly twelve; a pig, twenty or more; and a cow up to eighty. Only kings, cities, and the outrageously wealthy could offer a hecatomb of one hundred oxen, the most extravagant of all classical sacrifices. On the principle that a bit of cow is better than no cow at all, worshippers unable to spare a bull might content themselves (if not the bull) by offering the gods its testicles.

prisoners, and burn them to honor the gods. The Germans sacrificed men over a great bronze cauldron; when the cauldron was full, it was tipped over, and a priestess drew prophecies from the patterns made by the spilling blood. The Taurians sacrificed anyone unfortunate enough to be shipwrecked on their shores, impaling the heads of their victims on long lines of stakes beside the sea.[4]

The Greeks and the Romans believed that their distant ancestors also had performed human sacrifices. In several myths, the gods demanded human victims. Agamemnon, for example, was forced to offer his daughter Iphigenia to Artemis before he could sail for Troy, and Achilles saw fit to fling twelve sacrificed Trojans onto the funeral pyre of Patroclus.* Many cities celebrated rituals that had, or were assumed to have, roots in human sacrifice. In some cases, humans had been replaced by other victims. The Romans explained their odd habit of sacrificing a fish, an onion, and a hair after lightning strikes as the effective equivalent of human sacrifice. In other cases, human victims had been supplanted by effigies. Fourteen planks dressed as women were burned in a towering fire at one Greek festival. Every year, likewise, the Romans tossed straw puppets, bound hand and foot, into the Tiber. In some places, finally, a former human sacrifice had been commuted to a symbolic offering. The heads of wine bottles in Roman Gaul were sometimes struck off with swords, spattering wine like the blood of a ritually slit throat.[5]

Although there were instances of human sacrifice in the classical world, the evidence is scattered and disputed. Modern historians are skeptical, for example, about the ancient claim that an Athenian general sacrificed three members of the Persian royal family to Dionysus. Scholarly suspicion also surrounds the best candidate for regular human sacrifice in ancient Greece. In the remote region of Arcadia, high on a barren ridge of Mount Lykaion, stood an ancient sanctuary of Zeus. There, every four years, a boy was sacrificed in the dead of night upon a mound of blood-soaked ash—or so it was said. Archaeologists have yet to recover any unambiguous evidence.[6]

Most of the human sacrifices mentioned in Roman sources can also be chalked up to rumor or slander. The rebel Catiline supposedly

---

* A historical parallel to Achilles's sacrifice has been discovered at Lefkandi on the Greek island of Euboea, where—sometime around 950 BCE—a woman was apparently sacrificed and buried beside a prominent warrior-chieftain.

swore his coconspirators to secrecy over the entrails of a sacrificed boy (and then, for good measure, ate them). Augustus was said to have sacrificed no fewer than three hundred Roman captives to the deified Julius Caesar. There is no compelling reason to believe either of these stories. Occasionally, however, the Romans really did perform a human sacrifice. At least three times during periods of national crisis, four victims—two Greeks and two Gauls—were buried alive just outside the gates of Rome. The custom was finally banned, along with all other forms of human sacrifice, in 97 BCE.[7]

Human sacrifice, in short, was rare. Other forms of ritual murder were more widespread.* Some Greek cities, for example, chose one or two exceptionally ugly men as *pharmakoi*—scapegoats—each year. On a set day, these men were expelled from the city, being beaten, whipped, and/or stoned in the process. Sometimes—if we can believe our sources—they were killed. The ritual seems, however, to have become more humane over time. At one Greek city where a *pharmakos* was annually flung from a seaside cliff, the custom developed of supplying the victim with large wings and a flock of live birds on strings to slow his descent; after he crashed, birds and all, into the sea, he was picked up in a small boat and escorted outside the city's territory.[8]

Although the Roman scapegoating festival—which involved dressing an old man in animal skins and beating him with rods—was nonfatal, the Romans were more than willing to engage in ritual murder when it suited them. On the day a general triumphed, for example, it was customary for the enemy commander or king to be ceremonially strangled.[†] Even more dramatically, Roman generals could surrender their own lives to the gods to win critical battles.[‡] During a minor festival, finally, the blood of men killed in the arena was supposedly poured over a statue of Jupiter.[9]

---

* Human sacrifice involves offering a victim to a specific god or gods. Ritual murder is the broader category of killing in a religious context, without explicitly intending the victim as a gift to, or an act of communication with, the gods. The distinction, one imagines, was of little comfort to victims.

† A few generals made a point of being merciful. Pompey magnanimously spared most of the leaders displayed in his colossal third triumph, and Aurelian allowed the rebel queen Zenobia to live out her days in genteel captivity outside Rome.

‡ A Roman historian describes the ritual. The general put on his toga, covered his head, and stood on a spear. Repeating a formula dictated by a priest, he formally consecrated himself to the infernal gods. Then he mounted his horse and charged alone into the enemy lines.

The strange case of the priest-king of Nemi encapsulates the ambiguous status of ritual murder in the classical world. Lake Nemi, about 20 miles from Rome, lies in a deep volcanic crater ringed by woods. Its shady shores were a summer retreat of the Roman emperors; Caligula built two colossal pleasure barges, each nearly 250 feet long, so that he could cruise the cool waters in suitable magnificence. At a slight remove from this splendor lay an ancient grove sacred to Diana. The priest of the sanctuary, called the King of Nemi, was always an escaped slave. The only way to become King of Nemi was to kill the previous king in single combat. For centuries, as slaves fought and died in the quiet grove, scholars speculated about the custom, ascribing it to barbarian influence in the distant past. Caligula, drifting by on one of his vast barges, amused himself by hiring a thug to attack the current king. For most, however, the King of Nemi was merely an unpleasant reminder that the gods sometimes welcomed human blood.[10]

· 21 ·

Was the Oracle of Delphi
High on Fumes?

$\mathcal{O}$mens were everywhere. Any flight of birds or sudden breeze might be inspired. A casual word or cast die could be divine. Wisdom sprang daily to inspired lips; revelation fell nightly on the wings of dreams. For most mortals, however, the significance of all these signs was elusive. A professional seer or dream interpreter (or, in a pinch, a cheap street magician) could be hired to help. The single best way to learn the will of the gods, however, was to visit an oracle.

Individuals consulted oracles to inquire about their health, marriage prospects, travel plans, and odds of success in business (among much else). Delegations from cities and kings sought advice on the validity of treaties, the wisdom of political reforms, the best ways to avert plague or famine, and a host of other matters difficult or controversial enough to require divine wisdom. Whatever the topic, questions were generally posed in a formulaic manner that outlined two clear alternatives. The oracles' answers were often equally straightforward, though sometimes phrased in poetical or ambiguous language.[*1]

At some oracles, clients laid themselves on stone benches in "incubation" chambers—one shrine stipulated that they first wrap themselves in a bloody sheepskin—and slept there, hoping for prophetic dreams. Other establishments required more initiative. The intrepid soul who ventured to consult the Oracle of Trophonius, for instance, had first to cloister himself for several days, dining on sacrificial meat and bathing

---

* Probably the most famous example was given to the Lydian king Croesus. When Croesus asked the Oracle of Delphi whether he should attack the Persians, he was told that if he did, he would destroy a great kingdom. Croesus attacked and was defeated, destroying a great kingdom—his own.

112

in a local river. Once he had attained a suitable pitch of ritual cleanliness, he drank from two springs—one to make him forget the past, one to help him remember the future—and descended by rickety ladder to the bottom of a dry well. Thence he descended into a cavern and saw strange things in the dark. At length, shaken and disoriented, he crawled back to sunlight and was led to the Chair of Memory, where priests helped him interpret his visions.[2]

For a less harrowing experience, clients could visit oracles staffed by children. At a shrine of Fortune near Rome, a boy plucked wood blocks marked with words from a small box; at a sanctuary in Egypt, prophecies were drawn from the chatter of youths playing in a temple court. Other oracles relied on animals. One involved summoning schools of fish with a flute. Another featured a large snake, which specialized in verifying the virginity of young women.* A more versatile serpent, equipped with a human puppet head, presided over a popular oracle in Asia Minor. Other establishments featured talking skulls. Even these paled beside the eternal flame of Apollonia, a pillar of fire that signaled the will of the gods by engulfing or rejecting the incense thrown by petitioners.[3]

Though they lacked some of their competitors' glitz, the greatest oracles centered on an inspired medium, a man or woman who spoke with the voice of a god. The most ancient was the Oracle of Zeus at Dodona, where priestesses known as "the doves" listened to the rustling leaves of sacred oaks. The other leading oracles belonged to Apollo, the god most associated with prophecy. There was a famous oracle at Claros, where clients sacrificed beneath colossal statues of Apollo and his family before consulting the prophet in his subterranean chamber. There was another at Didyma, where a priestess of Apollo prophesied from the inmost chamber of a gargantuan temple, bathing her feet in the waters of a sacred spring. Greater than either of these, however, was the sanctuary of Delphi, home to the classical world's premier oracle.

The Oracle of Delphi stood at the center of a magnificent natural amphitheater in the mountains of central Greece. The Pythia—the priestess who served as the mouthpiece of Apollo—held one

* Women walked blindfolded into the sanctuary, carrying barley cakes. When they reached the snake's lair, they stooped and offered it the cakes. If it ate them, their virginity was confirmed.

The Temple of Apollo at Delphi. *Wikimedia Commons*

session every month.* On the appointed day, priests first ensured that the god was in an oracular mood by sprinkling a goat with cold water. If the goat shuddered, all was well (except for the goat, which was promptly sacrificed). Those who wished to consult the oracle then lined up in an order determined by the chumminess of relations between their native cities and Delphi. As each client reached the head of the line, he paid a consultation fee, offered sacrifice, and entered the Temple of Apollo. He then seems to have been led into an antechamber from which he could hear but not see the Pythia. He asked his question. And the Pythia—seated on a tripod, laurel branch in hand—answered with the voice of the god. Usually, her words were clear and coherent. But at least once, she shrieked and raved like a woman possessed.[4]

---

* Oracular sessions were not held during winter, when the god was presumed to be vacationing in more salubrious climes. Those who arrived between oracular days had to wait—unless they were Alexander the Great, who simply dragged the Pythia to her tripod.

Some ancient authors claimed that the Pythia owed her prophetic prowess to vapors seeping from the rock beneath her tripod.* According to one story, in fact, these emanations were responsible for the sanctuary's foundation. When the region around Delphi was first settled, it was said a mysterious crack was discovered in the ground. Every goat that approached the crack went into hysterics; any goatherd who followed spouted prophecies. As word spread, people began to gather around the crack. Some, however, were so overcome by clairvoyant ecstasy that they tumbled into the crevice and were seen no more. To put an end to such mishaps, it was decided to appoint an oracle who would approach the perils of prophecy with more professionalism. A first-century geographer described the site of the oracle as a deep cave where the Pythia, seated over a fissure streaming with vapor, gibbered in the grip of divine inspiration. A century later, the biographer Plutarch, a sometime Delphic priest, speculated that the oracle's decline could be traced to the disappearance of the divine vapor† that had inspired it from the beginning.[5]

When the French excavators of Delphi began clearing the Temple of Apollo at the turn of the twentieth century, they expected to uncover a cavern and steaming crack beneath it. Instead, they found a small sunken room with a floor of solid rock. An academic consensus quickly developed that the statements of ancient authors about Delphi reflected a literary tradition, not reality. The story about the spastic goats was identified as a legend devised to explain the forgotten origins of the oracle. The mysterious smoking crack was interpreted as an invention of authors who had never seen the oracular chamber. And the vapor described by Plutarch came to be understood as an imperceptible current of divine influence, not a literal gas.[6]

In the early 2000s, an interdisciplinary team of scholars revived the idea of an oracle under the influence. On the basis of new geological

---

* It is sometimes claimed that the Greeks used plants with psychoactive properties to heighten religious experiences, but there is no unambiguous evidence that they did so. The evidence for recreational drug use is equally scanty. Although the Greeks and Romans grew opium poppies, they seem to have used the narcotic milk only to relieve pain and induce sleep. Cannabis, likewise, was grown primarily to produce hemp for rope and cloth. The Scythians of Ukraine, who heated hempseed in their steam baths, are the only classical people known to have routinely "smoked" it.

† The Greeks knew that miraculous places were fragile: one spring, whose surface had shown spellbinding pictures of distant ships and harbors, was reportedly ruined forever when a woman washed her laundry in it.

surveys, they suggested that the famous crack beneath the Pythia's tripod was actually a fault in the bituminous limestone bedrock. Whenever slippage occurred along this fault, they theorized, friction vaporized some of the petrochemicals in the limestone, producing gases—methane, ethane, and ethylene—that wafted up to the surface and into the oracular chamber. Ethylene, once used as an anesthetic, could have produced the visions and fits described by ancient authors.

Could have—but probably didn't. Only trace amounts of ethylene or any other intoxicating gas are currently produced by the Delphi bedrock, and if levels had been significantly higher in the ancient world, we would expect clients of the oracle—who stood a short distance from the Pythia—also to have felt the effects. Since they did not, and since we have no records of sudden infernos in the sanctuary (ethylene is highly flammable), we should probably be skeptical. Not even the Delphic oracle dared to resolve academic disputes.[7]

How Long Did Paganism Survive?

The courier waited for the crowd to fall silent. Then, ostentatiously breaking the seal on the scroll he carried, he cleared his throat, tilted his head back, and began. The Great and Gracious Emperor Theodosius had decreed that the pagans occupying the Temple of Serapis were not to be punished, so long as they dispersed at once. (At this, cheers rose from part of the crowd. The courier, squinting severely, waited for them to fade before continuing.) But after deep deliberation and in the interests of the one true faith, the emperor had resolved that the Temple of Serapis was to be destroyed. Immediately.

Stunned silence. Then, all at once, a tide of sound as Christians cheered and pagans cried out in anger. Heedless of the tumult, soldiers filed up the marble steps of the sanctuary. One man, ax in hand, approached the great statue of the god Serapis. After a moment's hesitation, he swung at the gilded head. The ax struck with a hollow sound, sending fragments of gold leaf spinning through the air. Again and again the soldier swung until the wooden frame of the neck buckled and the head crashed to the floor. Serapis, guardian of Alexandria, had fallen.[1]

In 392 CE, when the great Temple of Serapis at Alexandria was destroyed, perhaps half the Roman Empire's inhabitants were Christian. A century before, the vast majority of the empire's population had

been pagan.* A century after, few pagans would remain. The causes and pace of this religious revolution defy easy summary. But since this is, for better or worse, a book of such things, an easy summary will have to do.

The rise of Christianity was expedited by the existence of the Roman Empire, whose scale and stability allowed missionaries and their letters to travel freely over a vast area. Language was equally important. Although Jesus and his first disciples (usually) spoke Aramaic, the native language of the early church was Greek, current throughout the eastern Roman provinces. Greek was also the language of the Jewish diaspora, whose communities supplied many of Christianity's first converts. Another critical precondition was the early imperial government's laissez-faire attitude toward most religious matters, which allowed the church to escape systematic persecution for the first two centuries of its existence.

During those first centuries, Christianity grew slowly but steadily. The Christian moral code was an important source of attraction. Traditional Greco-Roman polytheism had never been associated with any clear or single ethical system—the myths themselves, as we have seen, were morally problematic—and some pagans had long been drawn to the greater clarity offered by Judaism.† Christianity had a similar appeal, sharpened by the promise of eternal reward for those who abided by its precepts. For educated pagans steeped in philosophical currents that tended to emphasize divine unity, the monotheism of Christianity was an additional enticement.

The church's social network was at least as important as its teachings. After initial recruitment from Jewish communities, most Christian converts were drawn from those on the margins of classical civilization: slaves, freedmen, expatriates, and women. Excluded from the hierarchical society of their cities, these people found an appealing alternative in the egalitarian community of the church. Christian charity was another powerful incentive. Pagan benefactors tended to focus their generosity on the adult male citizens who comprised the political community. Christians, by contrast, gave freely to widows, orphans, and the poor.

---

* "Pagan" is something of misnomer, since "paganism" never existed as a coherent religion. Here, however, "pagan" is used as a term of convenience for the dazzling array of polytheistic traditions replaced by Christianity in and around the Greco-Roman world.

† For centuries, the monotheism and ethical code of Judaism had attracted pagan sympathizers. Relatively few of these "God fearers," however, actually converted, not least because they tended to be less than enthusiastic about circumcision.

Not all early Christians, however, came from the ranks of the needy. Almost from the beginning, a few wealthy people—in particular, imperial freedmen and aristocratic widows—were drawn to the church and supported it with their patronage.* Rich and poor, the faithful of every sizable city were supervised by a bishop whose activities lent even the largest Christian communities a degree of coherence unknown in traditional paganism.²

Since we hear little about missionaries in the second and third centuries CE, early Christianity is assumed to have usually spread informally, as converts won over their families and friends. Christian authors claimed that public cures, exorcisms, and other miracles convinced many souls and that martyrdoms during the empire-wide persecutions of the third and early fourth centuries gained widespread pagan sympathy. It was, however, the conversion of Constantine that finally set the church on track to dominate the Roman world.

The nature and sincerity of Constantine's Christianity have occupied whole cloisters of scholars. For our purposes, it matters only that Constantine consistently promoted the interests of Christianity from the time he ordered his soldiers to paint Christian symbols on their shields at the Battle of Milvian Bridge. Over the course of a long and busy reign, he freed Christians from all legal penalties, granted important privileges to the clergy, called the first ecumenical council, and built a series of monumental churches. These actions set the tone for the rest of Roman history.†

At the time of Constantine's conversion, perhaps 5 to 10 percent of the Roman Empire's inhabitants were Christian. Although there were large communities in Rome and a few parts of North Africa and Gaul, most Christians were concentrated in the cities of the Greek-speaking eastern provinces. Everywhere, the countryside remained largely pagan. The fourth century, however, witnessed a spectacular expansion of the Christian ranks. Every Easter, cities were filled with the white robes of

---

* At the end of the second century, for example, the Roman church was supported by Marcia, the favorite concubine of the emperor Commodus.

† The only non-Christian emperor after Constantine was Julian. During his short reign (361–363 CE), Julian ordered the restoration of temples, banned Christians from teaching positions and high political office, and tried to create a pagan religious hierarchy to match the Christian one (with the emperor himself, as pontifex maximus, at its head). All these measures died with him.

the newly baptized; every year, monks and proselytes drove deeper into the hinterlands.[3]

As Christian numbers and Christian confidence grew, the emperors closed temples, restricted sacrifices, and finally banned the public practice of paganism. At the same time, raids—often carried out by marauding bands of monks—destroyed temples in many cities. The final legal blows came during the reign of Justinian, who hounded the few remaining crypto-pagans from his court, closed the last working temples, and ordered every remaining pagan to accept baptism. Near the end of Justinian's reign, a mass burning of pagan texts and statues of the gods was staged in the Hippodrome of Constantinople as a sort of symbolic coda.[4]

The old ways endured, however, in rural areas. There had often been a cultural barrier between the cities of the classical world and the surrounding regions, particularly where the language of the countryside differed from the Latin or Greek of the cities. In many places, Christianity was slow to bridge the gap.* During the reign of Justinian, for example, the missionary John of Ephesus ("the idol smasher") found tens of thousands of pagan villagers in the hills of Asia Minor. A half century later, Pope Gregory I was still trying to convince peasants near Rome that they should stop revering sacred trees and despairing of ever converting the rustic pagans of Sardinia, who had bribed the local governor to leave their religious practices alone. As late as the ninth century, shepherds in remote parts of southern Greece still worshipped the old gods.[5]

Paganism lasted even longer in a few corners of the Near East. In 579, a Roman governor and local dignitaries were caught in the act of sacrificing to Zeus near the Syrian city of Edessa. Heliopolis, not far to the south, still had few Christians during the same period. The most enduringly pagan of all Roman cities, however, was the Syrian border town of Harran. The people of Harran worshipped a partly Hellenized pantheon dominated by the moon god Sin. By the sixth century, their stubborn devotion had won their city the nickname Hellenopolis ("Heathenville"). Roman emperors and Roman persecutors came and went; the Romans were replaced by the Arabs, and one caliphate by another. Through it all, the people of Harran remained loyal to their

---

* In Latin, "pagan" literally means "hick" or "bumpkin." Pagans in the eastern provinces, by contrast, tended to be called "Hellenes"—that is, "Greeks."

gods.* The Temple of Sin and its worshippers survived until the early eleventh century, when Harran was destroyed by nomads.[6]

By the time of Harran's destruction, Greco-Roman paganism had effectively vanished. Pagan practices and beliefs, however, left countless traces in the landscapes and mindscapes of medieval Europe. The most visible relics were the temples that still loomed over many cities. The Parthenon became the cathedral of Athens; the Pantheon was converted to a church of Mary and the Martyrs. Although temples usually became churches only after a period of abandonment, they sometimes passed directly into Christian use. In Athens, for example, a church of Saint Andrew was built in a sanctuary of the healing god Asclepius, and the incubation chambers—where worshippers slept, waiting for Asclepius to heal or advise them in their dreams—continued to function under new divine management. In Asia Minor, likewise, a healing spring sacred to Apollo was simply transferred to the Archangel Michael. Pagan statues also could be repurposed: until the end of the eighteenth century, villagers near Athens venerated a statue from an ancient sanctuary of Demeter as "Saint Demetra" and claimed that it protected their crops.[7]

Some pagan festivals also persisted.† The Lupercalia in Rome—a fertility rite that centered on naked and blood-spattered men lashing women with strips of goatskin—lasted until the end of the fifth century. The racy theatrical performances associated with the pagan Maioumas festival, popular throughout the eastern provinces, were even more enduring, though ecclesiastical disapproval eventually stripped the festival of its trademark nude swimming.‡[8]

As a living religion, Greco-Roman paganism had vanished by the Middle Ages. Yet it endured, and still endures, not only in odd corners of daily life—the days of the week, you'll recall, are named after the gods—but as an inescapable part of the classical legacy. In allusions and imitations, in art and literature, the gods, like so much and so little of the classical world, are with us still.

---

* In 830, after a passing caliph ordered them to become Muslims or die, the people of Harran claimed to be Sabians, a mysterious sect described in the Koran as People of the Book, and thus—like Jews and Christians—entitled to toleration and respect.

† It is sometimes claimed that Christmas was intended to replace a pagan festival of the sun customarily held on December 25. The date of Christmas, however, may have been selected for unrelated reasons. Early Christians—it has been theorized—assumed that Jesus, as a perfect being, must have led a mathematically perfect life. By this logic, since the date of the Crucifixion was calculated to have been March 25, Jesus also must have been conceived on March 25. His birth would have occurred precisely nine months later, on December 25.

‡ A few pagan rituals persisted even longer. Some Greek peasants, for example, maintained the ancient practice of pouring libations of wine over tombs into the twentieth century.

IV

SPORTS AND LEISURE

· 23 ·

Were There Professional Athletes?

*N*o need to be coy about this one: yes.

Like so many other aspects of classical culture, athletics emerged in the compulsively competitive world of early Greece. By the Classical period, every Greek city had a gymnasium where boys and young men sprinted around a short track, practiced throwing the javelin and discus, and paired off for wrestling and boxing matches.* Greek athletes exercised nude, coating their skin with olive oil to ward off sunburn and give their bodies a healthy sheen. At regular intervals, the more sprightly and ambitious of them competed in the contests attached to local religious festivals. And every summer, a fortunate few with talent and time to spare sallied forth to try their luck at one of the great games.[1]

The Olympic Games, the first Greek athletic competition, began as a regional festival of Zeus with a single event (the sprint). By the sixth century BCE, they had grown to incorporate every major sport and had become prestigious enough to draw athletes from every corner of the Greek world. In company with the three other Panhellenic festivals—the Pythian, Nemean, and Isthmian Games—the Olympics would dominate Greek sports for a thousand years. The leading competitors in these games were amateurs only in the modern sense of not

---

* Women were excluded from athletics in every Greek city except Sparta. On the theory that only strong mothers could give birth to strong sons, Spartan girls ran, threw, and wrestled, wearing the loose clothes that caused the Athenians to nickname them "thigh flashers" (the Athenians were especially amused by a dance they performed at festivals, during which they leapt and kicked their own buttocks). Inspired by the Spartan example, the emperors Nero and Domitian included footraces for girls in the Greek games they staged at Rome. After one of these, a young Roman aristocrat challenged a Spartan girl to a wrestling match. Our sources neglect to mention who won.

being salaried. In every meaningful way, they were professionals who dedicated years of their lives to athletics and were handsomely rewarded for doing so.

The Olympic Games (held, like their modern counterparts, every four years) encapsulate the range and professionalism of Greek athletics during the Classical period. Competitors had to arrive at least a month in advance and complete their training at Olympia. This allowed athletes to take the measure of their opponents and gave the ten judges ample opportunity to disqualify anyone not up to the standard of competition. At the end of the training period, the athletes swore that they would abide by the rules and do nothing to dishonor the festival. Then the games began.

The first event was the chariot race. As the crowd roared, dozens of four-horse chariots exploded onto the dusty track, wheels whirring, jockeys shouting, whips cracking in the air. Adding to the excitement was the virtual guarantee that chariots would crash; once at the Pythian Games, only a single chariot finished from a field of forty-one. At the race's end, the chariot's owner was recognized as the winner. The chariot driver, a man of much lower social status, was politely ignored. The chariot race was followed by a bareback horse race, which seems to have resembled a nudist Kentucky Derby (the jockeys were naked boys). Here again it was the owner who counted; at least once, a horse won after throwing her jockey.[2]

The pentathlon came next. The five events incorporated the favorite exercises of the gymnasium: discus, long jump, javelin, sprint, and wrestling. Winning any three events guaranteed victory. Although the competitors were the best all-around athletes at Olympia, the pentathlon was never especially popular. The running events were much more prestigious. The most eagerly anticipated race was the sprint (about 200 meters). The others were the long sprint (about 400 meters) and distance run (about 2.5 miles).*

Wrestling was the first of the fighting events. Since there were no weight classes in Greek athletics, champions tended to be massive.† The

---

* The most famous runner in ancient Olympic history, Leonidas of Rhodes, won both the sprint and the long sprint at four consecutive Olympics. On each of these occasions, he also managed to win the armored race, a rather comical event, held at the very end of the games, that required nude runners to dash up and down the track carrying a shield and wearing a helmet.

† Sheer physical intimidation also helped: in an inscription commemorating his victories, a wrestler boasted that every other man in the field forfeited the moment they saw him naked.

greatest of all Olympic wrestlers, the mountainous Milo of Croton, was strong enough to carry his own bronze statue into the Olympic precinct and heave it onto its pedestal. He won the wrestling title an incredible six times—at least once unopposed, since no man dared to face him.

Boxers, like wrestlers, were usually heavyweights. Unlike wrestlers, they faced a real risk of dying in the ring. Greek boxing gloves were made of sharp-edged leather, which tore skin with brutal efficiency. Typically, both fighters were dripping blood long before the match-ending blow. This could be fatal: once, during the final match of the Nemean Games, a boxer speared his hand into his opponent's side and tore out his entrails. Not all matches were so exciting. One champion just stood, guard up, for two days, and waited for his opponent to keel over from exhaustion.[3]

Dangerous (or tedious) though boxing sometimes was, it could never match the sheer savagery of pankration, the third and final fighting event. Pankration, the ancient counterpart of mixed martial arts, combined elements of wrestling and boxing with energetic kicking. Only biting and eye-gouging were banned—and these rules were not strictly observed. As might be expected, the pankration drew a special breed of competitor. One famous pankratiast reportedly hiked up the rocky foothills of Mount Olympus, hunted down one of Greece's last remaining lions, and beat it to death with his fists. Another was known as "Mr. Finger-Tipper" from his habit of breaking his opponents' fingers. A third great pankratiast met his demise in a championship match. Caught in a scissors hold and being vigorously throttled, he attempted to escape by breaking his opponent's toes. At last, unable to bear the pain, the man released his hold—and the great pankratiast fell dead to the ground. His corpse was declared the winner.[4]

Victors in the Olympics and the other Panhellenic Games were awarded a crown of woven twigs.* These modest wreaths conferred instant and enduring fame. Olympic victors were guaranteed a hero's welcome back home—one champion entered his native city at the head of a procession of three hundred chariots—and could count on such perks as free meals for life and front-row seats in the theater. Sparta granted Olympian victors the honor of fighting beside the king. The Athenians gave them cash. The real money for champion athletes,

---

* At Olympia, victors received crowns of olive leaves. At Pythia, they were crowned with laurel; at Isthmia, with pine. Celery garnished the brows of Nemean victors.

Two pankratiasts fighting under the watchful eyes of a referee. *Panathenaic prize amphora, now in the Metropolitan Museum of Art. Public domain*

however, was in the lesser games of the Greek world. Dozens of local competitions existed alongside the four Panhellenic games, and most of these contests compensated for their lack of prestige by offering valuable prizes.* Besides purses of gold or silver, victors might be awarded anything from wool cloaks to jars of expensive olive oil.[5]

---

* In the Roman imperial era, one Greek city paid a famous Olympic champion a whopping thirty thousand drachmas (enough to pay the annual salaries of one hundred contemporary legionaries) just to enter its games.

A talented athlete, in short, could hope to win both fame and financial security by competing in games across Greece. Already in the Classical period, a few champions were full-time professionals. The great wrestler and pankratiast Theogenes reportedly won more than a thousand prizes over the course of his career. If this is remotely accurate, he was a very wealthy man. For Greek athletes born into upper-class families, prize money was less important than the notoriety and respect that attended victory. Those from humbler backgrounds were more attentive to the bottom line. Some even acted like modern free agents, switching cities before the Olympics to maximize their earnings. Once they had passed their prime, a few star athletes entered politics. Most, however, became trainers in the gymnasia of their native cities.[6]

The number of Greek professional athletes grew steadily in the Hellenistic and Roman eras. So did the number of games. By the third century CE, there were more than five hundred athletic competitions in the eastern Roman provinces alone, almost all modeled on the ancient Panhellenic contests. The best athletes traveled constantly, combining victories in famous games like the Olympics with a lucrative selection of lesser contests.*

As athletes became more numerous, they began to organize regional guilds. Sometime in the early imperial era, the largest of these merged into the Sacred and Hercules-Worshipping Association of Traveling Athletes and Crown Winners. This organization scheduled games, supplied referees, and supported athletes across the Roman Empire. Its headquarters in Rome was graced by the presence of the Portico, the five high officials—all famous retired athletes—who ran the association. The members of the Portico were careful to maintain good relations with the emperors, going so far as to send Claudius a gold crown after his conquest of Britain. In return, the emperors appointed them to such honorific positions as "president of the baths" and "imperial masseuse."[7]

The Romans always regarded Greek athletics with suspicion. At best, they were a waste of time: "these wretched Greeks," Trajan growled to

---

* The most famous athletes were known throughout the Roman Empire. The mosaic floor of a tavern in Ostia, Rome's harbor, depicts a fight between the great pankratiasts Alexander and the Creeper ("Helix"—a stage name).

one of his governors, "are addicted to their gymnasia." At worst, their glistening nudity was a full-frontal assault on traditional values, distracting young men from military drills and other good Roman pursuits. The Romans had their own traditions of boxing, wrestling, and running—all decently clothed, thank you very much—but never developed competitive games. Only after the conquest of Greece, and then only occasionally, did Romans deign to participate in the Olympics.* Most infamously, Nero insisted on driving a magnificent ten-horse chariot in the Olympic race. By virtue of being emperor, he won, despite falling out of his chariot and failing to finish. Nero also attempted to establish Greek-style games in Rome. With more enthusiasm than tact, he imported gymnastic sand from Egypt, distributed gymnastic oil among the Roman elite, and forced everyone who was anyone to watch the events, which included literary competitions (the winning poem, to nobody's astonishment, was a hymn praising Nero). Five years later, when the games were held again, the Senate took the precaution of awarding Nero every prize in advance.[8]

Neither Nero's games nor the more enduring Greek festival established by a later emperor were ever popular. The Roman people didn't mind watching Greek athletic contests (the pankration, at least, was reliably exciting). But they always preferred the razzmatazz of gladiatorial combats and chariot races. Leaving the gladiators for a later chapter, we'll focus on the races. Rome's Circus Maximus could seat 150,000 spectators—three times as many as the Colosseum—and every one of those seats was filled during the races, which were held about sixty days a year. In some ways, the experience was reminiscent of a modern NASCAR race. There was fast food sold by vendors in stalls beneath the seats.† There were misting fans (pipes that drizzled cold water). There were T-shirt cannons, in the form of men flinging tokens into the stands that could be redeemed for anything from a toga to an apartment building. And, of course, there were the all-important racing teams.[9]

The races were organized by the four factions (teams), each named for its signature color: the Reds, the Whites, the Blues, and the Greens.

---

* The Roman dictator Sulla effectively moved the Olympics of 80 BCE to Rome. Subsequently, however, they were allowed to remain in Olympia.

† On special occasions, the emperors distributed free food among the spectators. At least once, fruits, nuts, and cakes were made to rain from the sky in the Colosseum as attendants handed out full cups of wine.

A mosaic showing a chariot race. Eight four-horse chariots are competing. Two chariots—one in lower left corner, one in the upper right—have crashed. The others are racing furiously around the central barrier. The lattice on the left side represents the starting gates. *Second-century mosaic, now in the Lugdunum Museum. Wikimedia Commons*

Each faction had its own horses,* chariots, and drivers. For most races, each of the four factions supplied a single four-horse chariot. There was, however, considerable variety both in the number of chariots in a given race—which ranged up to twelve—and in the number of horses drawing each chariot. Novices were assigned two-horse chariots, which were easy to control. Only seasoned veterans attempted more than four horses, though a few experts could manage as many as ten. However large the team, the chariot was always a light two-wheeled platform designed for speed and maneuverability.[10]

During the imperial era, it was customary to have twenty-four races in a day. Each followed the same pattern. The chariots lined up behind the gates, which were staggered to minimize the advantage of any starting position. The emperor or presiding official dropped a purple cloth, the opening mechanism was triggered, and the horses exploded from the gates. Up to the first turn, the chariots had to stay in their starting lanes. Past that point, it was a free-for-all. For seven breakneck laps (a total of about six miles), the drivers jockeyed and jostled for position. The most critical parts of each lap were the turns, where drivers attempted to save precious seconds by hugging the stone

---

* Horses were imported from stud farms in Spain, North Africa, and many other parts of the empire. They usually began racing when they were five years old and seem to have had lengthy careers. One horse, aptly named Winner, prevailed in no fewer than 429 races.

barrier. Any mistake there could smash a chariot to matchwood, leaving the driver—tied to the reins by his belt—to be dragged to a gruesome death.* Some drivers tried to keep the lead throughout the race; others surged forward in the final lap. In races involving multiple chariots from each faction, teammates worked together, with one or two defensive drivers attempting to block any rival who got too close to their champion. Sometimes factions even had a mounted coach, who galloped along the outside of the track and shouted advice to the drivers. At last, after fifteen minutes or so of dust and thunder, the winning chariot crossed the finish line. The victor was crowned, and the track cleared for the next race.[11]

Passions ran high in the crowd. Every faction had its legions of dedicated fans who wore the team colors to the races, bought miniature charioteer outfits for their children, and collected amulets stamped with the images of their favorite drivers. One Roman had the fact that he was a fan of the Blues inscribed on his tombstone. Another routinely sent carrier swallows back to his hometown to announce the latest winners in the circus. Some enthusiasts commissioned tablets cursing rival drivers and buried them at the starting gates and turns, where accidents were most likely.† A few went so far as to smell the dung of their faction's horses to make sure that they were being properly fed. Emperors were not immune to the madness. Caligula reportedly poisoned drivers who were making trouble for his beloved Green faction. Nero, another fan of the Greens, had the sands of the Circus Maximus sprinkled with glittering malachite. Caracalla ordered a general massacre of fans who cheered against the Blues.[12]

In this overheated atmosphere, champion drivers were akin to gods. After the death of a famous Red charioteer, a despondent fan flung himself on his hero's blazing pyre. Another fallen driver was commemorated with gilded busts throughout Rome. Although most drivers came from humble backgrounds—some started as slaves—success in the circus could transport them to dizzying heights. One famous

---

* In the event of a "shipwreck" (crash), a driver's only chance was to use the sickle-shaped knife he carried in his belt to cut himself free of the reins. If he managed to survive, he would plaster his battered limbs with boar dung. Exceptionally motivated drivers stirred pulverized dung into their drinks to speed the process of recovery.

† Drivers guarded against curses by wearing protective amulets (the image of Alexander the Great was supposed to be especially effective) and by hanging demon-discombobulating bells from their horses' traces.

driver, Crescens the Moor, started racing at the tender age of thirteen. By the time he died nine years later, he had won more than 1,500,000 sesterces. The greatest champion of all, Gaius Apuleius Diocles, retired at the age of forty-two, having participated in 4,257 races, won 1,462 of them,* and accumulated an incredible 35,863,120 sesterces in prize money.[13]

In late antiquity, a combination of changing tastes, escalating costs, and Christian disapproval put an end to Greek athletic contests and the gladiatorial combats. Chariot races, however, continued to be held in the Hippodrome (Circus) of Constantinople. There were now only two circus factions—the Blues and Greens—and loyalty to one or the other tore Constantinopolitans into squabbling camps. The most rabid fans on both sides wore special billowy tunics and sported a hair-style reminiscent of the modern mullet. They were also distinguished by a hearty willingness to start riots. Most of these were straight-forward slugfests between Blue and Green supporters. Occasionally, however, matters got out of hand. The most notorious incident, the so-called Nika Revolt, destroyed most of central Constantinople, nearly dethroned the emperor, and was only ended by the slaughter of more than thirty thousand rioters. The bodies were buried; the wreckage was cleared. And after a decent interval, the races resumed.[14]

---

* In 815 of these victorious races—as his exhaustively detailed career inscription tells us—he led from the beginning. He won 502 with a sprint in the final lap; 67 were the ancient equivalent of photo finishes.

· 24 ·

How Did They Exercise? Did They Jog or Lift Weights?

*I*f we can believe half the stories ancient authors told about him, Milo of Croton, the classical world's most famous wrestler, was superhumanly strong. He could repel anyone who tried to push him off a slippery greased discus. He could hold a pomegranate, without bruising the fruit, in a grip so firm that no man could budge a single finger. He could snap a ribbon tied around his forehead by holding his breath and making his veins bulge. He once went into battle dressed like Hercules, armed only with an enormous club. He ate twenty pounds of meat and twenty pounds of bread in a single day (and then swallowed stones from chicken gizzards, which were rumored to be the secret of his strength).* He complemented this hearty diet with a workout routine centered on deadlifting cows. After one of his victories, he carried a four-year-old bull on his shoulders around the entire Olympic precinct.† Then, naturally, he killed and ate it.[1]

The Greek athletic tradition epitomized by Milo shaped physical exercise in the classical world. In Greek gymnasia, as in the Greek games, boys and men stripped down and rubbed themselves with olive oil before working out. Their exercises, likewise, mirrored the events of the games. They threw the javelin and discus. They competed in sprints and the long jump. They wrestled and boxed and took turns punching

---

* The gluttony of combat athletes (who were almost always enormous men) was proverbial. Milo reportedly held a contest with a huge shepherd to see who could eat an ox faster. A famous pankratiast once consumed a banquet laid out for nine men.

† Since ancient Greek bulls weighed only five or six hundred pounds, a very strong man could have lifted one. It is unlikely, however, that anyone would have been able to carry a thrashing animal that size very far.

bags filled with sand. Between exercises, they stretched and limbered their limbs, often under the direction of a trainer.

Traditional Roman exercise was limited to military drills and (for the elite) hunting and riding. By the first century BCE, however, many Romans were working out in the Greek manner—the rich in recesses of their villas, the rest in courtyards attached to local baths. The Romans became especially enthusiastic about ball games adapted from the Greek gymnasium. One of the most popular involved three players in a triangular formation tossing small balls back and forth, catching with one hand and throwing with the other. The man who dropped the fewest balls won. Another popular game called for two groups arrayed around a single player, who had to pass a ball to his teammates while evading the flying tackles of the opposing team. Other ball games included a variant of volleyball and—in Roman Sparta—a team sport that looked remarkably like (American) football.

Over time, theories of exercise evolved. According to one Roman author, a healthy man could keep himself fit by sailing, hunting, walking, and making a moderate amount of love. A sickly man, by contrast, needed to prod his body into wellness by reading aloud, playing handball, walking up hills, and gamely pursuing a strenuous lifestyle. Another Roman author suggested that a sick person's health could be restored by both passive exercise (massage, carriage rides, long voyages) and activities ranging from riding to oratory.[2]

The great doctor Galen classified exercises into those that toned the muscles (such as digging, carrying heavy loads, and climbing ropes), those that encouraged speed and athleticism (such as running, boxing, ball games, and calisthenics), and those that increased strength (any activity done strenuously or with weights). But he especially advocated exercising with a small ball, which he regarded as the basis of a safe and versatile whole-body workout. Athletic trainers had their own ideas about fitness routines. By the Roman imperial era, champion athletes were expected to follow a four-day cycle: preparatory exercises on the first day, intensive exercise on the second, relaxation on the third, and moderate exercise on the fourth. Rigorous application of this scheme killed a famous Olympic champion, whose trainer made him follow his usual regimen despite a heroic hangover.[3]

Individuals tailored their workout routines to their tastes and talents. Alexander the Great liked tossing balls. Augustus worked up a light sweat by walking, riding, and playing the triangle ball game. Both Trajan and Hadrian regarded hunting as the finest form of exercise. When not philosophizing, Marcus Aurelius enjoyed boxing and wrestling. Other emperors sparred with personal trainers in mock gladiatorial matches, took lengthy swims, and jogged.[4]

Although short sprints were always part of the athletic repertoire, long-distance running was not popular. Greek and Roman men were much more likely to walk or (if wealthy) to ride for exercise. But since ancient doctors prescribed jogging for ailments ranging from flatulence to leprosy, a steady stream of puffing convalescents joined the gilded youth on the gymnasium track.* Then as now, some perverse souls actually enjoyed jogging. One Greek man, who started jogging for the health of his spleen, liked it so much that he began to run professionally and became an Olympic champion in the distance race. An epigram commemorates a scholar who passed his leisure hours loping along the porticoes and aqueducts of Rome. A few Roman ultrarunners even held exhibitions in the Circus Maximus, circling the track for hours on end. Some of these men, we are told, could run continuously for 150 miles.[5]

Since excessive muscle was assumed to oppress the body and weigh on the mind, few men wanted the rippling bulk of a laborer or gladiator. The ideal was a lean and toned physique—and to that end, many worked out with *halteres*. Originally designed to help athletes add distance in the running long jump, *halteres*—oblong pieces of stone or lead—were also used as dumbbells. Dumbbell exercises ("halter throwing") were developed for every muscle group. Since *halteres* seldom weighed more than ten pounds, they were used primarily to improve flexibility, stamina, and general fitness.† They seem to have been especially popular in the Roman world, where every bath complex had its row of puffing patrons heaving *halteres*.[6]

For those who insisted on serious strength training, several methods were available. The most straightforward was to lift stones. Gymnasia were supplied with rocks of graded weight, which athletes

---

* Most ran naked, though asthmatics were advised to wear a linen tunic to stave off the chill.

† Galen, for example, thought that exercises with *halteres* were especially useful for curing liver problems.

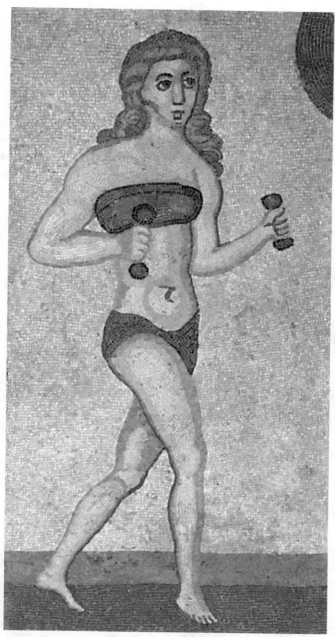

A Roman woman exercising with *halteres*. Fourth-century mosaic from the *Villa Romana del Casale*. *Author's photo*

lifted to the waist, shoulders, or overhead. An inscription describes gym rocks weighing forty, fifty, and one hundred (Roman) pounds.* The largest rocks were impressively massive. A 315-pound block of sandstone with a carved grip was discovered at Olympia, inscribed with the words "Bybon lifted me over his head with a single hand." A 1,060-pound rock found on the Greek island of Thera bears the inscription "Eumastas lifted me from the ground." When not grappling with rocks, some athletes toned their muscles by stringing powerful bows. As far as we know, however, only Milo made hefting heifers part of his workout routine.[7]

---

* The Roman pound was equivalent to 0.722 pounds avoirdupois (0.329 kg). In addition to the customary rocks, one Athenian gymnasium housed a huge bronze ball. Before competing, every athlete lifted the ball as high as he could and was assigned to a bracket on the basis of his performance.

Did They Travel for Pleasure?

$\mathscr{B}$eneath the royal necropolis, where carious peaks tumbled to a sunburnt plain, the colossus stood. Centuries of earthquakes and desert wind had reduced it to a shapeless hulk. But almost every morning, as dawn swept over the Nile, the colossus would sing. It was a song without words, sharp as the snapping of an otherworldly harp string.* The crowds of visitors who came to hear it were invariably impressed—so impressed that they did what people throughout history have done in the face of wonder and beauty: they left graffiti. The calves of the colossus read like a register: local dignitaries, passing soldiers, a scattering of provincial governors, and tourists from every corner of the Roman Empire.[1]

Travel in the classical world was inevitably slow, relentlessly uncomfortable, and surprisingly common. Merchants crossed and recrossed the Mediterranean, venturing as far as Sri Lanka in pursuit of pepper and profit.† Actors, athletes, and musicians journeyed from city to city, following the annual rounds of games and festivals. Scholars and students congregated in famous centers of learning. Pilgrims presented themselves to oracles. Officials shuttled from province to province.

---

* Local guides claimed that the colossus represented Memnon, the mythical son of Dawn, and that the song was Memnon's answer to his mother's light. The Colossus of Memnon actually depicted the great eighteenth-dynasty pharaoh Amenhotep III. Originally, it was one of two statues that flanked the main entrance to Amenhotep's mortuary temple, which fell into ruin before the Roman era. It began "singing" after it was badly damaged by an earthquake. The sound, probably caused by dew escaping from deep cracks in the stone, ceased after the statue was restored in the third century CE.

† A merchant from what is now western Turkey made no fewer than seventy-two voyages to Italy over the course of his career.

The Colossus of Memnon. The left leg is still covered with ancient graffiti. *Author's photo*

Slaves were sold. Soldiers marched. And a trickle of tourists set out for parts unknown.[2]

Leisure travel was limited in Classical Greece, where famous sanctuaries like Delphi and great festivals like the Olympics were almost the exclusive goals of long-distance journeys. Tourism was much more widespread in the rich and stable Roman Empire. The great biographer Plutarch, writing around the end of the first century CE, describes a meeting with two friends who had recently returned from long tours abroad. One had traveled through Egypt, visited the cave dwellers along the coasts of the Red Sea, and voyaged beyond the Persian Gulf on the trade route to India. The other man had been commissioned by the imperial government to explore remote islands off the coast of Britain that were rumored to be haunted by demons.*[3]

Whenever possible, long journeys were made by sea. Since there were no passenger ships, travelers booked passage on merchant vessels heading in the right direction. Most had to sleep on deck, and all were responsible for their own food and bedding. Passengers were also expected to help the crew in the event of bad weather, which could wreck even the largest vessels. One Roman author describes how he and six hundred fellow passengers were pitched into the sea when their vessel broke apart in a gale.† Only eighty survived to be rescued by a passing ship the next morning. Pirates could be an even greater danger, especially during the first century BCE, when they were bold enough to sack cities and kidnap Roman senators (including a young Julius Caesar).[4]

It was unusual for an ancient ship to sail faster than about 5 knots (approximately 6 miles per hour), or more than 125 miles in a day. But with a good wind, a ship setting out from the ports of Rome could reach North Africa in as little as two days, the French Riviera in three, and the Strait of Gibraltar in seven. Heading east from Rome or Naples, Greece might be only five days away, and Egypt only nine. These, however, were best-case scenarios. Contrary winds added weeks or months to a voyage, and for nearly half the year—from November to March—few captains would put to sea. These limitations, combined with the various dangers and discomforts of sea travel, encouraged many ancient tourists to make at least part of their journey overland.[5]

In Classical Greece, land travel meant walking or riding a donkey. Only the richest could afford horses, and the poor quality of the roads often made wagons impractical. Thanks to vastly better highways

---

* The islands turned out to be inhabited only by a few soggy druids.

† Most Greek and Roman merchant ships used in long-distance trade probably displaced between one hundred and four hundred tons—about as much as a modern harbor tugboat. A few, however, were considerably larger; the barges that carried Egyptian grain to Rome might be 180 feet long and displace 1,200 tons. These oversize vessels could carry up to a thousand passengers.

(and cheaper horses), passenger vehicles were much more common in the Roman world. There were many types. Two-wheeled carriages were typically light and swift, designed for one or two passengers and minimal baggage. Though heavier and slower, four-wheeled carriages were more spacious and—if the owner had money—luxurious. Roman emperors and senators pimped their rides with gold statues, silk upholstery, swivel seats, and built-in gaming boards.* Since even the swankiest examples lacked shock absorbers, however, riding in one of these rolling palaces was a rattling experience. It was much more comfortable to travel in a cushioned and curtained litter, which made it possible to nap, read, and write on the road.[6]

On foot or in a litter, a good pace was about twenty miles a day.† Heavy carriages were only slightly swifter, probably averaging about twenty-five miles a day. A light carriage might be twice as quick but was still unlikely to break five miles per hour; Caesar's single-day sprint of one hundred miles in a carriage was remembered as exceptional. Riding was the only way to go significantly faster. Since saddles were rudimentary and stirrups nonexistent, however, riding long distances was uncomfortable. And because of their relatively small size‡ and lack of shoes,§ ancient horses could not be ridden as fast or as far as their descendants. The record for a day's ride, with frequent changes of mount, was two hundred miles.[7]

Whether ensconced in a litter or jolting along in a carriage, it was a good idea to travel with a large group or at least with a few armed slaves. Highwaymen lurked in dark forests, lonely mountain passes, and even hotels (they occasionally took over remote inns and used them as bases for attacking unsuspecting travelers). Waylaid travelers lost their valuables and sometimes their lives; one especially brutal brigand was notorious for cutting off his victims' legs and letting them bleed

---

* The most impressive carriage of all was the one built to carry the body of Alexander the Great, a gilded temple-shaped monstrosity drawn by sixty-four bejeweled mules.

† Professional message runners—more useful than horses in the mountainous and largely roadless Greek world—were much faster. The famous Athenian runner Phidippides managed 155 miles in two days, and Alexander the Great's messenger supposedly ran almost as far in a single day.

‡ In Classical Greece, horses probably averaged about 4.5 feet (13.2 hands) at the withers. Roman horses tended to be slightly taller, but most were still only the size of a large modern pony.

§ The Romans sometimes equipped their horses with hipposandals—metal boots that encased the entire hoof—for long or hard rides. Horseshoes, however, were a late antique invention.

to death. Local authorities responded in kind, staging manhunts and hanging or crucifying robbers by the side of the road.[8]

No matter how dangerous the road, the hotel was usually worse. The great majority of Greek and Roman inns were filthy, cramped, and crawling with bedbugs. The food wasn't very appealing either; some innkeepers were said to slip the flesh of murdered guests into their stews. Travelers who could afford to avoid hotels usually did so. Some Roman notables bought lodges on the roads between their villas and the capital, staffed them with slaves, and slept in them as they journeyed to and fro. Whenever possible, wealthy travelers stayed in the homes of friends and acquaintances. If none was available, a slave was sent ahead to the next town, where he would inform the owner of the largest house that *someone important* was in need of a room.[9]

As mentioned earlier, the Classical Greeks normally confined their travel to the great sanctuaries that hosted oracles and games. The Romans were more ambitious tourists. For wealthy Romans, the default vacation destination was the Bay of Naples. Although the island of Capri, owned by the emperors, was off-limits to the public, tourists could revere the Grotto of the Sibyl at Cumae, sample athletic contests and theater performances at Naples, or abandon themselves to the torrid pleasures of Baiae, sin city of the classical world.

Those who wanted a serious dose of culture headed to Greece. In Athens, tourists marveled at the artistic treasures of the Acropolis and visited the most fashionable philosophers. At Sparta, they indulged in the less exalted pleasure of watching the annual "endurance contest," during which boys lay upon an altar and competed to see who could be whipped the longest without crying out. The mountain sanctuary of Delphi, glittering with the offerings left by centuries of pilgrims, was another favorite destination, as was the magnificent ivory statue of Zeus at Olympia, one of the Seven Wonders of the World. The remains of another wonder could be seen at Rhodes, where tourists tried to wrap their arms around the thumb of the fallen Colossus. Between the famous cities and artistic treasures, visitors paused to appreciate mementos of the Greek myths, including the clay from which Prometheus had molded mankind and a loving replica of Helen of Troy's breast.[10]

In Asia Minor (modern Turkey), tourists flocked to the famous statue of Aphrodite at Knidos, which stood in a marble pavilion perfumed by flowering trees. This sculpture was agreed to be the most alluring of Greek masterpieces (local souvenir sellers produced a titillating array of commemorative erotic pottery).[11] For any Roman traveling through Asia Minor, however, the main attraction was the city of Ilium, which stood on the reputed site of Homer's Troy. Since the Romans claimed descent from the Trojan hero Aeneas and his followers, they sometimes thought of Ilium as a sort of ancestral home. The Ilians, happy to profit from this fantasy, led visitors to the site of every episode in the Trojan War, up to and including the tomb of Achilles.

Tourists could relive history in Ilium and stock up on erotic crockery at Knidos. But for a real taste of the exotic, they visited Egypt. Most began by sailing to Alexandria. After docking in the shadow of the city's towering lighthouse—more than three hundred feet tall and visible up to thirty miles away—they wandered the broad boulevards lined with porticoes for miles on end. The pious sacrificed in the immense temple complexes. The scholarly took in lectures at the famous library. The curious visited the monumental tomb of Alexander the Great.[12]

From Alexandria, tourists secured passage on boats heading up the Nile. The first destination was usually Memphis, where the sacred Apis bull could be seen moseying around its enclosure. A short distance away, visitors watched local villagers, working for tips, climb the sheer face of the Great Pyramid. Some tourists continued up the Nile to modern Aswan, where the more daring shot the rapids of the First Cataract in an ancient version of whitewater rafting. Most, however, went no further than Thebes (modern Luxor), where they gaped at the colossal Karnak Temple, strained to hear the colossus sing, and lighted torches to explore tombs in the Valley of the Kings. In one tomb, more than a thousand ancient graffiti have been discovered. These confirm that, when it came to the pleasures of travel, the Greeks and Romans felt much as we do. One etched message summarizes them all: "wonderful, wonderful, wonderful!"[13]

· 26 ·

How Was the Colosseum Built in Less Than a Decade?

The numbers are impressive: 617 feet long, 512 feet wide, 170 feet high; eighty entrances, seating for fifty thousand or so spectators. The amenities were equally remarkable. A sail-like awning, furled and unfurled by a detachment of imperial marines, sheltered the upper decks from the sun. An elaborate barrier of ivory and gold, punctuated by sniper stations, protected the lower rows from leaping carnivores. Alcoves beneath the seats held lavatories and water fountains.* Along the edges of the sandy arena, dozens of trapdoors waited to unleash exotic beasts and gladiators from a warren of subterranean corridors and cells. The Colosseum, in short, was a triumph of Roman engineering. Astonishingly, almost the whole vast structure, from the flapping awnings twenty stories above the arena to the lamplit labyrinth beneath it, was constructed in a few years.[1]

In the Greek world, large building projects tended to be agonizingly slow. The great Temple of Olympian Zeus at Athens, for example, was begun around 520 BCE but not finished until 131 CE—and then only with a serious infusion of imperial funding.† The Temple of Hera at Samos, begun around 530 BCE, was still under construction when a marauding Gothic tribe put the project out of its misery a millennium later.[2]

---

* The Colosseum also may have had sprinklers to cool fans in hot weather. Other Roman entertainment buildings of the same vintage were equipped with nozzles that emitted a saffron-scented mist. A poet describes sprinklers integrated into the bronze statues around a theater's stage.

† When Hadrian dedicated the temple, he saw fit—for reasons best known to himself—to decorate it with an enormous stuffed python.

143

Although the greatest building projects of the Roman emperors were larger and more complex than any Greek temple, they were completed much, much more quickly. Justinian's Church of Hagia Sophia, with its awesome central dome and vast expanses of glittering gold mosaic, was finished in five years. The bathing block of the Baths of Caracalla—a building that covered more than six acres and whose main rooms were more than one hundred feet tall—was done in four.*

Roman emperors had three critical advantages over other ancient builders. First and foremost, they were Roman emperors—undisputed masters of nearly a quarter of the human race and capable of calling on labor and resources beyond the wildest dreams of any king or city council. Second, they had access to mass-produced building materials. By the end of the first century CE, every large marble and granite quarry in the Roman Empire was under state ownership. These quarries—located as far afield as Greece, Tunisia, and Egypt—exported columns, blocks, and prefabricated statues hundreds or thousands of miles to the capital. The remotest quarries of all, in the burning wastes of Egypt's Eastern Desert, produced fifty- and one-hundred-ton granite columns for Rome's temples and baths.† Equally important for the construction process, if less dramatic, were the imperially owned brickyards in and around the Tiber valley, which turned out millions of square, thin bricks in three standard sizes every year. The cocktail of water, lime, and volcanic powder that we call Roman concrete was the final factor that allowed the emperors to build so quickly. Unlike modern concrete, it was not poured, but laid in thin layers over bedded rubble. It set, however, as hard as its modern counterpart—and in some cases, even harder.‡ Concrete allowed the Romans to build soaring vaults and audacious domes. But it was most commonly used as a time-saving filler in walls and foundations.

---

* These construction times are made even more impressive by the fact that the Romans typically built only eight months of the year, since winter rain and frost complicated the setting of mortar and concrete.

† Pompey's Pillar, a three-hundred-ton column from the same quarries, still stands in Alexandria. In keeping with the scale of the quarry system, the barges that carried Egyptian stones were gigantic. The largest on record, built to bring a 230-ton obelisk from Egypt to Rome, is said to have carried (besides the obelisk) some 2,600 tons of grain and no fewer than 1,200 passengers.

‡ Counterintuitively, Roman concrete is most durable when exposed to salt water. The interaction of pozzolana and lime with seawater produces crystals of a rare mineral called aluminum tobermorite, which cause the concrete to actually grow stronger with age.

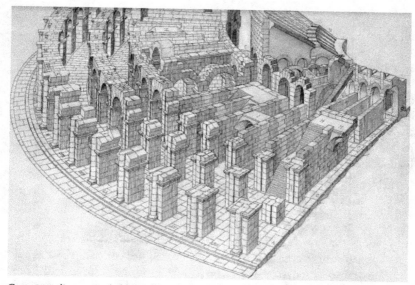

Cutaway diagram of the Colosseum's first level, showing the stone piers that supported the building. *After Le Moniteur des architects 9 (1875), pl. 12*

Vast resources, mass-produced materials, and concrete gave Roman emperors the means to build on a massive scale. Politics supplied the motivation. Public construction in the capital was an important way for emperors to advertise their legitimacy and demonstrate their commitment to the welfare of the Roman people. Vespasian, the emperor who began the Colosseum, was the founder of a new dynasty and thus particularly motivated to build something spectacular.

The Colosseum was constructed by private contractors under imperial supervision. Each contractor employed a permanent staff of skilled slaves and freedmen, who directed large teams of unskilled day laborers.[3] Although the number of laborers varied, it is likely that more than ten thousand men were involved at peak times.[4] The gargantuan first task was to excavate an oval trench—twenty-five feet deep and two hundred feet wide—beneath the footprint of the planned amphitheater. Since the trench had to be cut through bedrock and saturated subsoil, digging alone may have taken the better part of a year. Once the spoil was clear, the walls were lined with wooden forms, and the trench was filled with a colossal ring of concrete.*

As soon as the foundation had set, work began on the super-structure. The walls of most large Roman buildings were made of brick-faced concrete. Both the perimeter wall and the interior support columns of the Colosseum, however, were built of massive stone blocks bonded with iron clamps. The decision to use so much stone reflects the builders' awareness that Roman concrete, for all its strength, tended to deform at points of great stress. To avoid risking a collapse, all major load-bearing elements were made the old-fashioned way.

The stone used was travertine, a heavy limestone quarried east of Rome and ferried to the city by barge. More than one hundred thou-sand cubic yards (bonded with an estimated three hundred tons of iron clamps) eventually would be built into the Colosseum—and all of it, cut into blocks that averaged four tons in weight, was lifted into place with a few dozen simple cranes. Each of these machines consisted of a heavy wooden frame supporting a block and tackle. Once a stone had been secured to the rope running through the block and tackle, it was raised by men turning a windlass or walking in a giant treadwheel.[†5]

The vaults and substructures that would support the seats rose in tandem with the perimeter wall. Although the key structural elements were travertine, both tufa (a soft local stone) and concrete were used extensively. Throughout, the builders carefully managed structural weight, mixing pumice into the concrete in the vaults of the upper levels to ease the stress on the walls and foundations.

As the perimeter wall neared its final height, the marble seats were laid on the concrete crowns of the vaults, and craftsmen began to install the building's amenities. Plumbers ran lead pipes through the building, opened a branch line from the nearby Claudian Aqueduct, and installed the water fountains. Sculptors created statues of gods and heroes for the arches of the second and third stories, and metalworkers crafted gates to fill the arches of the first. The corridors were plastered and painted,

---

* Despite its immense strength, the Colosseum's concrete foundation had a serious weak-ness: only the northern half was supported by bedrock. The southern half was laid on loose sediment, leaving the portion of the amphitheater above it susceptible to earthquake damage. During the Middle Ages, this part of the building would be virtually destroyed by a series of tremors.

† Roman cranes could handle impressive loads. The marble capital of Trajan's Column, which weighs fifty-three tons, was lifted more than one hundred feet to its final position.

the masts and canvas of the awning were maneuvered into position, and then—at last—all was ready.*[6]

The man stumbled forward, narrowly avoiding collision with the large and surly-looking person just ahead of him in line. Stopping himself in time, he fixed the folds of his toga. Then he craned his neck back again and gaped. Like everyone else in Rome, he had watched from a distance as the new amphitheater's walls rose. Standing beneath those walls, however, was something else entirely. The rising sun lent a rosy tinge to the cliff of masonry, and the bronze statues in the arches blazed like sparks or falling stars or . . . An unpoetic shove from behind shattered his reverie. The line was moving again.

Hustling forward, he fished the entry token[†] from his coin purse and presented it to the bored-looking slave at the table. The slave examined his token. Then, with the ghost of a shrug, he handed it back and motioned the man past the white-cloaked guards. Faintly relieved—the Praetorians always made him anxious—he made his way to the entrance marked on his token and merged with the flood streaming up the broad stairs.

A few minutes of jostling, a few more flights of stairs; then solitude, sunlight, and his section. When he reached his row, he paused. Marble benches shimmered on either side. The sands of the arena sparkled far below. Overhead, the awnings framed a perfect oval of blue sky. Rome, he reflected, really was the center of the world.

---

* Well, almost all. When the Colosseum was dedicated in 80 CE, the labyrinth of corridors, cages, and lifts beneath the arena was left unfinished. This was probably deliberate. Among the grand and gory spectacles staged during the hundred days of games that marked the building's dedication were several that required flooding the arena. One of these aquatic extravaganzas involved dozens of horses and bulls performing an elaborate synchronized swimming routine. Another culminated in a miniature sea battle between fleets of small ships. It would have been very difficult to stage these spectacles if the subterranean tunnels had been in place.

† "Tickets" for the Colosseum were the tokens (ivory, metal, or terracotta) known as tesserae. These seem to have usually indicated the entrance, section, and row. Though free, the tesserae were distributed in blocks to prominent men and organizations. Any ordinary Roman who wanted to watch the games had to beg, borrow, or steal his token from one of these brokers.

· 27 ·

How Were Animals Captured
for the Colosseum?

$\mathcal{H}$e squinted, shielding his eyes with a cupped hand. For hours, he had watched the line of sunlight creep closer, illuminating the hats of the senators in the first rows,* the perspiring worthies in the second tier, and finally his own section. Keenly aware of the sweat soaking his toga, he shifted on the marble bench, trying to find a more comfortable position. He succeeded only in impaling his back on the knees of the man behind him. Resigning his rear to numbness, he turned his attention back to the arena.[1]

The games, at least, had been worthwhile. There had been some first-rate executions. One criminal had been given the wings of Icarus, strung on a wire high overhead, and dropped into the arena. Another had been dressed as the mythical bard Orpheus and tied to a stake. Dozens of tame animals had been placed around the prisoner in a circle, as though listening. Then a bear had risen from a trapdoor and torn "Orpheus" apart.† The hunts also had been very fine. A team of women dressed as Amazons had stabbed a charging lion, and a famous gladiator had killed a great white bear with a single thrust of his spear.‡[2]

And now a new wonder: the voice of the announcer rang over the arena, proclaiming that the emperor had brought from farthest

---

* Only senators were allowed to wear sun hats at public spectacles. Everyone else had to sweat it out.

† Animals were frequently used in arena executions, though elaborate mythological dramas like those described here were relatively rare. It was much more common to tie the condemned to stakes and unleash dogs, bears, lions, or leopards on them. Alternatively, criminals might be given ineffective weapons and forced to defend themselves against starving predators.

‡ The best arena hunters were capable of stunning bears by punching them in the face, blinding charging lions with their cloaks, and killing elephants with a spear.

Ethiopia a creature not seen since the reign of the divine Augustus: the terrible and tremendous rhinoceros! As the crowd buzzed excitedly and the organist played a triumphant tune, a strange beast shambled onto the arena: bull shaped, but larger than any bull, with the wrinkled hide of an elephant and two wicked horns on its snout. An anxious-looking trainer in a smudged tunic emerged beside it. Cracking a long whip, he drove the beast toward the center of the arena. As he did, heavy doors grated and a huge bull trotted out. The man sat up expectantly. He had seen bears battle bulls, bulls batter elephants, and—once, gloriously— lions lacerating tigers. This promised to be a fight to remember.

The bull stopped a few dozen yards from the rhinoceros, snorting and pawing. For a long moment, the rhinoceros stared at the other animal, ignoring its trainer's whip. Then it charged with astonishing speed, lowered its mighty head, and threw the bull over its shoulder. Its opponent vanquished, the rhinoceros slowed to a trot, ears twitching at the sound of fifty thousand Romans cheering themselves hoarse.[3]

The games at which the rhino appeared were staged sometime in the 80s CE. In their wake, the rhino became a celebrity. It appeared on coins, starred in poems, and was even featured in the decoration of a temple in the Forum. From these adoring portraits, we can tell that it was a white rhinoceros, probably captured in what is now South Sudan or Uganda, some four thousand miles from Rome. Although few others came quite so far, the rhino was only one of the hundreds of exotic animals brought to the Colosseum every year. No fewer than nine thousand animals were killed during the Colosseum's dedicatory games. A generation later, over the 123 days of games commemorating the conquest of Dacia (modern Romania), eleven thousand were slaughtered.

To meet this immense demand, animals were imported from every corner of the known world. Bears were shipped from as far away as Scotland. From northern Europe came elk, bison, and the fierce aurochs, a now-extinct species of wild cow. Tigers were taken in northern Iran and India. Egypt produced crocodiles and hippos. Other parts of North Africa provided lions, leopards, panthers, hyenas, and elephants. Sub-Saharan Africa sent gazelles, giraffes, ostriches, zebras, apes, and the occasional rhinoceros.

Some arena animals were captured by soldiers. Roman troops netted gazelles in Egypt, stalked lions in Algeria, and bagged bears and bison in Bulgaria. A few men became semiprofessionals; one German centurion managed to capture fifty bears in six months. Most of the animals that appeared in the Colosseum, however, were caught by local groups of experienced hunters. In parts of North Africa, these men were organized into guilds. Elsewhere, they were probably freelancers hired to provide a certain number of animals by a given date.[4]

Hunting methods varied by species. Herbivores like deer and gazelle were frightened into long nets by teams of men with dogs and torches. Bison, which could charge through any net, were funneled into valleys lined with greased hides, where they lost their footing and rolled into an enclosure. Ostriches were ridden down and lassoed by cowboys. Lions were taken in pit traps baited with lambs or kid goats. Leopards were drugged—it was said—by dumping wine in their watering holes. Tiger cubs were reportedly seized by hunters on fast horses.*[5]

Capturing the animals was the easy part. The hard part was getting them back to Rome and keeping them alive until the games. During the first stages of the journey, herbivores were led along with ropes. Carnivores were confined in ventilated wooden boxes, which were loaded onto ox-drawn carts. Within the imperial borders, hunters were authorized to use the heavy wagons of the postal system. These vehicles, which had a maximum capacity of about twelve hundred pounds, could comfortably accommodate a crated carnivore or two. Conveniently, every town through which the hunters passed was obligated to feed the animals for up to a week.[6]

In African ports where merchants specialized in shipping animals for the games, there were ships designed to hold large animals. But most animals seem to have been crammed into the holds of bulk cargo

---

* Hunters, we are told, would steal a female tiger's cubs from her den and gallop off with them. When she realized her cubs were gone, the tigress would pursue the hunter. But just as she caught up with him, he would drop one of her cubs. The tigress would stop to rescue it, taking it back to her den. Then she would resume her chase. Just as she got close enough to pounce, the hunter would drop another cub, and she would stop again. By the time she returned, the hunter would be safely out of reach with the remaining cub or cubs. In a variation of this technique, a hunter would drop a mirror instead of a cub as the tigress approached. Mistaking her reflection for one of her cubs, she would stop and worry the mirror while the hunter escaped. There is, of course, no reason to believe that tigers were actually captured this way; the story probably evolved from the fact that most of the tigers shipped into the empire from Iran and India were females and cubs.

A disgruntled-looking antelope being loaded onto a ship. Note the ventilated transport crates on deck. *Fourth-century mosaic from the Villa Romana del Casale. Author's photo*

vessels for the long journey to Italy. On arrival, elephants and other herbivores were sent to imperial estates outside the capital.* The rest proceeded directly to Rome, where they were kept in a large enclosure with high stone walls and rows of wooden pens and cages.† A few of the more telegenic specimens were exhibited in the city center. During the reign of Augustus, for example, a reservoir was built to exhibit Nile crocodiles to the Roman people, and the Egyptian handlers put on regular shows for onlookers, netting the crocodiles and flipping them onto a basking platform.[7]

As they awaited their moment in the arena, some animals were trained to entertain. Lions were taught to gum their trainers' hands

---

* Thanks to inscriptions, we know that the animals on the imperial estates were overseen by men with titles like "elephant handler," "camel keeper," and "master of herbivores."

† During some periods, the animals were briefly kept in riverside cages before being shipped to the vivarium. In the first century BCE, a famous sculptor visited these cages to make sketches of a recently arrived lion. He was so intent on his work, however, that he failed to notice he was being stalked by an escaped leopard.

and play fetch with live hares. Monkeys learned to wear miniature soldier's uniforms and ride goats around the arena. The most aggressive predators were sent to the school of the beast fighters, where they were conditioned to overcome their fear of humans. Those that showed exceptional savagery would be used to execute prisoners. A few even received stage names.*[8]

Sometimes predators were given live prey: one anecdote mentions a goat being dropped into a tiger's cage (to the frustration of its trainers, the tiger befriended the goat). If games were underway, predators received the remains of animals killed in the arena. Otherwise, they apparently lived on butcher's meat. This could be quite expensive: Caligula once ordered prisoners fed to the animals to cut costs. Beyond the logistics of feeding, there was the sheer difficulty of keeping exotic animals alive in a strange environment. One late Roman official lamented that most of the crocodiles he had imported at great expense from Egypt were too sick to eat.[9]

The day before they appeared in the games, herbivores were moved to the outskirts of Rome, and carnivores were prodded back into their traveling crates. That night, the animals were brought to the Colosseum. Elephants and other large animals, which would enter the arena through one of the ground-level entrances, were penned nearby. Everything smaller than a bull was herded into the tunnels beneath the arena, where hundreds of slaves manned a bustling underworld of cages and lifts. Just before the games, the animals were given some final primping and prepping—festive garlands might be wrapped around their paws, or gold dust sprinkled on their fur. Then, at last, they were hoisted up to the arena in a slave-powered elevator. Virtually all were killed within a few minutes of reaching their final destination.†[10]

---

* Favorite names included "Victor" (Winner), "Crudelis" (Savage), and "Omicida" (Murderer).

† Death was not quite the end. As soon as the animals were dragged from the arena, tusks, skins, and other valuable bits and pieces were removed for sale. A few delicacies, like elephant heart and ostrich brain, went to the emperor's table. Most of the meat, however, was given to the Roman people (bear, incidentally, was considered more nutritious than lion or leopard). The meat often seems to have been distributed by a sort of lottery. During intermissions in the games, tokens were thrown into the audience. Those who managed to catch a token with the image of an animal could redeem it for a given quantity of arena meat at the end of the day. Sometimes, to cut out the middlemen, Roman citizens were allowed to hunt for themselves. One emperor created an artificial forest in the Circus Maximus and populated it with a thousand ostriches, a thousand deer, a thousand boars, and many other animals. He then allowed the people to enter the forest and kill as many animals as they could drag away.

The beast hunts allowed the emperors to showcase their generosity, demonstrate their world-spanning power, and advertise Rome's domination of nature itself. But they did so at a terrible ecological cost. By the time the last games were held in the Colosseum, the leopards of Turkey, the tigers of Iran, the hippos of Egypt, and the North African forest elephant had all been hunted to or near extinction. Not all victims of Roman imperialism were human.

Were Gladiators Fat? How Deadly
Was Gladiatorial Combat?

$\mathcal{W}$e don't know how the gladiator fell. Maybe a net caught his ankles; maybe a flickering trident bit his side. Somehow, he found himself gasping on the bloody sand. Over the ringing of his ears, he heard the crowd roar. Then his helmet was wrenched off. A slap of air, the dazzle of light—and a trident, blurring toward his head. The gladiator's punctured skull, discovered eighteen centuries later near the ancient city of Ephesus, tells the story of his death. The rest of his bones, analyzed by forensic anthropologists, trace the longer tale of his life. He had died in his twenties. And he had lived—apparently for years—on a fattening diet of beans and porridge.[1]

A gladiator had little control over his diet or any other aspect of his existence. Most gladiators were slaves, captured in war or condemned in court. The rest were freeborn volunteers, motivated by desperate poverty or misguided enthusiasm. Whatever their origins, gladiators resided in a prisonlike compound known as a "school." There, except for the few times each year that they faced the hazards of the arena, they spent their days training. A new gladiator began by practicing basic swordplay against a dummy or wooden stake. Once the master of the school had evaluated his abilities, he was assigned to one of the dozen or so fighting styles.* He would spend months honing his skills under the direction of an experienced trainer before his first match. Throughout the training process, his body was kept in good fighting order. His

---

* Exceptionally talented fighters would learn additional weapons. The leading members of a gladiators' guild in second-century Rome claimed to be masters of no fewer than six fighting styles.

muscles were eased by expert masseuses. If he was wounded, he received medical care.* He could count on eating often, if not well.[2]

Gladiators were fed bean soup and barley gruel, mashed together and dished out in enormous quantities. This high-protein paste was unique to gladiators. Other Romans mocked it, calling gladiators "barley boys." Soldiers never touched the stuff, and professional boxers and wrestlers, who might be expected to have a similar diet, guzzled meat instead.†[3]

So why were gladiators—and only gladiators—given barley and beans? The scientists who analyzed the gladiator bones in Ephesus suggested that the diet was intended to encourage weight gain; a few inches of fat would have shielded a gladiator's vital organs, allowing him to sustain spectacular flesh wounds without losing the ability to fight. The idea that gladiators were overweight soon trickled into the mainstream media and is still routinely cited online.[4]

There is, however, no reason to assume that the heroes of the arena were out of shape. That gladiators ate a potentially fattening diet is clear. That this diet actually made them overweight is not. It is intrinsically unlikely that the masters of the gladiator schools, where the training emphasized speed and endurance, would have wanted, let alone encouraged, their men to become heavy. In all probability, gladiators were served beans and barley simply because these foods were nutritious and cheap. Ancient authors describe gladiators as men bulging with muscle;‡ and unless we attribute the trim and powerful fighters who strut across so many Roman mosaics to artistic license, we can safely assume that gladiators, if not as toned as modern athletes, were far from out of shape.[5]

---

* The quality of this care varied. The grateful men of one school set up a statue of the doctor who treated their wounds. Galen, on the other hand, noted that the gladiator doctors of his native city killed most of their patients.

† The training diet for combat athletes—boxers, wrestlers, and pankratiasts—was based on pork, ideally acorn fed. Beef was an acceptable alternative. Goat meat, which produced goatish-smelling sweat, was not. When preparing for competitions, athletes devoured enormous servings of meat—sometimes three pounds or more—along with great hunks of doughy bread.

‡ Galen, admittedly, claims that the gladiators' food made their flesh soft, but he seems to mean only that they became more vulnerable to disease.

Thick or thin, gladiators knew how to put on a show. Like modern professional wrestlers, gladiators chose stage names that ranged from menacing ("Blade") to sexy ("Loverboy") to ironic ("The Gentleman"). Matches were promoted weeks in advance with painted advertisements, hand-drawn programs, and full-length portraits of famous fighters. The venues themselves were spectacular. Nero had flakes of glittering moonstone scattered over the sands of his amphitheater and sent an expedition to the Baltic to gather amber for the nets that protected the first rows. There was even theme music: a mosaic from Libya shows a full arena band, complete with a bored-looking woman in a wig playing the water organ.[6]

Unlike pro wrestling matches, gladiatorial combats weren't staged.* They were, however, carefully stylized. Some gladiatorial fighting styles were copied from Rome's enemies; the war chariots of Gaul and Britain, for example, inspired the *essedarii*—gladiators who battled from speeding chariots driven by steely-nerved slaves. Other styles were created for the arena, like the *andabatae*, who wore helmets without eyeholes and fought by sound. All were designed to maximize spectacle.[7]

The various fighting styles fell into light-armored and heavy-armored groups. Since like-armored men tended to produce long and boring fights—one Roman poet describes a duel between two heavy gladiators that went on until nightfall—matches almost always pitted a light fighter against a heavy one. In the imperial era, the most popular pairing was between a *retiarius* and a *secutor*. The *retiarius* was a light-armored gladiator equipped with a weighted net and fisherman's trident. The heavy-armored *secutor* had a large rectangular shield, a helmet with narrow eye slits (to keep trident thrusts at bay), and a stabbing sword. The *retiarius* darted from side to side, trying to immobilize his opponent with the net and spit him with the trident. The *secutor* parried casts and thrusts and attempted to maneuver his nimble adversary into stabbing range.[8]

Matches were planned months in advance. When an emperor or local notable decided that his games needed gladiators, he contacted the masters of the local schools and arranged to rent a given number of their

---

* Cheating was far from unknown in ancient athletics. A number of Olympic contenders attempted to bribe their competitors, and a papyrus from Roman Egypt describes a fixed wrestling match. Accusations of cheating occasionally forced chariot races to be stopped and rerun in the Circus Maximus.

Two scenes of a match between a *retiarius* named Astyanax (left) and a *secutor* named Kalendio. The men in white tunics are referees. The lower panel is a combat scene, showing Kalendio lunging toward his opponent. In the upper panel, Kalendio has fallen, and both of the referees have rushed forward. The inscriptions on top tell us how the match ended: Astyanax "vicit" (won); the crossed "O" next to Kalendio's name indicates that he was killed. *Third-century mosaic now in the National Archaeological Museum in Madrid. Wikimedia Commons*

fighters.* To make matches exciting, pains were taken to pair fighters with similar skill levels. During the early imperial era, a six- or seven-tier

---

* Gladiators received part of the money paid to the school owner regardless of whether they won or lost. According to one inscription, enslaved gladiators were granted 20 percent of the lease money, and free gladiators 25 percent. Victorious fighters were given additional prizes ranging from crowns to sacks of coins.

system for ranking gladiators emerged. The lowest rank was for first-time fighters.* The next rank was for those who had survived their inaugural fight. Above these were four or five "training groups." Members of the top group, who were likely to have won at least ten fights, had an internal hierarchy based on record. Matches between champions of this caliber were the highlight of any games that could afford them.[9]

Gladiators fought in the afternoon, often after a morning of beast hunts. There seem to have been about a dozen matches per day, each lasting an average of ten to fifteen minutes. Fights took place under the watchful eyes of two referees—probably retired gladiators—who wore distinctive striped tunics and used long switches to signal fouls. These men ensured that both combatants followed the rules and may have even called timeouts if a fighter was badly wounded or visibly exhausted.

Some fights were terminated by a fatal blow.† A few were declared a draw, usually after evenly matched gladiators had fought to a standstill. The majority, however, ended when one of the gladiators—disarmed, wounded, or simply unable to continue—raised a finger in the gesture of submission. The head referee then stopped the match and looked toward the sponsor of the games. The sponsor, in turn, listened to the audience. Those who wanted to spare the defeated gladiator called out *missum!* (pardon!) and waved handkerchiefs. Those who thought otherwise shouted *iugula!* (cut his throat!) and jabbed their thumbs at their necks. If the cries for death prevailed, the victorious gladiator struck a fatal blow. A few unfortunates were subjected to a more theatrical execution. A slave dressed as the demon Charun materialized in the arena carrying a sledgehammer. Gliding past the referees, he lifted his hammer high, paused for effect, and brought it down on the doomed man's skull. The corpse was then dragged from the arena behind a slave costumed as Mercury, guide of the dead.[10]

Most of the gladiators killed after their defeat died because they had failed to please the crowd. The Romans were connoisseurs of

---

* Beneath even the lowliest gladiators were the *gregarii* (gang fighters), unruly mobs of prisoners and convicts who battled each other before the one-on-one matches. These bloody brawls could be massive. Caesar once staged a battle with five hundred men (and twenty war elephants) on each side. Nearly a century later, in a spectacle organized by the emperor Claudius, an army of condemned men attacked a purpose-built "town" defended by British captives.

† A few famous fights ended with the deaths of both gladiators. When this happened during the reign of Claudius, the emperor was so impressed that he had a set of knives made from the men's swords for his personal use.

combat. Some fans, preferring the fast footwork and dexterity of the light-armored gladiators, were "little shield men." Others were "big shield men" and cheered for the sturdy defense and raw power of the heavy-armored types. In some cities, there were full-fledged fan clubs for the different fighting styles. During a match, the audience worked itself into a frenzy, cheering, shouting advice, and calling out *habet!* (he's done!) when a fighter was wounded.* Spectators knew a good fight when they saw one—a character in a Roman novel complains about gladiators "fighting by the book"—and respected skill and bravery.† If a defeated gladiator had fought well, they usually called for him to be spared.[11]

When the crowd called for mercy, the sponsor of the games was likely to listen. Gladiators were hired for a small fraction—perhaps 5 or 10 percent—of their estimated value. If they died in the arena, however, the sponsor had to pay their full value to the master of their school. Only an extremely wealthy man could afford to allow indiscriminate slaughter. Indiscriminate slaughter, admittedly, sometimes occurred. One inscription mentions an afternoon in which eleven matches were held—and eleven gladiators died. Another describes games in which every gladiator had to fight "for his life." Such bloodbaths, however, were rare. Most sponsors preferred to minimize casualties,‡ and some went so far as to issue blunted weapons before a fight.[12]

Even gladiators were reluctant to kill their opponents. This was partly an expression of comradery, since the combatants in a match often came from the same school. But it was also a matter of professional pride. In their funerary inscriptions, gladiators boast that they "saved many souls" or "hurt no one." One gladiator's epitaph, in fact, claims that he killed an opponent specifically because the man was filled with "unreasoning hatred"—in other words, he was murdering people

---

* Such audiences did not take kindly to interruptions: in the early fifth century, a monk was stoned to death for leaping into the arena of the Colosseum and trying to stop a gladiatorial match. Or so the pious legend goes.

† The popular association of gladiators with courage and virility went far beyond the arena. It became customary, for example, to run a spear dipped in gladiator blood through a bride's hair, on the theory that this would encourage fertility. Gladiator blood was also an accepted cure for epilepsy. Even the bloodstained sand on which gladiators fought was thought to have magical and medicinal properties.

‡ Even the emperors—who could afford to kill as many gladiators as they liked—sometimes encouraged mercy. Nero staged a long series of bloodless gladiatorial combats, and Marcus Aurelius presided over matches in which every weapon was blunted. Commodus, who fancied himself a gladiator, fought with a wooden sword, and never killed an opponent.

he didn't have to. The spectators, for their part, appreciated fighters who could demonstrate their skill without slaughtering every opponent. A Roman poet wrote an epigram praising a gladiator who "always wins, but never kills."[13]

Defeated gladiators, in short, were often spared. To judge from the fight records preserved on gladiators' tombstones, perhaps one in five matches ended in death. Although a few champions managed to rack up more than one hundred victories, the typical gladiator who survived until retirement faced a total of ten or fifteen opponents during the course of a five- or six-year career. Most gladiators who died in the arena probably did so in their first or second fights. The more experienced they became, the likelier they were to survive. A high-ranked gladiator had learned how to win; if he lost, he was very expensive to kill.[14]

V

WAR AND POLITICS

· 29 ·

How Were War Elephants
Used in Battle?

He blinked sweat out of his eyes, whispered a prayer, and braced. Ten thousand miles he had marched with King Alexander. Times beyond counting he had held the line, facing death down a splintered pike. But he had never seen anything like this. Across a steaming field, hundreds of elephants were charging. Spattered mud hung in the air. Sunlight flashed on the beasts' bladed tusks. And then pikes snapped and men screamed and an elephant was among them, twenty feet away, impaling, killing. Reaching out with its trunk, it caught a man around the waist, lifted him, flung him to the ground with a sickening crunch. Spattered to its flanks in blood, heedless of the spears hanging from its sides, it tore deeper and deeper into the ranks. Shouts from behind snapped the soldier's head around. Another elephant. He blinked sweat out of his eyes, whispered a prayer, and braced.[1]

In the end, the elephants were driven back. In the end, Alexander won, as he always did. But the terrifying charge of the elephants on that day in 326 BCE, at what would come to be known as the Battle of the Hydaspes, changed the course of Greek warfare. Alexander and his generals had encountered elephants before. Only after witnessing the carnage at the Hydaspes, however, did they begin to consider using the animals for themselves. Alexander died before he could try, but his generals would marshal ever-larger elephant herds in their struggles to control the fragments of his empire. At the epochal Battle of Ipsos, which ended the first phase of their wars, nearly five hundred war elephants took the field.

For two centuries, elephants were a fixture of Mediterranean warfare. They scattered Roman cavalry on the plains of southern

Italy, crested the Alps with Hannibal, and charged the Maccabees in the Judean Hills. But then, almost as quickly as they had appeared, elephants vanished from the battlefields of the classical world. To understand why, we need some background about how they were used in war.

The Greeks and Romans knew two varieties of elephant: the Asian elephant, which they associated with India, and a now extinct species or subspecies of African forest elephant, which was found throughout North Africa.* The most important difference between these varieties was size. A male Asian elephant averages between nine and eleven feet at the shoulder and weighs five or six tons. North African forest elephants were considerably smaller, with males probably averaging slightly less than eight feet at the shoulder and three tons in weight.

There were several methods of capturing elephants. In India, tame females were used to lure wild elephants into a corral. In North Africa, pit traps were dug.† An alternate method involved driving an entire herd into a closed valley. After several days of being trapped without food, the elephants would become docile enough to be led away.

Captured elephants were led away on chains, preferably held by other tame elephants. If they were to be transported by sea, a suitable vessel had to be found. The Ptolemaic kings of Egypt built special barges to bring elephants up the Red Sea. Elsewhere, the largest available ships were probably requisitioned.‡

Once the elephants had disembarked, they were taken to the stables where they would be trained. Males and females were separated (when they could smell females, male elephants had a habit of knocking down walls to get at them) and led to their stalls, where they were fed a rich blend of barley, raisins, and vegetables.[2]

Training a war elephant required years of careful supervision. Each animal was given a suitably warlike name—"Ajax" was a popular choice—and assigned a driver. These men were specialists, occasionally recruited from as far away as India. They formed close bonds with their

---

* The Greeks and Romans never used the massive African bush elephant, which was both less accessible (as a native of central and southern Africa) and more difficult to train.

† It was rumored that as soon as an elephant fell into one of these traps, the other members of its herd would pile brush and earth into the pit to help their comrade escape.

‡ Whatever the vessel used, the voyage was seldom relaxing for anyone involved, since elephants tended to panic when they realized that they were being led over water. One author claims that when elephants disembarked from a ship, they went down the gangway backward to avoid seeing the water on either side.

mounts.* The loyalty of elephants to their drivers was legendary. Once, for example, when a driver was wounded and fell from his seat during a furious street battle, his elephant scooped the man up in its trunk, laid him across its tusks, and charged through the enemy to safety, trampling all who stood in the way.[3]

In the course of its training, an elephant learned to obey the calls of its driver and to interpret the taps of his crooked staff. It was taught to face the noise and missiles of an enemy army, sometimes by being subjected to volleys of slingstones. It was accustomed to the weight and fit of its battle armor and—in some cases—trained to fight alongside the infantrymen who would accompany it into battle.[4]

On campaign, elephants marched behind the army, probably with the baggage train. Pace was not an issue: even a heavily laden elephant could walk faster than a man or mule. Elephants could, however, become problematic when crossing a wide river or a mountain pass. Their dislike of being transported over water required generals to either find a shallow ford or build special rafts covered with soil and turf. And since elephants cannot easily bend their knees, steep slopes required the construction of either steps or—on at least one occasion—gigantic transport sleds.[5]

Shortly before they were deployed, the elephants were equipped for battle. Massive helmets, often topped with luxuriant plumes, were fitted over their heads. Spears, swords, or razor-sharp spikes were fastened to their tusks. When needed, armored platforms with room for up to four spearmen or archers were strapped to their backs. Finally, on the cusp of battle, the elephants were given a deep drink of wine to fortify their courage.

Cautious generals, or those with only a few animals, might keep their elephants in reserve or on the wings. But most commanders placed them in the front lines. The elephants were typically stationed in a single row, fifty to one hundred feet apart. A small squadron of archers or slingers might be attached to each elephant. Considerable distance, however, was left between the elephants and the rest of the army to give the animals space to retreat or maneuver.

When the action began, the elephants surged forward. If the enemy also had elephants, they attacked these first. Sometimes, the

---

* Close enough, apparently, to discover that putting one's head in an elephant's mouth cured headaches.

A war elephant with an armored platform on its back. *Statuette from Pompeii, now in the Naples National Archaeological Museum. Photo by Jona Lendering, Wikimedia Commons*

enemy elephants would panic and retreat. If they did not, the elephants dueled, locking tusks and pushing with their foreheads while their riders jabbed at each other with long spears. Once one elephant succeeded in forcing the other to expose its flanks, it gored its opponent with bladed tusks.[6]

If or when there were no other elephants to contend with, the elephants charged the enemy lines. They were particularly effective against cavalry, since horses—if not specially trained—were terrified by the sight and smell of elephants.* An elephant charge was equally unsettling for infantry. The sheer weight of armored elephants could break any formation, and they were capable of inflicting terrible damage once they were inside the lines, impaling men with their tusks, throwing them with their trunks, and crushing them underfoot. One Roman author describes watching a badly wounded elephant crawling forward on its knees, grabbing armed men by their shields and hurling them high in the air.[7]

Yet for all their strength, war elephants were far from invulnerable. Besides supernatural assistance—one bishop, we are told, summoned a horde of gnats to sting the trunks of the elephants besieging his town—there were many ways of blunting or repelling an elephant charge. Before battle, generals could use captive elephants (or life-sized models with trumpeters inside) to accustom their men and horses to the animals' appearance and scent. If defending a position, commanders might fend off enemy elephants by digging trenches, making wagon barricades, or creating minefields of iron caltrops. Once battle began, charging elephants could sometimes be frightened by trumpet blasts or turned back with barrages of slingstones, arrows, fire darts, or ballista bolts.[8]

If these measures failed to stop the elephants, there was always the berserker charge. We hear about soldiers hacking off trunks, hamstringing legs, and being crushed as they impaled elephants on their spears. One king created an anti-elephant corps of soldiers with nail-studded shields and helmets, and the late Roman army—which had to contend with the elephants of the Persians—maintained troops of heavy cavalry with spiked armor. There were even anti-elephant "tanks" consisting of wagons on which poles with long pikes, grappling irons, and/or torches were mounted. But the real acme of pachyderm prevention was the flaming pig. Elephants were leery of fire and unsettled by porcine squealing. The combination of the two was thought to be unstoppable. Eventually, however, generals discovered a simpler method of dealing with an elephant charge. A well-prepared army, it was found, could

---

* Sixteen war elephants once destroyed a massive barbarian army simply by appearing on the battlefield: as soon as the barbarians' horses caught wind of the elephants, they panicked and bolted back into their own lines, scythed chariots in tow.

simply open gaps in its lines to let the animals through, keeping them from plunging into the ranks on either side with volleys of slingstones and arrows. Once the animals were past the lines, they could be surrounded and killed.[9]

For a competent general, in short, fending off elephants was difficult but far from impossible. And elephants had other liabilities on the battlefield. Their bulk made them difficult to use in forests (where they got stuck in trees), cities (where they got stuck in gates), and rough terrain (where they got stuck everywhere). Even more serious was their tendency to panic and wreak havoc among their own armies. Any injury was liable to send an elephant into a blind rage; when one elephant lost control, all others in the vicinity usually followed suit.

A frenzied elephant had no interest in distinguishing friend from foe. During one battle, for example, when a young war elephant cried out in pain, its mother—who was fighting nearby—immediately ran to the rescue, trampling every soldier in her path. The driver of a rampaging elephant had only two options: to let it run amok or to kill it by driving a chisel into its spine. Neither alternative was appealing. The tendency of elephants to cause damage to their own side became proverbial to the point that they were sometimes called "double-edged weapons" or "the common enemy."[10]

For this reason, after some early experiments, the Romans stopped using elephants on the battlefield. They continued, however, to feature them in their arenas.* One troupe of performing elephants became especially famous. During an exhibition at the emperor's games, these elephants wore plus-sized tunics and wreaths, reclined on gargantuan couches next to their trainers, and staged a banquet. On another occasion, four of them carried a litter in which a fifth elephant pretended to be a woman in labor. They imitated the dances of stage mimes, scattering flowers with their trunks. And when the program called for it, they held mock battles. Entering the arena in full armor, they struck a series of combat poses, hurled spears with their trunks, and dueled before delighted crowds. In the Roman imagination, at least, war elephants lived on.[11]

---

* They also continued to find them useful. Elephants moved heavy objects (Hadrian once harnessed twenty-four to move a colossal statue), graced imperial processions, and even were ridden as mounts by the occasional pretentious aristocrat.

· 30 ·

How Were Fortified Cities Captured?

$\mathcal{T}$he Romans would break through soon. The Persian officer could hear them now over the rattle of falling stones, barking orders in their uncouth tongue. It was time. Moving to the brazier, he stirred the coals to life and motioned the engineers into position. As the light of Roman torches began to flicker along the tunnel roof, he dropped the precious pieces of sulfur and naphtha into the brazier. Tendrils of oily smoke snaked upward. The engineers pumped their bellows, and the smoke thickened, rising with fatal inevitability toward the Roman tunnel.

Shouts, screams, desperate coughing. Then silence.

After a few moments, the officer tied on his cloth mask and led a patrol up to the Roman tunnel. At least twenty men lay dead around the breakthrough, suffocated by the smoke. The rest had fled—for now. Ordering his men to heap the Roman corpses into a makeshift barricade, he watched the engineers prepare fuel for the fire that would collapse the tunnel—and with any luck, the wall of the city above.[1]

This episode took place beneath the Roman frontier settlement of Dura-Europos in 256 CE. A detachment from the Persian army besieging Dura had tunneled under the western wall of the city in an attempt to undermine it. Realizing what was happening, the defenders started a tunnel of their own to intercept the attack. The Persians, however, heard the Romans coming and pumped suffocating smoke into their tunnel as soon as they broke through.[2]

The brutal ingenuity on display under Dura was characteristic of ancient sieges. Although the goals of a siege remained the same from

168

the beginning to the end of classical history, the techniques evolved constantly—as, of course, did the fortifications they were meant to circumvent.*

In the *Iliad*, the Greek hero Patroclus tries to storm the walls of Troy by simply climbing them—and fails only because Apollo swats him down. Even in Classical Greece, many cities were content with a simple mudbrick circuit wall, and some had no fortifications at all. The Spartans flatly refused to build walls, on the theory that their warriors were all the defense they needed. It was only during the fourth century BCE, as professional armies and artillery made sieges increasingly worrisome, that cities in mainland Greece began to protect themselves with sophisticated stone fortifications. Walls were built taller and thicker than ever before and equipped with artillery platforms and outworks. Soon, new model defensive circuits guarded the cities of old Greece (including Sparta), the far-flung colonies of the Hellenistic world, and the fledgling metropolis of Rome.[3]

The Romans, famous for the instant fortifications of their legionary camps, absorbed everything the Greeks could teach them about defensive architecture. But during the long, drowsy summer of the Pax Romana, when sieges and raiders were banished to the fringes of a Mediterranean-spanning empire, city walls came to seem ornamental or unnecessary. The chaos of the third century ushered in a new era of wall building. On the nervous edges of imperial control, frontier towns and legionary camps were crowned and carapaced with walls. And at the center of things, an awesome triple line of defenses, studded with hundreds of towers, guarded the new city of Constantinople.

Although Constantinople came close, no city was impregnable. The greatest weapon was the simplest: hunger. Once a besieger managed to cut off supplies of food and water, it was only a matter of time before the defenders began to suffer. Effectively blockading a large city, however, was far from easy. If it had a harbor, ships were needed; one Hellenistic king recruited an entire fleet of pirates to shut down the port of Rhodes. Even if the city was landlocked, a heroic amount of military

---

* Castles—in the sense of aristocratic strongholds—were uncommon in the classical world. The closest equivalents were the fortified villas of late Roman notables, which were sometimes built on a daunting scale. The most impressive example, constructed as a retirement home for the emperor Diocletian, covered nearly ten acres, had perimeter walls up to eighty feet high, and eventually housed an entire medieval town. The natural habitat of the Greco-Roman aristocrat, however, was the city. Consequently, the greatest classical fortifications were city walls.

engineering might be necessary. Julius Caesar encircled the Gallic town of Alesia with a wall ten miles in circumference and twelve feet high—and then, when he learned of an army coming to the city's relief, constructed another wall, thirteen miles around, to protect his camps.[4]

Starvation, however, was a tardy ally. Some cities had enough food to hold out for years, and few large armies could be provisioned so long. To force the issue, generals typically tried to intimidate a city into surrender with some combination of military exercises and bloodcurdling threats. If these failed, a surprise attack was often attempted. This might be low-tech—during one such assault, a centurion had three of his men hoist him onto the rampart of a Gallic town—but typically the attackers at least had scaling ladders.* Armies with more sophisticated siege trains might employ the pulley-powered device known as the sambuca, which lowered fortified ladders loaded with soldiers onto enemy ramparts. Although most scaling ladders were wooden, some were rope or leather nets with hooks designed to catch the tops of walls. One Greek inventor even devised a ladder made of inflatable tubes.[5]

If human pyramids and balloon ladders failed to do the trick, it was time to bring in the heavy artillery. The most common siege engine was the ballista, a torsion device powered by twisted bundles of dried animal sinew.† Ballistas could fire either bolts or stones. Bolt-throwing ballistas were rated by the length of the missiles they hurled, which ranged from foot-long darts to twelve-foot javelins. Stone-throwing varieties, likewise, were classified by the weight of the ball they were designed to cast. Miniature models, which could be carried by a single soldier, threw bullet-sized pellets; the monsters carried in the siege trains of emperors and kings fired stone balls weighing up to 165 pounds.‡ The effective range of a midsized ballista seems to have been about 160 to 180 yards. During the Roman siege of Jerusalem, however, one oversize machine

---

* These ladders were fitted to the height of the city wall. There were several methods of determining a wall's height. If it was built of regular masonry, one could simply count the courses of stone or brick. Alternatively, a string with measuring marks was tied to the head of an arrow, which was then shot at the top of the wall. The more geometrically inclined measured the wall's shadow at a given hour and compared it to the shadow cast by a ten-foot rod.

† In a pinch, hair (either horse or human) could be used for the springs, though neither packed the same punch as sinew.

‡ Machines of this size could also hurl lighter missiles impressive distances. One Roman general reportedly catapulted the head of an Armenian nobleman into a beleaguered city, where—by luck or good aim—it landed in the middle of an enemy council of war.

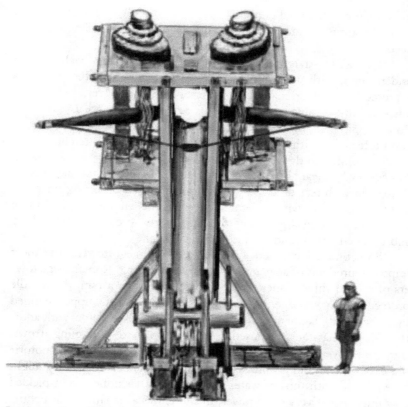

Reconstruction drawing of a large Roman ballista, with a legionary for scale. *Wikimedia Commons*

threw sixty-pound stones up to 450 yards. An even larger engine, known as "the thunderbolt," could reportedly shoot a spear over the mile-wide Danube.* In late antiquity, ballistas began to be supplemented by the vertical-armed catapults called onagers, which had enormous throwing power. One, nicknamed "the crusher," reportedly cast missiles weighing

---

* Being struck by such a missile meant instant and grisly death. One ancient author describes how a man's head, torn off by a ballista stone, was flung hundreds of yards. Another mentions a barbarian pinned to a tree by a bolt.

more than two hundred pounds.* Like ballistas, however, onagers were primarily antipersonnel weapons. To breach walls, other engines were needed.[6]

The most straightforward way to destroy a city wall was to undermine it with picks and crowbars, preferably under the shelter of a protective shed or mantelet. Battering rams, however, were much quicker. Simple rams were logs with a fire-hardened end. Deluxe versions capped the log with iron, suspended it from a wooden frame, and protected it with a wooden roof. There were even interchangeable heads—pointed to drive through mudbrick, hooked to tear out stones. Besiegers who meant business might invest in a truly gargantuan model. A Roman architect describes a 105-foot ram, which swung on ropes eight inches thick; with its protective shed, this engine weighed more than 125 tons. The largest rams on record were more than 150 feet long and required a thousand men to maneuver them.[7]

Sometimes, rams were incorporated into siege towers, the most imposing products of ancient battlefield engineering. Roman siege towers often had three stories, the lower story housing a ram, the middle protecting a drawbridge for storming the walls, and the upper manned by archers and pikemen. Some towers were even extendable, with additional levels that could be raised on pulleys. To ward off flaming arrows, they were covered with fresh hides, metal sheeting, or—in one notorious case—screaming prisoners. As an additional precaution, they might be equipped with tubs of water and fire hoses fashioned from pickled cow intestines. Every siege tower, in short, was a remarkable structure. But the "city takers" of Demetrius the Besieger loomed over all the rest.[8]

Demetrius the Besieger, one of the Hellenistic world's most adventurous kings, was always eager to deploy the latest military gadgetry. As his nickname suggests, he became famous for his massive and innovative siege engines. During the inaugural siege of his career, at the city of Salamis in Cyprus, he constructed a gargantuan siege tower, which he dubbed "the city taker." Each of the tower's nine stories hummed and shook with ballistas throwing rocks and bolts. No fewer than two hundred men were required just to operate the machines. Once the tower had been hauled into position, it rained death on the

---

* The mangonel, or traction trebuchet, was introduced to the Mediterranean world at the end of the sixth century, probably by steppe nomads familiar with Chinese technology. The awesome counterweight trebuchet, the most powerful siege engine of the pre-gunpowder era, appeared in the twelfth century.

ramparts of Salamis, clearing the walls of defenders—and clearing the way for Demetrius's victory. The following year, while laying siege to the rich and powerful city of Rhodes, Demetrius constructed an even larger "city taker." This structure was 125 feet tall, with a base 60 feet to a side. Although it weighed 180 tons, it rolled easily on its eight wheels, which were mounted on casters to allow both forward and lateral movement. The front and sides were plated with iron and peppered with portholes for stone- and bolt-throwing ballistas. When the tower was rolled forward (a task that involved 3,400 men), its engines swept every defender from the vicinity and reduced a long stretch of wall to rubble.[9]

If a more stable assault platform was needed, a siege ramp was constructed. Working behind hide or wicker shields, the attackers heaped earth and rubble to a level even with or higher than the city walls. This could be done with incredible speed: Caesar's legionaries managed to build a ramp 330 feet wide and 80 feet high in only twenty-five days. The most famous ancient siege ramp, raised by the Tenth Legion to subdue the fortress of Masada, rose to a height of 225 feet. Though less imposing, siege mines could be equally effective. Often, like the Persians at Dura-Europos, attackers dug beneath the foundations of a city wall and set fire to the tunnel supports, hoping to create a breach. Alternatively, they might attempt the riskier strategy of digging into the beleaguered city and sending a party of commandos to open the gates.[10]

For every cunning stratagem and clattering siege engine, there was a countermeasure. Mines, for example, could be detected by laying a bronze shield on the ground and listening for reverberations. Once the tunnel had been located, the defenders dug a countermine or simply dropped pots filled with bees, wasps, or burning feathers through holes in the roof.* Scaling ladders were thrust back with forked poles, and clambering soldiers neutralized with stones, arrows, or pots of scorpions. Siege engines were set ablaze with fire arrows and hacked to bits during sorties. The blows of battering rams were cushioned with hanging sacks of wool, blunted by rocks that knocked off their metal heads, or stopped short with a clawlike instrument known as "the wolf." Siege towers were burned, fended off with beams, and impaled with rampart-top rams. Even Demetrius's mighty "city taker" was vulnerable. The Rhodians subjected the tower to a thunderous barrage of ballista bolts,

---

* A particularly enterprising group of defenders managed to drop several enraged bears into a Roman mine.

damaging the iron sides and starting several fires.* When it continued to advance, they channeled a stream of sewage into its path, causing it to bog down in fetid muck.[11]

By way of summary, it might be helpful to trace a siege from beginning to end. In 359 CE, during one of his invasions of Roman Syria, the Persian king Shapur II besieged Amida, a fortified city on the banks of the Tigris. The future historian Ammianus Marcellinus, then an officer in the Roman army, was with the seven legions trapped inside the walls.† At the beginning of the siege—as Ammianus later recorded in his history—King Shapur himself, resplendent in his gilded war crown, rode up to the gates and demanded the city's surrender. The Romans refused.

The Persians then tried intimidation, surrounding Amida and standing in silence for an entire day as their horsemen and war elephants paraded back and forth. When this failed, they mounted two general assaults on the walls. The Romans repulsed both with arrows and onager-flung stones. Now committed to a siege, the Persians began to build two ramps and a pair of towers with ballistas. In response, the defenders worked feverishly to raise and strengthen the walls opposite the ramps. A Roman deserter led seventy Persian archers into the city via a secret passageway. Before they could do serious damage, however, the traitor and his raiding party were pincushioned with ballista bolts.

The final assault came several weeks later. The siege towers were hauled up the ramps, and the massed Persian infantry advanced under the cover of wooden sheds. As the ballistas in the towers wreaked havoc on the ramparts, wave after wave of attackers, supported by war elephants, surged against the walls. Roman onagers smashed the towers, and Roman fire arrows stampeded the elephants. But the Persian attacks continued until a section of the city wall, destabilized by attempts to heighten it, suddenly collapsed. Persian soldiers surged through the breach, and the battle devolved into the timeless brutality of a sack.[12]

---

* When Demetrius ordered his men to gather the missiles that had struck the tower, they counted eight hundred fire arrows and fifteen hundred ballista bolts.

† Fourth-century legions were much smaller than those of the early imperial era; these formations had only about a thousand men each.

Were There Secret Police,
Spies, or Assassins?

*I*t had been a splendid banquet. The dinner was unimpeachable, the service timely, and the wine Italian. Around the agent's couch, in fact, that excellent wine was still flowing freely, and the conversation had become correspondingly . . . honest. The officer on the couch opposite was feeling especially frank. "When I was a boy, an astrologer—said he was a Persian—cast my horoscope and told me that I'd be emperor someday." The officer paused for a swig. "You know what? Maybe he was right. I'd be a hell of an emperor. Can tell you one thing—wouldn't have any *agents* running around and poking their noses into people's business." He struck a pose, wine sloshing from his goblet as he raised it overhead. "So long live me, your future emperor! May I be luckier than Augustus and better than Trajan*—and less of a prick than our good lord Constantius!" The drunker guests laughed. The agent smiled and raised his cup. After a polite interval, he slipped outside. Within an hour, the incident had been reported. Within the day, word had been sent to Emperor Constantius. Within a week, every guest at the party had been arrested for treason.[1]

Although there were no professional secret police in the classical world, there were plenty of enthusiastic amateurs. The most numerous and least interesting of these were informers. Since dedicated police forces did not exist, authorities relied on citizens to report crimes, and since those who provided useful information were rewarded for their services, such citizens were seldom in short supply. Under paranoid

---

* The Roman Senate greeted new emperors with the acclamation "May you be more fortunate than Augustus and better than Trajan!"

regimes, informers were ubiquitous and deadly.* But they were essentially opportunists, with no special training or missions.[2]

The men closest to our idea of secret police were affiliated with the Roman postal service, an empire-wide network of way stations and hostels designed to speed the travel of messages and messengers on official business. During the early imperial era, many of the couriers shuttling through the stations of the imperial post were the soldiers known as *frumentarii*. Originally, *frumentarii* had specialized in securing grain supplies for the legions. But over the course of the first century CE, they assumed a much broader role centered on conveying messages from the emperor to provincial officials. Along the way, they became part-time informers and secret policemen. Emperors used them to read senators' mail, arrest dissidents, and hunt the occasional Christian. Sometimes they even operated in plainclothes: one Roman author describes *frumentarii* walking around in disguise, striking up casual conversations with passersby, and arresting anyone unwise enough to criticize the emperor.[3]

Around the end of the third century, the *frumentarii* were replaced by the *agentes in rebus*. *Agentes*—sometimes called *curiosi* ("snoops")—began their careers as couriers in the postal service. Once they had carried their share of imperial letters, they graduated to management positions in the postal system. Finally, they were granted the power and pleasure of auditing senior government officials. *Agentes* were normally no more (or less) sinister than other bureaucrats. Under some of the more suspicious emperors, however, they became tireless and terrifying informers, notorious for extorting bribes and leveling treason charges against the rich and powerful. They could even be a menace in retirement: as a sort of hobby, one former agent spent his free time spying on a bishop, whom he eventually denounced to the pope.[4]

Spying was most prominent during military campaigns, when scouts infiltrated enemy lines. Usually, these men had no special training. One Roman general, for example, sent several of his officers into an enemy camp disguised as slaves. There they "accidentally" released a skittish horse, which they proceeded to chase into strategically interesting places. The professional military of the Roman Empire, however,

---

* One Greek tyrant compelled his city's prostitutes to report treasonous pillow talk.

developed semipermanent units of skilled scouts. During Trajan's Dacian Wars, one such squadron was sent on a lightning mission to capture the enemy king, and nearly succeeded.* The leader of another squadron was commended for killing a German chieftain in single combat.[5]

Roman scouts were also responsible for peacetime reconnaissance. Regular patrols swept twenty miles or more beyond the frontiers, making rendezvous with local contacts. Northern Britain had a special unit of *arcani* (secret men) who gathered intelligence about the hostile tribes beyond Hadrian's Wall.† Occasionally scouts were sent deep into the unknown. Expeditionary parties ventured into the Sahara, sailing up the Nile as far as the impenetrable Sudd swamp. On the empire's northern fringe, likewise, soldiers investigated remote islands off the coast of Britain.[6]

In civilized settings, the Greeks and Romans had other means of gathering information. Diplomats were expected to snoop around when they were sent to a foreign court, and even in Persia—where they were shadowed by Greek-speaking minders—they usually managed to learn a great deal. Friendly merchants were another valuable resource, as Julius Caesar discovered when planning his invasion of Britain. If all else failed, a bright-eyed and expendable lackey could be launched into enemy territory. One Roman general dispatched a subordinate into the mountains of Armenia to observe an advancing Persian army and confer with a sympathetic governor. Another instructed his secretary to disguise himself, visit a nearby city, and gather evidence about an enemy fleet.[7]

We know little about professional spies, beyond the fact that the later Roman Empire maintained operatives in Persia. These men, skilled enough to penetrate even the royal palace, often disguised themselves as merchants. Living in rented rooms, they peddled cheap goods, traveled from city to city—and listened. In times of war, they sometimes dressed as soldiers to infiltrate military camps. The Persians knew the same tricks. During one border skirmish, the Romans apprehended a man in legionary uniform who admitted to being a Persian spy sent to

---

* The king thwarted the scouts by committing suicide. His head—carried back to Trajan as a sort of consolation prize—was escorted back to Rome and flung down the steps where bodies of executed criminals were traditionally exposed.

† The *arcani* were disbanded in the late fourth century when it was discovered that they had been selling Roman military secrets to the tribes they were supposed to be spying on.

mingle with troops along the frontier.* There were even agents in the government: one Roman official fed intelligence about the locations and planned movements of the legions to Persian contacts before fleeing the empire.[8]

Spies communicated with their handlers by a variety of methods. At short range, they employed homing pigeons, dogs with letters sewn into their collars, or bits of parchment wrapped around arrows. Longer distances required a trustworthy or oblivious messenger with inscribed slips of tin worked into his sandals, sheets of papyrus sewn into his cloak, or a fake bandage on one leg.[†] If the spy was worth his salt, the messages were coded. A few letters in innocuous-seeming sentences might be dotted or written in a particular way to spell new words. Vowels could be substituted or replaced by prearranged patterns of dots. The whole message might be written in invisible ink.[‡] Another method was to carry a small bone with twenty-four holes, one for each letter in the Greek alphabet. Passing a thread through the holes would spell a message, which could be concealed by winding additional thread around the bone.[9]

The best-attested ancient assassins were poisoners. The Greeks and Romans had a practiced understanding of dozens of toxins, from relatively benign opium—a useful medicine in low doses—to deadly and swift-acting aconite, the "queen of poisons." Fear of poisoning was so prevalent that some Roman aristocrats found it worthwhile to have a trained "taster" sample every dish before it reached rich and vulnerable gullets. One Hellenistic king kept a whole garden of poisonous plants, which he tended and studied obsessively. Another was prudent or paranoid enough to take minute doses of poison every day in an effort to build up his immune system.[10]

---

* Centuries earlier, a barbarian king sent a band of Roman deserters to assassinate the emperor Trajan. The plot failed when one of the deserters, arrested for suspicious behavior, confessed under torture.

† There were even more complex methods. Tiny scrolls of inscribed lead foil were rolled into earrings. Messages were written on inflated animal bladders, which were then deflated and hidden in oil flasks. At least once, a messenger's head was tattooed with cryptic phrases.

‡ The late Roman bureaucracy had a proprietary and exceedingly complicated script, which it was illegal to imitate. To prevent forgery of their signatures, likewise, Roman emperors wrote with a special purple ink. Unauthorized use was punishable by death.

Nero's arch-poisoner Locusta was the classical world's most notorious practitioner of the venomous arts. In the space of a single year, she prepared the aconite-coated mushrooms that eliminated Emperor Claudius (Nero's stepfather), mixed the poison that killed Claudius's son, and made herself so indispensable that Nero provided her with a villa and apprentices. Like the other poisoners mentioned in our sources, however, Locusta merely readied the murderous means. We catch only occasional glimpses of those who did the actual poisoning. One German chieftain promised to personally do away with one of his rivals if the Romans would send him a good poison. And on several occasions, intriguingly, a mysterious ring of assassins struck down victims by jabbing them with poisoned needles on Rome's crowded streets.[11]

Most classical assassinations, however, belonged to the stab-in-the-back variety. Daggers appear to have been the weapons of choice among the *frumentarii*, whom the emperors sometimes used to dispose of political enemies.* Although most of their assassinations were domestic, the Romans became fairly prolific killers of foreign leaders. A first-century general arranged a fatal accident for a German chieftain, and Marcus Aurelius put a bounty on the head of a troublesome war leader. But the golden age of classical wet work was late antiquity, when the Romans tried to assassinate their way to success in a dangerous political landscape.† A favorite tactic was to invite the target to a banquet, get him drunk, and knife him.‡ Good faith, it would seem, was a luxury even Roman emperors were unable to afford.[12]

---

* Not all Roman aristocrats were easy targets. One man—famous as a lion hunter—managed to kill the entire squad of assassins sent to dispose of him, and nearly escaped to Persia.

† The later Roman Empire also became rather adept at kidnapping. Troublesome foreign leaders were detained at dinners, seized during church services, and plucked from their palaces by raiders.

‡ The most famous assassination plot in late Roman history was a failure. In 449 CE, the most menacing of the Romans' many enemies were the nomadic Huns, united by their fearsome king Attila. The Huns had ravaged the Eastern Roman Empire for a decade, alternating savage raids on the Balkans with demands for vast tribute payments. At last, the imperial chamberlain arranged a meeting with an important Hun chieftain and promised him an immense fortune if he could find a way to kill Attila. The chieftain agreed to bribe Attila's bodyguards and was sent back with a small party of Roman diplomats. As soon as he returned to Attila's presence, however, the chieftain lost his nerve and confessed everything. Enraged, Attila sent messengers to Constantinople, demanding the head of the chamberlain who ordered his death. The emperor, naturally, denied any involvement.

Why Didn't the Romans Conquer Germany or Ireland?

If you squinted, the town could almost be in Italy. It had an orderly grid of streets. It had a forum, complete with porticoes and a basilica. It even had gilded statues of Augustus and his generals. But the buildings were roofed with wooden shingles, the columns of the porticoes were tree trunks, and those orderly streets were filled with Germans wearing the armor of imperial auxiliaries, carrying bundles of vegetables, entering wooden versions of Roman townhouses.

The town was never finished. In fact, to judge from the ruins—located near the village of Walgirmes, in what is now west-central Germany—most of the space within its palisade walls remained empty. Before any further work could be done, the Romans withdrew from the region, and the town was abandoned. Its remains, however, show how close Germany came to being incorporated into the Roman Empire.[1]

During the early imperial era, the Romans had, or seemed to have, the military might to conquer all of northern Europe. The empire employed more than four hundred thousand full-time soldiers. At the core of this vast military establishment was the heavy infantry of the legions. The legionaries were complemented by auxiliaries, locally recruited units of light infantry and cavalry. Both legionaries and auxiliaries served for twenty years or more and were subjected to rigorous training and brutal discipline.* By way of compensation, they

---

* One Roman general allegedly executed two of his soldiers for daring to set aside their swords while digging a trench. Sentries found sleeping at their posts, likewise, were beaten to death. Occasionally, commanders made an example of units that had failed to perform in combat by decimating them—executing every tenth man. Since this sort of thing wasn't great for morale, however, most generals settled for shaming underperformers by issuing them barley bread (as opposed to wheat), denying them the right to wear their military belts, and/ or forcing them to pitch their tents outside the camp walls.

received good food, medical care, regular pay, and—in the case of the legionaries—a massive discharge bonus intended to ensure a comfortable retirement. For the men who spent two or three decades of their lives in its service, the Roman army was a world unto itself, with its own settlements and laws, a complex internal hierarchy,* and intense esprit de corps.†[2]

The morale, training, and raw power of the legions were impressively displayed during campaigns. A Roman army marched in a careful column. Scouts led the way, followed by pioneers who cleared and levelled the road. The general and officers came next, then the standard-bearers and trumpeters. Behind trooped the rank and file, with the baggage train in their midst. Every night, the soldiers constructed a camp with palisade walls, precisely placed ovens and latrines, and neat rows of leather tents. The same overawing orderliness prevailed in combat. At the beginning of a battle, auxiliary archers and slingers unleashed a glittering shower of missiles, the artillery thrummed into action, and the legionaries hurled their javelins. Then, as the archers and slingers continued to rain death and the cavalry moved to flank the enemy formation, the legionaries drew their short stabbing swords.[3]

There were many tactics for the messy remainder. Faced with a vast army of British tribesmen, one general launched a frontal assault and a line-smashing cavalry charge. Confronting mounted nomads with the chainmail and lances of medieval knights, another general arranged his men on a hillslope and drove off the charging horde with a barrage of missile and artillery bolts. A third commander, fighting barbarian cavalry on the frozen Danube, ordered his men to stand on their shields for traction and tear riders from their horses.[4]

The Dacian Wars showcased the Roman military at peak efficiency. The Kingdom of Dacia, centered in what is now Romania, was rich, well organized, and ruled by a king who sent large armies—equipped with the dreaded *falx* (war scythe)—to raid Rome's Balkan provinces. After an initial punitive expedition, the emperor Trajan decided to wipe

---

* We encounter such hyperspecialized jobs as *hydraularius* (water-organ player), *ad camellos* (camel master), and the indispensable *pullarius* (keeper of the sacred chickens). There appear even to have been licensed prostitutes for individual units.

† The epitaph of an anonymous centurion epitomizes the ambitions of a Roman soldier: "I wanted to hold the corpses of Dacians [barbarians], and I did. . . . I wanted to march in glorious triumphal processions, and I did; I wanted the salary of a *primuspilus* [high-ranking centurion], and I got it."

Dacia from the map. He ordered the legionary engineers to construct a colossal bridge over the Danube—3,800 feet long and 140 feet high from foundations to deck*—and marched units from no fewer than eleven legions across. The winding reliefs of Trajan's Column, set up to commemorate the conflict, capture scenes from the campaign. Roman soldiers besiege Dacian fortresses. The Dacian capital is taken. Dacian chieftains surrender; more strongholds fall. The Dacian king, surrounded by Roman cavalry, commits suicide. The last Dacian cities are taken and burned. Dacian captives are led away to slavery.[5]

By Trajan's reign, it was imperial policy to station troops along the edges of the empire. The greatest concentrations were always in the north, along the banks of the two rivers—the Rhine and the Danube—that marked the limits of Roman control in central Europe. Both the idea and the realities of this frontier developed gradually. Republican Rome had expanded by leaps and bounds as ambitious nobles and fractious neighbors pushed and pulled the legions into a series of fresh conquests. With less to gain from such rampant expansion, the emperors adopted a more defensive foreign policy, foraying into new territories only to seize easy revenue sources and bolster their prestige.

The conquest of Germany was difficult to justify on those terms. As the Romans defined it, Germany was a vast territory east of the Rhine and north of the Danube, shading off from the familiar sun-dappled hills of the Rhineland to the obscurity of the Baltic. The Germans, it was thought, could be differentiated from the Gauls by their dislike of cities, from the nomadic tribes of the Eastern European plains by their settlements, and from all peoples by their distinctive language and culture. The Germans were acknowledged to be respectable warriors. Like other northerners, they fought without order or discipline, but they fought bravely, and—the Romans grudgingly admitted—well. They only became a serious threat, however, when whole tribes migrated in search of new lands, or charismatic chieftains mounted large-scale raids into Roman territory.[6]

During his conquest of Gaul, Julius Caesar twice invaded Germany, throwing wooden bridges over the Rhine to show local tribes that the river was no barrier to Roman arms. There were no attempts

---

* Not that Roman soldiers needed bridges. During the reign of Hadrian, one thousand auxiliaries splashed across the Danube in full armor. A half-century later, during Marcus Aurelius's campaigns, a single intrepid soldier swam across the river to free some Romans in barbarian captivity.

to actually conquer Germany, however, until a generation later, when Augustus decided to tidy up his northern frontiers. A series of talented generals crossed the Rhine and campaigned as far east as the Elbe, creating alliances with local tribes, establishing military bases, and founding the town at Waldgirmes as an administrative center. Soon, what is now the western half of Germany was well on its way to becoming a province. Then, on a rainy summer afternoon in 9 CE, disaster struck.[7]

The three legions that made up the Roman army of Germany were slogging along a muddy track. At the head of the line, engineers struggled to bridge the deep ravines that gashed the path. The soldiers behind slipped and stumbled in deepening muck. Suddenly, German war cries sounded from the surrounding woods, and arrows and spears began to whistle from the brush. Unable to engage their opponents, the Romans hastily built a walled camp. They continued their march the next morning—and the Germans, invisible among the trees, followed, picking off soldiers and pack animals. Another anxious night, another fortified camp, another day of attrition. On the morning of the fourth day, as the disintegrating army resumed its desperate march, a storm broke. Half-blinded by rain, staggering down a narrow strip of land between a high ridge and an impassable marsh, the Romans found their way blocked by a large German force. When it became clear that they were trapped, some soldiers, including the general, committed suicide. Others tried to fight their way out. All but a handful died. The Battle of the Teutoburg Forest, as it is now known, destroyed two decades of patient province building in Germany. The surviving Romans withdrew to the Rhine.[8]

From the first to the fifth centuries CE, more than two-thirds of the Roman army was stationed along the Rhine and Danube. These rivers were not frontiers in the modern sense. They were, rather, the central arteries of military occupation zones, which separated the area of provincial administration from an ill-defined belt of tribal territories assumed to respect and acknowledge Roman power. Starting in the late first century, however, the military camps along the rivers became permanent. Even small emplacements were strongly fortified—one Roman author describes a camp for four hundred soldiers protected by tall brick ramparts, broad ditches, and wall-mounted ballistas.* The walls

---

* The turreted walls of a legionary fort, which often contained fifty acres or more, enclosed a sprawling headquarters complex (complete with a shrine for the standards and a subterranean strongroom for the soldiers' pay), a hospital, a bath, granaries, elaborate houses for the officers, and orderly blocks of barracks.

that began to appear along stretches of the frontier were even more impressive. In the angle between the upper Rhine and upper Danube, the emperors built and rebuilt lines of walls and trenches more than a hundred miles long. Though less monumental than Hadrian's Wall in Britain, they had the same basic function: to monitor and control the steady stream of Romans and barbarians passing through the frontier zone.[9]

The Romans never abandoned Germany. Patrols continued to circle forest tracks beyond the Rhine and Danube, stopping at night in friendly villages and purpose-built outposts. German chieftains crossed the rivers to attend banquets held by legionary commanders. Whole tribes were sometimes invited to settle on Roman soil. Far from being a line of exclusion, the frontier attracted merchants and migrants from both sides of the border. Since the soldiers in the camps had to be fed, German farmers tended fields, herds, and vineyards under legionary contracts. And since all those thousands of soldiers were well paid, towns populated largely by Germans grew up beside the bases to help them spend their money.[10]

Although Roman campaigns in Germany were rare after the first century, the presence of hundreds of thousands of Roman troops along the Rhine and Danube profoundly changed German society. The regions closest to the bustling frontier zone were integrated into the Roman economy. Roman coins and Roman goods circulated freely; towns were laid out with Roman street grids; Roman-style villas rose. Many local men spent years as auxiliaries, learning Latin and developing a taste for things like fish sauce and wine. Germans farther from the frontier tended to be less friendly, largely because there was no better way for an ambitious chieftain to gain honor and followers than a lightning raid on Roman territory.* Roman wealth, pilfered or earned, fueled the emergence of powerful German leaders. In this sense, the mighty legions of the Rhine and Danube frontiers slowly created the enemies they were meant to destroy.[11]

---

* Loot from a few of these raids has been discovered at the bottom of the Rhine. The most famous find, the so-called Neupotz hoard, consisted of more than a thousand pieces of metal, including gold and silver vessels, cult images stolen from temples, and shackles for Roman prisoners.

So why didn't the Romans conquer Ireland? We might answer that question with another: what possible reason could the Romans have for conquering Ireland? For the emperors, annexing a new territory was only worthwhile (a) if it presented a legitimate threat to imperial security, (b) if it promised to produce plenty of taxable income, and/or (c) if it could provide a hearty helping of prestige with minimal military heartburn. Ireland met none of these criteria. By all accounts, in fact, it was an unprepossessing place. The weather was cold and stormy. The grass, though lush, was said to have the regrettable property of causing cattle to explode. And the natives were reported to be gluttonous, incestuous, and cannibalistic, sometimes all at once. On the plus side, there was a decided lack of snakes.*[12]

During the late first century, an ambitious governor of Britain briefly considered conquering Ireland. He interrogated local merchants about the island's harbors, acquired a fugitive Irish chieftain, and predicted that a single legion would smother all resistance. But the emperor was uninterested, and the plan came to nothing.† As in the case of Germany, however, the proximity of the empire changed the course of Irish history. Steady trade with Britain and Spain brought Roman coins‡ and Roman trade goods. The Latin alphabet inspired the creation of the Irish ogham script. And Christianity made its triumphal entry, not least through the efforts of a British councilor's son by the name of Patrick. Roman conquest didn't always require legions.[13]

---

* The idea that Irish grass was explosive probably derived from misunderstood accounts of frothy bloat, a disorder common in cattle that graze on alfalfa and clover. Rumor and a readiness to believe the worst of distant peoples account for the description of the Irish as inbred cannibals.

† On the basis of stray passages by first-century authors and scattered finds of Roman artifacts in the vicinity of Dublin, some scholars have speculated that a small expeditionary force actually sailed to Ireland. The evidence, however, is inconclusive.

‡ The fifth-century Coleraine hoard, discovered in an Irish peat bog, included about 1,500 silver coins from Roman mints, probably acquired through some combination of trading and raiding. One recent article suggests that the coins were tribute from Roman Britain, paid to Irish pirates.

VI

LEGACIES

What Happened to the City of Rome after the Empire Collapsed?

*W*hen I was a young and wayward graduate student at the University of Michigan, I fell into the habit of exploring abandoned buildings in Detroit. I especially liked the Lee Plaza, an Art Deco masterpiece that was once one of the city's finest apartment buildings. After scrambling in through the rubble-filled basement, I would wander the grand public rooms, steps stirring clouds of plaster dust. Then I would follow a long procession of stairs to the windy roof. One December morning, I paused in an apartment on the fifteenth floor, where a gaping hole in the wall framed a panorama. Falling snow shrouded the horizon, hiding the distant skyscrapers of downtown. Most of the houses in the neighborhood below had been demolished years before. The survivors straggled, swaybacked and gray, over an urban prairie. As I stood there, listening to the whisper of snowflakes on brick and broken glass, I remember thinking: *Rome must have felt like this after the fall.**

Rome was the biggest, dirtiest, and most dangerous city in the classical world. It was also the most magnificent. Even emperors were impressed. In 357 CE, when Constantius II visited Rome for the first time, he was awestruck. He marveled at the vast bath complexes, where pools smoked beneath walls of glass. He squinted appreciatively at the towering walls of the Colosseum. He was overwhelmed by the Pantheon. And these were only a few of Rome's wonders. At the time of Constantius's visit, the population was probably around seven hundred

---

* Please don't construe this anecdote as an endorsement to explore abandoned buildings. It's usually dangerous and/or illegal, and the pictures are almost always underwhelming.

thousand—fewer than the million or so of the early imperial era but still greater than that of any other city on the planet.* These teeming multitudes patronized Rome's 424 temples and 861 baths, occupied its 1,790 aristocratic houses and 46,602 apartment buildings, and were laid to rest in cemeteries radiating miles beyond the city walls.[1]

The next half millennium, however, was not kind to the capital of the world. Rome was sacked by barbarians, burned in a civil war, pillaged by both sides during Justinian's Gothic Wars, ravaged repeatedly by plague, flooded ad nauseam, and sacked again for good measure by Saracen pirates. For much of this period, the city was reduced to the status of a frontier outpost ruled from distant Constantinople. Only pilgrimage and the prestige of the pope[†] prevented Rome from sinking into obscurity. By the ninth century, the population had fallen by more than 95 percent, leaving thirty to forty thousand residents scattered through the ruins of a city built for a million.

Some of Rome's buildings were destroyed violently. During the first sack of Rome, aristocratic mansions and structures in the Forum burned.[‡] Gilded roof tiles were stripped from the great Temple of Jupiter during the second sack. Overall, however, the raiding parties seem to have caused surprisingly little destruction, and at least some of the damage was later repaired: a fifth-century inscription commemorates the restoration of a statue "overturned by the barbarians." The Gothic Wars caused more lasting devastation. Notable casualties included the colossal marble statues atop the Mausoleum of Hadrian, which the Roman defenders catapulted onto barbarians attempting to scale the walls.[2]

Most of the urban fabric was undone by less dramatic means. Thanks to extensive use of brick-faced concrete, large Roman buildings were, by premodern standards, remarkably solid. They were, however,

---

* On a whim, it was said, the eccentric emperor Elagabalus once ordered his slaves to collect cobwebs throughout Rome. When they returned to the palace carrying ten thousand sticky pounds, he remarked that one could judge from this how great the city was.

† "Pappas"—a colloquial term for "father" in Greek—was a term of affection for bishops in the Greek-speaking eastern provinces of the empire. In the west, however, only the bishop of Rome received this title, partly because the language of the Roman church was, until the third century, Greek rather than Latin. (For centuries, the Christian community in Rome was composed primarily of Greek speakers from the east. The first Latin-speaking bishop of Rome was Victor [r. 189–199], and it was only under Damasus [r. 366–384] that Latin replaced Greek as the city's liturgical language.) "Pappas" gradually became the Vulgar Latin "papa," from which our word "pope" derives.

‡ Visitors to the Forum still can see coins melted into the marble floor of the Basilica Aemilia by the heat of the fire.

Pieces of Roman marble built into a medieval house. *The façade of the tenth-century House of the Crescentii in Rome. Author's photo*

far from immune to weathering. Once their roofs collapsed, water worked into masonry joints and cracks in the concrete fill, pulverizing the mortar. By the beginning of the seventh century, Pope Gregory the Great could lament "every day, we watch buildings decayed with age fall down."[3] During windstorms and hard frosts, Rome must have echoed with the thunder of collapsing walls.

The pace of decay was quickened by natural disasters. Serious earthquakes rattled the city in 801 and 847, cracking walls, toppling columns, and laying low many a lofty vault and dome. Floods were more frequent and almost as destructive, particularly to the blocks of tottering ancient apartments near the river. A flood in the early eighth century is reported to have sent many of these buildings crashing into the muddy water.[4]

The greatest enemies of Rome's monuments, however, were the Romans themselves. Despite the reduced size of the medieval city, constant small-scale construction, papal patronage of church building, and a thriving export trade in marble created a persistent hunger for scrap metal and building materials. The ruins provided a seemingly inexhaustible supply of both.

The forests of bronze sculptures in Rome's public places were especially vulnerable to plunder. The process had already started by the beginning of the sixth century, when an official complained of drowsy night watchmen ignoring the sounds of thieves wrenching statues from their bases. Later, Byzantine emperors and their officials periodically harvested statues for scrap. The worst pillager was Emperor Constans II, who visited the city in 663. Over the course of his two-week stay, men from his entourage gathered all the bronze statues they could find, hacked them into manageable pieces, and hauled the metal to boats waiting on the Tiber.* Marble statues were treated no better. Sometimes they were hauled to building sites, smashed with sledgehammers, and used as rubble fill in foundations and walls. More commonly, however, they were burned in kilns to produce lime for mortar. When the House of the Vestals in the Roman Forum was excavated, a pile of marble statues fourteen feet long, nine feet wide, and seven feet high was discovered near one of these kilns, stacked and ready for burning.[5]

Ancient buildings were torn apart in the same spirit. Although the scavengers had little use for the concrete and rubble cores of foundations and thick walls, they stripped almost everything else. The fine marble veneers were often the first to go, both because they were straightfoward to remove and because they made excellent lime. Iron and bronze fittings were other easy pickings. There also was constant demand for dressed stone. One eighth-century pope personally supervised the demolition of a decrepit Roman temple for its usable blocks. This was unusual only in being recorded: for the next millennium, virtually every stone used in Rome's churches and palaces would be plucked from the nearest convenient ruin.[†6]

A few prominent Roman buildings were preserved by being converted into churches. Even consecration, however, was only partial

---

* Some of this loot may have surfaced in 1992, when divers near Brindisi discovered the remains of a huge trove of bronze statues, ranging in date from the second century BCE to the third century CE. Every statue had been cut up for scrap. It has been suggested that the metal was dumped when one of Constans's ships either sank or jettisoned part of its cargo.

† One of the last buildings dismembered this way, a temple of Minerva near the Roman Forum, provides a sense of how creatively stone could be recycled. One huge block of marble became part of the high altar of St. Peter's Basilica. The columns and architrave were cut into thin slabs and used to decorate a new fountain. The remaining stone was built into the walls of the Borghese Chapel in Santa Maria Maggiore.

protection. The Pantheon, for example, became a church in 609. But when that scrap-happy emperor Constans II showed up a half century later, the pope was powerless to prevent him from stripping the building's gilded roof. Nearly a millennium later, another pope melted down the massive bronze trusses of the Pantheon's porch and had the metal (which weighed more than 450,000 pounds) cast into 110 cannons.*

You are a ninth-century pilgrim. The journey was long, the road was hard, and the inns were grim even by ninth-century standards. But you reached Rome safely, and having visited the most famous relics, you've decided to take a stroll through the ruins.

Staff in hand, you walk along a street of decaying apartment blocks, each one as tall as the church in your native village. To your surprise, the lower stories of some buildings are still occupied.† Most, however, are gutted shells, and a few have collapsed onto the street. At the street's end looms the Colosseum. A fellow pilgrim at your hostel told you that the building was originally a temple of the sun, where Christians were sacrificed to the old gods. Whatever it used to be, the Colosseum is falling apart now. Huge heaps of stone blocks, shaken down by earthquakes, cover the pavement on one side of the building. Lime kilns smolder among the rubble.‡ On the other side of the building, slightly better preserved, houses and shops have been squeezed into the lowest row of arches.[7]

From the Colosseum, you follow a path through the columns of a collapsed temple. Passing beneath a marble arch, you find yourself

---

* There were many other instances of papal pillaging. In 630, Pope Honorius I stripped the gilded bronze roof tiles from the Temple of Venus and Rome and used them to repair the roof of St. Peter's Basilica. Some of these tiles survived until 1613, when Pope Paul V melted them down to make the colossal statue of the Madonna that still stands in front of Santa Maria Maggiore. Another Renaissance pope destroyed two sets of bronze Roman doors to make the statues of Saints Peter and Paul now atop the Columns of Trajan and Marcus Aurelius.

† Some of the great mansions of the late Roman elite also remained in use through the ninth century, at least in modified form. Pope Gregory I, for example, converted his ancestral mansion into a monastery (still extant as San Gregorio Magno al Celio).

‡ Selective pillaging of the Colosseum's stone seems to have begun even before 523, when the last games were staged in the arena. The marble seats were early victims, as were the iron clamps holding the travertine blocks together. The worst damage, however, occurred during the late Middle Ages, when a severe earthquake destroyed nearly half of the building. The huge heap of travertine left by the collapse—nicknamed "the Colosseum's thigh"—took more than four centuries to haul away. In 1452, a single busy contractor carried off 2,522 cartloads of stone.

between hills of tumbled brick. To your left are the half-buried but-tresses and buckling roofs of the old imperial palace.* But you turn right, where a faint track leads into an enormous brick building.† Entering cautiously—this is the sort of place where demons lurk—you peer into the dim interior, which smells faintly of manure. As your eyes adjust to the gloom, you make out the fragments of a gargantuan statue in one corner. You also notice, however, that sunlight is slanting through huge cracks in the vaults overhead, and decide not to explore further.[8]

Back outside, you continue toward the Forum. Ahead, you can see the red walls of the Church of Saint Hadrian, once—according to the guide you hired in the Vatican yesterday—the house of the Senate. (You aren't quite sure what the Senate was but gather that it was impor-tant.) Next to the church, a few shops and houses have been built into a tottering two-story colonnade. The huge hall behind them is in ruins. So are all the other temples in sight.‡ Walking beneath another arch, you emerge onto the Forum square, a rectangular plaza bounded by tall columns. A few columns, you notice, still carry battered bronze statues.

There are more ruins beyond Saint Hadrian's—half-collapsed temples and broken porticoes jutting from orchards and fields of wheat. Beyond them, you glimpse the wonder your hostel keeper advised you see: the column of the good emperor Trajan. You head toward it, and after a few minutes among the wheat fields, you reach the door of the huge ruined building§ in front of the column.

You step through the door and emerge in what was once a vast hall. The roof, however, is long gone, and trees have forced their way through the marble floor. Weaving through the thickets, you make your way to the column's base. As your hostel keeper claimed, the column is carved from top to bottom with scenes of Trajan's wars against the

---

* Though stripped of its last bronze statues by a cash-strapped governor in 571, the palace continued to be used for at least another century by a few functionaries, who kept offices in corners of the vast and decaying complex. The severe earthquakes of the early ninth century probably destroyed the towering reception rooms, leaving a moonscape of heaped stone and tile. A twelfth-century traveler described the ruins as a marble quarry for Rome's churches.

† The Basilica of Maxentius.

‡ The notes of a pilgrim who visited Rome around the year 800 suggest that the buildings of the Forum were then still standing, though badly decayed. It was probably the earthquakes of the ninth century that destroyed most of the surviving buildings and buried the ancient pavement under debris.

§ The Basilica Ulpia.

heathen. And just as he said, there is a door at the column's base. You enter and start up the steps within. The stairway is narrow and dark. Your breath comes ragged. Sweat stings your eyes. All discomfort, however, is forgotten the moment you reach the platform at the column's top.

Rome spreads like a figured mosaic beneath your feet. To one side is the great building you walked through, nearly as tall as the column itself. Starlings call from nests in the rafter holes. On the other side is a roofless temple* with columns thicker than any oak. The Forum crouches in the middle distance, overlooked by the gaunt Temple of Jupiter, arch-devil of the old gods. Beyond are windrows of ruinous apartments, stretching off toward the wilds of the Campagna. You would like to linger. But the sun is setting, and the streets are dangerous at night. Your footfalls echo as you descend the stairs.

---

* The Temple of the Deified Trajan.

· 34 ·

What Happened to the Body of Alexander the Great? Has the Tomb of Any Roman Ruler Been Discovered Intact?

$\mathcal{A}$lexander was dead. After a night of hard drinking—and a thirty-two-year-old who has conquered the known world can drink very hard indeed—the king had woken with a fever, which steadily worsened. Within six days, he was bedridden. Within eight, he had lost the ability to speak. On the tenth, he breathed his last. Rumor soon improved on the facts. Alexander, it was whispered, had been poisoned with strychnine. No, his wine had been turned deadly with water from the River Styx. One of his generals had killed him. No, it was an agent working for the Spartans. Or maybe Aristotle. Only one thing was certain: Alexander was gone, and the world was about to change.[1]

Change it did, rapidly and untidily, as Alexander's former subordinates battled for mastery of his empire. Ptolemy, the canniest of these rivals, stole Alexander's remains and brought them to Alexandria, capital of the kingdom he had established in Egypt. There, beneath the great mausoleum known as the Soma, the conqueror's embalmed body whiled away the centuries in its crystal sarcophagus,* clad in magnificent armor.[2]

Alexander's tomb became a famous tourist attraction. Julius Caesar made a point of visiting. So did Augustus, who planted an awkward kiss on Alexander's cheek, breaking the mummified nose.† All this, however, was nothing compared to the obsessive fandom of Caracalla,

---

* A cash-strapped member of the Ptolemaic dynasty had Alexander's original golden casket melted down. The replacement, which survived until late antiquity, was fashioned from either glass or alabaster.

† Other emperors were less reverential. Caligula stole the breastplate from Alexander's corpse and liked to saunter around Rome in the great conqueror's armor.

who drank from Alexander's cups, modeled his statues on Alexander's portraits, and informed the Senate that he was Alexander reborn. When Caracalla visited the Soma, he tenderly draped his purple cloak over the conqueror's wizened body. Then he removed his jeweled rings, dropping them one by one into the sarcophagus.[3]

Caracalla is the last person known to have visited the Soma. Some historians believe that Alexander's tomb was destroyed by a catastrophic fire in 272 CE. If it survived this disaster, it may have perished in a sack a generation later or during the earthquake and tsunami of 365. One late fourth-century author implies that the tomb still existed in his time. Another, however, rhetorically asks whether anyone knows where Alexander lies.[4]

Today, at least, nobody does, though there is no shortage of theories. In 2004, for example, British researcher Andrew Chugg made headlines by announcing that Alexander was in Venice. Sometime in the fourth century, he claimed, the conqueror's body had been secretly transferred from the Soma to the nearby Church of St. Mark. There the remains remained for a half millennium or so, until two merchants—mistaking Alexander for St. Mark himself—brought them to Venice. Forensic examination of the bones now beneath the high altar of St. Mark's Cathedral, Chugg insisted, would reveal the truth.*[5]

The truth, however, is already clear. There is no reason to think that Alexander reposes by the Rialto. Nor (as other interested parties contend) should we seek him in Egypt's Siwa Oasis or Greece's Amphipolis Tomb. The ruins of the Soma lie somewhere beneath central Alexandria. It is there, if anywhere, that Alexander will be found.

In 14 CE, toward the end of the month recently renamed in his honor, the body of Augustus was carried into the Forum. The coffin, crowned by a wax effigy, was followed by members of the imperial family, impassive behind the death masks of their eminent ancestors. Behind came men costumed as the heroes of Roman history, citizens personifying the nations Augustus had conquered, and the massed ranks of the senatorial and equestrian orders.

---

  * If Alexander really is in Venice, his mummy hasn't aged well. When St. Mark's reliquary was opened in the early nineteenth century, the remains were found to consist of little more than a skull and a few shattered bones.

The emperor's bier was set on the rostra, and a long, somber man—Tiberius, Augustus's successor—delivered a long, somber eulogy in the Forum square. Then the procession reassembled and snaked through the streets to the stubbly brown lawn of the Campus Martius. Followed by the Roman people in their hundreds of thousands, the marchers drew into formation in the center of the campus, where a tall pyre had been erected.* After the pallbearers slid the emperor's coffin into its appointed place, the high priests circled the pyre, spiked caps gleaming. They were followed by the five thousand soldiers of the Praetorian Guard, who flung military decorations onto Augustus's coffin. Finally, a chosen group of centurions lit the pyre from beneath. As the flames rose, an eagle, released from a hidden cage, soared heavenward.[6]

Five days later, when the pyre had finally cooled, Empress Livia and a small band of retainers walked barefoot through the cinders to recover the emperor's bones.† The remains were washed with wine and sealed in a golden urn. Then, gliding through clouds of dust, the mourners turned toward the great mausoleum Augustus had built for himself forty years before.[7]

The Mausoleum of Augustus was a vast circular structure whose roof—modeled on the burial mounds of the distant past—was planted with evergreens and crowned by a colossal statue. The burial chamber beneath was lined with dozens of niches for funerary urns. Here, for more than a century, the remains of emperors and their families were laid to rest. The mausoleum was full by the reign of Trajan, whose ashes were placed in a small chamber beneath his namesake column. Trajan's successor Hadrian constructed a new mausoleum, circular like Augustus's but with marble walls and a whole gallery of rooftop sculpture. A ramp wound up to the elaborate burial chambers, in whose niches the next hundred years of emperors were ensconced. After Hadrian's Mausoleum filled, emperors and their families were buried in widely scattered tombs, often outside the city of Rome.

Like rich and conspicuous burials the world over, the tombs of the emperors attracted looters. Virtually all were robbed and ruined

---

* Two centuries after Augustus, the body of Septimius Severus was cremated on a pyre with five stories, each packed with incense and decorated with tapestries, paintings, and ivory statues. Even the austere soldier-emperors of late antiquity were cremated in style: the place where the tetrarch Galerius was burned, for example, was found to contain fragments of silver vessels.

† The bodies of eminent Romans were sometimes wrapped in flame-resistant asbestos shrouds to ease the separation of their bones from the ashes.

in late antiquity. The golden urns in the Mausoleums of Hadrian and Augustus were melted down and the ashes within scattered.* Only a few fragments have survived: a single alabaster urn, the marble block that housed the ashes of Caligula's mother, and the sarcophagus lid— reportedly from the tomb of Hadrian—that serves as the baptismal font of St. Peter's Basilica.[8]

The most impressive relics of Rome's imperial burials are two enormous sarcophagi now in the Vatican Museums.† Both are made of porphyry, a hard purple stone found only in the mountains of Egypt's Eastern Desert. One of the sarcophagi, decorated with figures of mounted soldiers, was likely carved for Constantine. But since Constantine ended up being buried in Constantinople, it was occupied instead by his mother, Helena, whose remains reposed within until they were displaced by an upstart medieval pope. The other sarcophagus, which probably held the remains of Constantine's daughter Constantia, lay in an imposing mausoleum—now the church of Santa Costanza— until the fifteenth century.[9]

As the postmortem peregrinations of Helena and Constantia's sarcophagi suggest, medieval and Renaissance Romans were not shy about disturbing imperial burials. Only occasionally, however, is any record preserved of how or why a tomb was opened—and the few accounts that do exist are usually unreliable. Take, for example, the legend surrounding the destruction of Nero's tomb. After his disgrace and suicide, Nero was quietly cremated by his childhood nurses.‡ Since burial in the Mausoleum of Augustus was out of the question, the ashes were deposited in the family tomb of Nero's father. Over the centuries, a vast walnut tree grew from the ruins of the tomb. This tree (locals claimed)

---

* The later histories of the imperial mausoleums are interesting in themselves. The Mausoleum of Augustus was fortified, destroyed, refortified, and subsequently converted (at different times) into a garden, bullfighting arena, and theater. The Mausoleum of Hadrian was integrated into Rome's defenses in late antiquity and served as the fortress of the popes until the nineteenth century.

† From the second century onward and for mysterious reasons, the Roman elite turned from cremation to inhumation. Instead of urns, they were now interred in imposing sarcophagi, often carved with episodes from mythology or scenes of their lives. (It was assumed, incidentally, that stone coffins caused flesh to decay more quickly; in Greek, "sarcophagus" means "flesh eater." The limestone of Assos, now in western Turkey, was reportedly capable of consuming an entire corpse—except the teeth—in forty days.)

‡ One of these nurses, Claudia Ecloge, chose to be buried beside the villa where Nero had committed suicide. Her simple tomb was discovered there in the nineteenth century.

The Sarcophagus of Helena. *Fourth-century porphyry sarcophagus, now in the Vatican Museums. Author's photo*

was infested with demons, who amused themselves by beating up passing pedestrians. At last, a pope put an end to the peril. Shortly before Easter, he led a great crowd to the base of the infernal walnut. After exorcising it, he sank an axe into its roots—whereupon, we are told, a great crowd of demons took flight from its branches. The tree was thrown down, and beneath its roots was discovered the urn containing Nero's remains. The urn was destroyed, the ashes were dumped into the Tiber, and the church of Santa Maria del Popolo was built on the spot.[10]

An equally colorful and equally unreliable tale describes the discovery of a Roman sarcophagus in eleventh-century Marseilles. Gilded letters on the lid identified the occupant as Maximian, an emperor remembered for his persecution of the Christians. The sarcophagus was found to be filled with perfumed oil, beneath which the corpse lay, pallid and incorrupt. On the advice of a local bishop, the body was flung into the sea, which boiled and churned at the touch of its unsanctified flesh.* Although some details of this story are obviously fabricated, it is possible that the people of Marseille really did discover an intact Roman corpse bathed in unguent. In 1485, for example, the opening of a sarcophagus near Rome disclosed the perfectly preserved body of a Roman woman, coated with aromatic paste.† The body was brought into Rome, where the whole city marveled at its condition. There may, in short, be a kernel of truth in the story about the discovery of Maximian's tomb. But we can never be sure.[11]

The only imperial burials reliably known to have been discovered intact were found beneath the chapel of Santa Petronilla, a late antique mausoleum attached to Old Saint Peter's Basilica. In 1458, a marble sarcophagus was discovered beneath the chapel floor. Within were two silver-plated coffins, each containing a body wrapped in cloth of gold. These were almost certainly the remains of the empress Galla Placidia and her son Theodosius. Sixty years later, as the chapel was being demolished, more sarcophagi came to light. One of these, which held a body draped in golden cloth, may have belonged to an imperial prince. The final and most momentous discovery took place in 1544, when the granite sarcophagus of Maria, wife of the fifth-century emperor Honorius, was uncovered. The empress was robed, veiled, and shrouded in cloth of gold. Two silver chests lay beside her—one filled with gold and crystal vessels, the other with jewelry and gems. Tragically, the entire treasure has vanished; the jewels were stolen or given away, and the gold vanished into the melting pots of the papal mint.‡[12]

The early Byzantine emperors were buried at the Church of the Holy Apostles in Constantinople. The tombs were concentrated in two mausoleums adjoining the main church. One of these was a circular building dominated by the great sarcophagus of Constantine. The other

---

* Not all imperial corpses were treated so summarily. When the body of Constantius I, one of Maximian's co-emperors, was (reportedly) discovered in York a few centuries later, it was reburied with royal honors by King Edward I.

† When the crusaders opened the sarcophagus of the Byzantine emperor Justinian, they found his body perfectly preserved, probably by similar means.

‡ Since the Renaissance, the burials of a few figures with tangential connections to emperors have been found. In 1884, an aristocratic family tomb was discovered just outside Rome. On the floor, littered with the shattered remains of cinerary urns, was discovered a funerary altar for L. Calpurnius Piso, heir to the imperial throne for four days during the civil wars of 69 CE. More recently, a cache of jewelry, including pieces of a golden diadem, came to light in the mausoleum of the tetrarch Galerius's sister, located near the Serbian village of Sarkamen.

was a cruciform structure centered on the tomb of Justinian. Both were crowded with marble and porphyry sarcophagi. After the eleventh century, when the mausoleums of the Holy Apostles were finally filled, new constellations of imperial burials emerged in the Monasteries of Christ Pantokrator and Constantine Lips.[13]

The imperial tombs of Constantinople were despoiled, desecrated, and destroyed—in that order—by a Byzantine usurper, the crusaders, and the Ottomans. The mausoleums of the Holy Apostles were demolished by the Turks soon after the fall of Constantinople. The two monasteries in which many of the later Byzantine emperors were buried still survive, but both have been converted into mosques, and their tombs were removed long ago.* From twelve centuries of sepulchral pomp, only a few broken sarcophagi remain.[14]

A single imperial tomb, however, may have survived to be uncovered by archaeologists.† In 1929, after the Fenari Isa Mosque—the former Monastery of Constantine Lips—was gutted by fire, several late Byzantine burials were discovered beneath the floor. Most had been looted and emptied. But one, beneath a simple marble slab, was intact. It contained only a skeleton surrounded by the nails of a decayed wooden coffin. From the context of the burial, the excavators deduced that the bones belonged to Emperor Andronicus II, who had been deposed and forced to live as a monk.[15]

An even more surprising survival is the body of Theodora, a ninth-century empress venerated by the Eastern Orthodox Church for her role in restoring the adoration of icons. When Theodora's tomb in the Holy Apostles was destroyed, her remains were saved and sent into Greece. They ended up in Corfu; there, every year, the body of the empress is carried in a procession to mark the Feast of the Triumph of Orthodoxy. Visitors to Corfu can pay their respects to the empress—or at least to most of her. Theodora's head is rumored to have gone missing.

---

* The body of the eleventh-century emperor Alexios Komnenos was salvaged from its original resting place in the Pantokrator Monastery and brought to the church of Theotokos Pammakaristos. Subsequently, however, Alexios seems to have been misplaced.

† Though not exactly "imperial," the tombs of several members of the ruling dynasty of the Despotate of Epirus, a Byzantine successor state, were uncovered in the Greek Monastery of Varnakova during the early twentieth century.

Why Did Latin Evolve into Multiple Languages? Why Didn't Greek?

*T*he Greek and Latin languages are willfully complex, pitilessly gram-matical, and impressively durable. Greek has outlasted three millennia. And Latin, which first emerged as a literary language in the third cen-tury BCE, is now spoken by more than a billion people. Or rather, some sort of Latin is. Since the early Middle Ages, Latin has diffracted into dozens of regional varieties. The most prominent became the Romance languages: Spanish, Portuguese, French, Italian, Romanian, Catalan, and various dialects. As an illustration of the common ancestry and mutual differences of these tongues, consider the phrase "the man gave my book to a friend."*

Latin	homo meum librum amico dedit
Italian	l'uomo ha dato il mio libro a un amico
Spanish	el hombre le dio mi libro a un amigo
French	l'homme a donné mon livre à un ami

The Italian, Spanish, and French words for "man," "gave," "book," and "friend" obviously derive from Latin. But differences are equally apparent. In Latin, since nouns have case endings that indicate their function in a sentence, word order is more or less free; *homo meum librum amico dedit* means the same thing as, say, *homo amico librum meum dedit*. In the Romance languages, by contrast, nouns lack those telltale endings, and their interrelations are identified by prepositions and position in the sentence. Latin relies on context to determine whether a noun is definite or indefinite—"the book" as opposed to "a

---

* Feel free to be inspired by this sentence.

book." In the Romance languages, definite and indefinite articles signal the distinction.* Our Latin phrase differs from its descendants, finally, in the way it forms its verb. Italian, Spanish, and French, like English, frequently use auxiliary verbs to indicate the past tense;† something we gave in the past is something we *have* given. Latin, however, has little love for auxiliaries.

Even at the Roman Empire's height, Latin was never monolithic. Like any other language, it varied with place, context, and speaker. And like any other language, it was constantly evolving at a pace and in ways determined by both internal and external factors. The only form of the language that remained stable was the artificial and learned dialect we call Classical Latin. This was essentially a literary standard, reserved for formal oratory and high-style composition. Among the educated class, however, it served as a touchstone of linguistic correctness. Elite education was founded on memorization and imitation of the texts that defined Classical Latin. Although the vast majority of the empire's population did not receive such schooling—only about 10 percent of Roman adults were literate—the power and prestige of the educated elite ensured that spoken Latin everywhere was influenced by Classical models. There were, of course, regional variations—Romans from Spain, for example, had a notoriously thick accent—but as long as a unitary, empire-spanning aristocracy dominated both politics and high culture, these differences remained relatively insignificant.[1]

The fall of the Western Roman Empire shattered the old elite.‡ There was still a literate class, but it was smaller, less educated, and concentrated in the church. The prominence and social prestige of Classical Latin faded accordingly. At the same time, a steep decline in long-distance travel allowed regional variations in spoken Latin to develop unchecked.

Over the next few centuries, as the literate few continued to learn a more or less classicizing Latin, the various dialects of spoken Latin

---

* The definite article ("the") in Italian, Spanish, and French evolved from the Latin pronoun *ille* "that." The indefinite article ("a"; "an") developed from the Latin *unus* "one."

† Our Spanish example does not employ an auxiliary verb in the preterite tense. It does, however, in the perfect: *el hombre le ha dado mi libro a un amigo.*

‡ Latin continued to be the dominant language in most parts of the former Western Empire, and it was quickly adopted by the new Germanic ruling class. The great exception was Britain, where a more traumatic and protracted conquest resulted in the replacement of Latin by Old English. Later, Arabic would displace Latin across North Africa, and Slavic languages would drive Latin out of the Balkans.

diverged steadily from the ancient models. Yet they continued to be regarded as Latin until the early ninth century, when educational reforms associated with the court of Charlemagne brought about the realization that the spoken and written forms of the language had become essentially different; in 813, a church council decreed that local sermons were to be delivered in the "simple Roman language" instead of formal Latin. The earliest recorded recognition of the distinctions between the various Romance dialects dates to the end of the tenth century, when a pope's epitaph mentioned his mastery of French, Italian, and Latin.[2]

The firm establishment of the Romance dialects as legitimate languages occurred after the turn of the millennium, especially during the explosion of vernacular literature that accompanied the renaissance of the twelfth century. Latin continued to be regarded as the sole suitable vehicle for serious scholarship until the early modern period. But it was now, firmly and finally, a fossil language, confined to learned discourse and the nightmares of schoolchildren.

What if the Western Roman Empire had survived another thousand years? We might imagine any number of political scenarios, but we can be sure of one thing: the Western Empire would have used Latin to the bitter end. Spoken Latin probably still would have evolved in the direction of the Romance languages, but since the imperial elite would have continued to uphold the classical standard, the change would have been much slower. And since there would have been only a single reference point for linguistic correctness, the Romance languages themselves—in the sense of recognized and prestigious alternatives to Latin—would never have come into existence.

This thought experiment actually took place in the Eastern Roman Empire, which survived its western counterpart by nearly a millennium. As a result, its language—Greek—never strayed too far from its ancient roots. This is neatly exemplified by our inspiring sample phrase "the man gave my book to a friend:"[3]

Ancient Greek   ὁ ἀνὴρ ἔδωκε τὸ βιβλίον μου τῷ φίλῳ
       ho anēr edōke to biblion mou tō philō
Modern Greek   ο άντρας έδωσε το βιβλίο μου σε έναν φίλο
       o ántras édose to vivlío mou se énan phílo

The complex pitch accent of ancient Greek has evolved into a simple stress accent, and beta has taken on a "v" sound. There also have been significant grammatical changes.* But the basic structure and vocabulary of the language have changed relatively little through two and a half millennia.

The durability of Greek is rooted in a long imperial career. Alexander the Great and his successors established Greek as the language of politics and prestige throughout the eastern Mediterranean. The Romans made no efforts to change this and governed in Greek from Bulgaria to Libya. Despite its official status, Greek never developed a single standard of linguistic correctness. By the first century CE, government, business, and unpretentious literary works (like the New Testament) employed the dialect known as Koine or "common" Greek.† High-style literature, however, was usually composed in Attic—an obsessively conservative imitation of the great authors of Classical Athens.[4]

The Byzantine Empire retained, if only in Constantinople, the essentials of the Roman educational system, founded on memorization and imitation of a small canon of ancient masterpieces. Although spoken Greek drifted steadily away, shifting its sounds and simplifying its syntax, literature continued to be written in stylized Koine or the author's best stab at Attic, and the unchallenged prestige of the ancient models prevented a rupture between literary and vernacular usage.

The Greek language, in short, was saved from developing into multiple languages by the persistence of the Eastern Roman Empire and its schools, which continued to endorse ancient paradigms of "good" Greek. Thanks to the Greek Orthodox Church and Greek nationalism, this dynamic survived Byzantium itself. Greek has retained a vital connection with the classical past.‡ So, less directly, have the

---

* In our phrase, for example, take a look at the indirect object (the friend to whom my book is given). In ancient Greek, the indirect object is signaled with a dative case ending. But in modern Greek, the dative case has disappeared, and a prepositional phrase is used instead.

† Almost all dialects of modern Greek derive from Koine. The single exception, Tsakonian, is a distant descendant of the Doric dialect of ancient Sparta.

‡ Another Byzantine legacy is lingering tension between everyday spoken Greek and literary archaism. Until 1976, the Greek government insisted on a highly formal and classicizing Greek in all official communications. This brought about the promulgation of some very archaic-sounding neologisms, such as τεχνητός δορυφόρος (*technetos doryphoros*)—literally "artificial spear bearer"—for "satellite."

Romance languages. So, more distantly still, has English, whose vocabulary is about half Latinate—yet another instance of how deeply and unconsciously we draw on antiquity.

Can Any Families Trace Their Ancestry Back to the Greeks or Romans?

*M*y ancestors were Greeks and Romans. They listened to Socrates in the Agora. They marched to India with Alexander. They dueled in the Colosseum. They were martyrs and persecutors, Spartans and Athenians, senators and emperors. And if you have even the tiniest dollop of European DNA, so were yours.

Every person has two parents, four grandparents, eight great-grandparents, and so on, ancestors theoretically doubling with each generation. Extrapolate the numbers to ten generations, and you have 1,024 eight-times-great grandparents. Venture back a millennium—say, thirty-two generations—and you find yourself with more than four billion forebearers. The actual tally is much smaller, since we've been mating with our more-or-less distant relatives since time immemorial.* The entire human family, in fact, is impressively inbred. Statistical models estimate that all humans share at least one common ancestor born sometime in the past 3,500 years. And genetic sampling indicates that any European alive a thousand years ago is now—if he or she left descendants—likely an ancestor of almost *every* living European. If

---

* The technical term is "pedigree collapse." A demographer once estimated that an English child born in the middle of the twentieth century would have some 31,000 ancestors in the fifteenth generation—about 1,000 fewer than the 2^{15} you would mathematically expect. Roughly 1,000 of the child's fifteenth-generation ancestors, in other words, would be duplicates, related through more than one lineage. In the thirtieth generation, the child would have just under a million actual ancestors, as opposed to the billion produced by simply doubling the numbers each generation. Since the England of thirty generations before the child's birth (roughly the mid-eleventh century) had only about 1.1 million inhabitants, this would mean that the child was related to some 86 percent of the whole medieval population (some of the child's ancestors would of course have lived outside England, but you get the point).

some branch of your family is rooted in the Mediterranean world, in short, you are all but guaranteed to be a much-displaced cousin of any given Greek or Roman.[1]

It is one thing to know that much of the world's population is descended from the Greeks and Romans. It is another to actually trace the lines of descent. Most of the family trees preserved in ancient sources were grounded in elite ambitions, not reality. Noble Greek families liked to claim gods and heroes as their founders:* as late as the fifth century CE, a bishop boasted of descent from Hercules. Aristocratic Romans were equally bold genealogists; Julius Caesar hailed Venus as a many times great-grandmother. In the yawning gulf between themselves and the gods, however, few aristocratic families could confidently trace their lineage back much more than a century. Grim demographic realities ensured that the male lines of most families failed quickly. And even when families survived longer, the fact is attested only if enough members managed to stumble into the historical record. Otherwise, the sole clues to ancestry are names.[2]

Although they often mentioned their fathers in public contexts—Plato, for example, might describe himself as "son of Ariston"—Greeks of the Classical period had only a single name. Male Roman citizens, by contrast, usually had three: a praenomen (personal name), nomen (clan name), and cognomen (family name).† Helpfully for later historians, these conventions spread throughout the empire. Less helpfully, the system changed as it grew. From the first century onward, the cognomen displaced the praenomen as the personal name, and the nomen began to lose its significance. The empire's noble families complicated matters further by adding the names of distinguished relatives

---

* A Greek historian visiting Egypt once informed a coterie of Egyptian priests that he was descended from a god in the sixteenth generation. The priests refused to believe him, since their temple archives contained no records of such intimate immanence.

† In the name Gaius Julius Caesar, for instance, "Gaius" is the personal name, "Julius" indicates membership in the Julian clan, and "Caesar" denotes the Caesarian family. (Caesar's contemporaries, incidentally, called him either Gaius Julius or Gaius Caesar; only relatives and very close friends would have ventured to address him as Gaius.) Roman women—excluded from public life, and thus from any apparent need for public recognition—were usually given only a single name: the feminine form of their father's nomen. Thus Caesar's daughter was simply named Julia. (If Caesar had fathered two daughters, he would have referred to them as either Julia Maior and Julia Minor (older Julia and younger Julia) or Prima Julia and Secunda Julia (first Julia and second Julia).)

and benefactors to their own; one senator accumulated no fewer than thirty-eight.*[3]

Among the western senatorial aristocracy, the traditional nomenclature persisted into the sixth century. Then things fell apart. Decades of warfare destroyed most of the ancient Italian families, and chronic political instability elsewhere was attended by the steady rolling of notable heads. The families that managed to survive gradually stopped using their ancient names. In part, this was because many adopted the naming conventions of the new Germanic elite.[†] More generally, however, it reflected the fact that families no longer had much reason to commemorate the details of their lineage. In the brave new post-Roman world, all they or anyone else cared about was the fact that they had been aristocratic back to the limits of living memory.[4]

Even in Gaul, where there was considerable social continuity, genealogical knowledge was limited (not least among the ruling dynasty, which claimed descent from an amorous sea monster). Some ancient clans must have survived—there have been various attempts to connect Charlemagne with the Roman aristocracy of late antique Gaul—but we simply lack the evidence to follow any family's fortunes through the chaotic collapse of the classical world.[5]

The same holds true for Byzantium. During the fifth and sixth centuries, when the Eastern Roman Empire provided a relatively peaceful and prosperous contrast to the shattered west, Constantinople became a haven for wealthy refugees from western cities. The invasions and chaos of the seventh century, however, destroyed many of these ancient families. The rest were gradually absorbed by a new aristocracy with no conscious connections to the Roman past.

Since the later Byzantine aristocracy endured to the threshold of the modern era, the fortunes of its greatest clans can be traced relatively easily; we know, for example, that a princess from Byzantium's last

---

* This polyonymous paragon was Quintus Pompeius Senecio Roscius Murena Coelius Sextus Iulius Frontinus Silius Decianus Gaius Iulius Eurycles Herculaneus Lucius Vibullius Pius Augustanus Alpinus Bellicius Sollers Iulius Aper Ducenius Proculus Rutilianus Rufinus Silius Valens Valerius Niger Claudius Fuscus Saxa Amyntianus Sosius Priscus. As far as we can tell, his friends just called him Sosius Priscus.

† During the early eighth century, for example, Senator, a man from an old Italian family, married a Lombard woman named Theodelinda. Their daughter's name, a combination of her parents', was the Germanic-sounding Sindelinda.

imperial family was a grandmother of the first Safavid Shah of Iran, and thus an ancestor of both the Mughal emperors of India and the modern sultans of Brunei.[6]

There has always been particular interest—academic and otherwise—in the descendants of Constantine XI, the last Byzantine emperor. Constantine was killed during the Turkish capture of Constantinople, and his body was never identified. Legends arose about the emperor being turned to marble and hidden in a cave, where he would sleep until the day came to redeem his people. For the time being, however, the Byzantine throne devolved to his bickering relatives. One of Constantine's brothers ended up in Rome, where he tried to win the pope's favor by giving him the head of the Apostle Andrew. One of Constantine's nieces married Ivan III, grand prince of Moscow (Ivan the Terrible would be her grandson). But it was Andreas, the eldest of the last emperor's nephews, who was generally considered—at least by himself—to be the heir to Byzantium. His reign proved inglorious. Disowned by the pope, Andreas wandered across Europe with a ragtag retinue, desperately seeking a patron. At last, he was reduced to hocking his imperial title to the king of France. When the king reneged on their deal, Andreas repossessed his birthright and ultimately bequeathed it to the king of Spain. For all intents and purposes, however, the Byzantine imperial line died with him in 1502.*[7]

We are about twenty generations removed from the fall of Constantinople, fifty generations from the end of the Western Roman Empire, seventy generations from Julius Caesar, and eighty generations from Socrates. On such a scale, heredity is meaningless. None of us has any special claim to be a descendant of the ancient Greeks or Romans. But we are all recipients—willing, witting, or otherwise—of their

---

* Thanks to earlier dynastic marriages, there was already plenty of Byzantine blood circulating in Western Europe. In 1197, the Byzantine princess Irene married Philip, king of Germany. One of their daughters married the king of Bohemia, producing children whose descendants would join the Hapsburg and Brandenburg royal families. Another of Philip and Irene's daughters became an ancestor of the ruling house of Castile, and thus of many Spanish, Portuguese, French, and English monarchs. In 1284, likewise, the Byzantine emperor Andronicus II married Yolande of Montferrat, an Italian noblewoman. One of their sons returned to Italy to become the Marquis of Montferrat. Although the male line of his dynasty died out in the sixteenth century, earlier generations had married into a whole host of noble houses, eventually becoming ancestors of the Italian royal family. Otto I, the (very German) first king of Greece, was descended from two Byzantine imperial families via a thirteenth-century princess.

wisdom and absurdities. To the extent we understand that inheritance, and in the sense we choose to accept it, we are their heirs.

Apppendix

A Very Short History of the Classical World

Author: So—you're looking for a crash course in Greek and Roman history?

Reader: *I guess so.*

Then buckle up, hypothetical reader, for an irresponsibly short survey of the whole grand narrative: who did what, why they did it, and whether it all matters.

THE GREEKS

OK . . . so why were the Greeks such a big deal?

Why, you mean, do we still study the writings and doings of a bunch of squabbling city-states that flourished two and a half millennia ago?

Sure.

In short, century after century of cultural elites have decided that the Greek heritage matters, and we—as heirs or voyeurs of the Western tradition—tend to follow suit. There are a whole host of historical reasons, but it boils down to the fact that the Greeks produced a durable canon of literary masterpieces and an impressive array of philosophical and political concepts. In fact, our word "political" derives from the Greek *polis*.

What's a polis?

A polis was a city-state governed by and for its citizens, the free adult men who made up its political and military class. Although the typical polis was quite small (many had fewer than a thousand citizens), every polis aspired to autonomy. As a result, the Greek world was divided into hundreds of mutually suspicious little states. This fragmentation sparked endless skirmishes and petty wars. But it also encouraged competition, creativity, and innovation.

Cool. Which polis was the most important?

There was a constant struggle for supremacy, so it varied over time. In the decades leading up to the Persian Wars, Sparta probably had the most clout, at least on the Greek mainland.

What made the Spartans so successful?

Early in their history, the Spartans conquered a large territory and effectively enslaved most of the inhabitants. Thus freed from the need to work (and finding themselves outnumbered by their serfs), the Spartans had the means, motive, and opportunity to become Classical Greece's most professional soldiers.

What about Athens?

Like Sparta, Athens was a large, wealthy, and powerful polis. There, however, the similarities ended. Sparta was located in a mountain valley; Athens stood beside the sea. The Spartans shunned commerce; the Athenians lived by it. Sparta retained a conservative oligarchy; Athens evolved a radical democracy. You get the idea. Despite their differences, however, the Athenians and Spartans were sometimes firm allies, most famously during the Persian Wars, the greatest crisis in Greek history.

I suppose you want me to ask . . .

What happened during the Persian Wars? In 490 BCE, the Persian King of Kings Darius launched a punitive raid against Athens. To everyone's surprise, the Athenians defeated the Persian expeditionary force at the Battle of Marathon. The Persians returned ten years later under the personal leadership of Darius's son Xerxes. Faced with the largest army the world had yet seen, many Greek cities capitulated. A coalition led by Athens and Sparta, however, decided to resist. A small allied force under the command of the Spartan king Leonidas failed to hold the Persians at the narrow pass of Thermopylae. But a few weeks later, the Athenians crippled the Persian fleet at the Battle of Salamis, turning the tide of the war. The allies destroyed the Persian army the following year. After this victory, the Athenians embarked on an unprecedented golden age, which would define what we call the Classical period (that's Classical with a capital *C*)—the century and a half of Greek history between the Persian Wars and the death of Alexander the Great.

Why was the Athenian golden age so important?

Because Classical Athens was responsible for most of the cultural achievements we associate with the ancient Greeks. Tragedy became a sophisticated art form, capable of plumbing the depths of human motivation and divine indifference. Philosophy, in the person of a chronically unemployed stonemason's son named Socrates, began to shed new light on questions of human ethics and knowledge. Sculpture scaled new heights in the marble reliefs of the Parthenon. Last but not least, the first true work of history, a sprawling account of the Persian Wars, was composed by the genial and uncritical Herodotus.

Why did the Athenians accomplish so much?

On the most fundamental level, because they had the time and money. After the Persian Wars, the Athenians acquired a lucrative little empire centered on the Aegean Sea. The revenues from their subject cities financed the development of a direct democracy, in which every male citizen was allowed and expected to take part. Under the guidance of Pericles, a gifted statesman and orator, the same flow of money underwrote the construction of the Parthenon and drew ambitious intellectuals from every corner of the Greek world.

What were the Spartans doing during this period?

For the most part, brutalizing their serfs and resenting the Athenians. The Spartans always had regarded the Athenians as rivals; as Athenian power grew, so did their anxiety. Within a few decades of the victory against the Persians, mutual distrust had hardened into cold war. The inevitable open conflict between Athens and Sparta, which we call the Peloponnesian War, broke out in 431 BCE.

Why does the Peloponnesian War matter?

Because it destroyed the Athenian Empire, and because it inspired the work of Thucydides, arguably the greatest ancient historian. Originally an Athenian general, Thucydides traced the grinding cost and growing brutality of the Peloponnesian War with coolness and precision. He lived long enough to recount the Athenians' disastrous attempt to conquer Sicily. He died, however, before he could analyze the final years of the war, when the Spartans, now taking money from the Persians, built a fleet and dismantled the Athenian Empire. The war effectively ended in 405 BCE, when a Spartan admiral executed the rowers of the last Athenian fleet on a lonely beach.

How long did the Spartans dominate Greece?

Only for a few decades. Then Epaminondas, a general from the second-tier polis of Thebes, shattered the Spartan army and freed the Spartans' serfs. Epaminondas, however, was killed in battle before he could consolidate his position, creating a power vacuum that would be filled by Philip II, the talented and ambitious king of the Macedonians.

You dropped a lot of names there. So who were the Macedonians?

Northern Greeks, who ruled a large but usually anarchic kingdom. Philip II was the first Macedonian king to unify his realm and intervene decisively in the affairs of the Greek city-states to the south. By the time of his death, Macedon was indisputably the greatest power in Greece.

Why was Philip so effective?

Partly because he was a skilled diplomat, but primarily because he had developed a new military formation: the Macedonian phalanx. For centuries, the armies of the Greek cities had been organized in hoplite phalanxes—deep formations of heavy infantry armed with circular shields and eight-foot spears. Philip massed his troops in similar deep formations but equipped them with pikes up to eighteen feet long. The pikes of the first five ranks projected beyond the front of the formation. As the enemy struggled to break through this iron hedge, the superb Macedonian cavalry exploited the weaknesses that developed in their lines.

What happened to Philip?

Philip defeated the armies of Athens and Thebes and began to plan a grand campaign against the Persian Empire. But he was assassinated before his preparations were complete, leaving the Macedonian throne and Persian crusade to his son Alexander, a short and stocky twenty-year-old with a raspy voice, odd-colored eyes, and dreams of conquering Asia.

What made Alexander great?

He was that rare and dangerous thing: a military genius. Alexander launched his invasion of Persia in 334 BCE. Over the course of a campaign that lasted ten years and covered more than 10,000 miles, Alexander faced the vast armies of the Persians, the nomadic horsemen of central Asia, and the war elephants of the Indian kings—and never lost. Along the way—to the delight of future biographers—he ran naked around the tomb of his idol Achilles, drunkenly burned the Persian capital to the ground, and took an Indian arrow through the lung, among other adventures. When it was all over, Alexander, at age thirty-one, was master of an empire that stretched from Bulgaria to Pakistan. Then, while planning vast new campaigns, he abruptly died from some combination of alcoholism and malaria (or, if you believe ancient conspiracy theories, because he was poisoned by Aristotle).

What happened after Alexander's death?

Alexander's generals tore his empire apart in a generation-long struggle for dominance. Once the dust of their wars finally settled, it revealed a profoundly changed and vastly enlarged Greek world, divided among three major kingdoms and a shifting cast of smaller states. The Hellenistic period—as we call the era between Alexander's death and Rome's absorption of the eastern Mediterranean—had begun.

Did any Hellenistic king try to imitate Alexander's conquests?

Every Hellenistic king tried to imitate Alexander, at least to the extent of copying his hairstyle and pretensions of divinity. Only a few, however, attempted anything remotely like Alexander's career of conquest. Probably the most notable was Pyrrhus, ruler of a small kingdom in northern Greece. Pyrrhus had a strong sword arm (he once split a man in half lengthwise with a single blow), a feisty troop of war elephants, and outsized ambitions. When he learned that a Greek colony in southern Italy was having problems with some barbarians who called themselves the Romans, he decided to launch an Alexander-style campaign in the West.

How did that go?

Not very well.

THE ROMANS

How much do we know about the early history of Rome?

Much less than we would like. The Romans claimed that their city was founded by Romulus and Remus, twin sons of the war god Mars and an Italian princess. Shortly after their birth, an unscrupulous uncle left the twins to die on the banks of the swollen Tiber. But they were nursed by a she-wolf, raised by a shepherd, grew to strapping manhood, and overthrew their uncle. Then the young heroes founded the city of Rome at the place where that accommodating she-wolf had suckled them.

Uh–huh. What actually happened?

Rome grew up at a ford of the Tiber River, a natural crossing of trade routes. The famous seven hills, rising from the riverside marshes, were easily fortified and attracted settlers from the surrounding countryside. During the eighth century BCE, the hilltop villages began to coalesce into a larger settlement, which quickly became one of the most important cities in central Italy. Sometime around 500 BCE, the aristocrats of the growing city overthrew their king and established a new government: the Republic.

How did the Republic work?

Although it had popular assemblies and elections, the Roman Republic was always government by and for the elite. The whole political system was designed to allow wealthy families scope for power sharing and competition. By the fourth century BCE, the chief officials were the two consuls. These men presided over a government in which virtually every position was both annual (held for a single year) and collegiate (held by multiple incumbents) to limit the power of ambitious men. Real authority was vested in the Senate, the advisory council whose three hundred members, chosen for life, filled every important office.

How did the Republic become so powerful?

Roman aristocrats were locked in a constant struggle for prestige, especially for the prestige conferred by military success. So almost every year, the legions marched out to campaign against their neighbors. If we can believe later Roman authors, they usually won. These victories were secured by the Roman custom of integrating former enemies into their political and military system: the elites of conquered cities were granted Roman citizenship, and their armies brigaded with the legions as "allies." This policy provided the Republic with both influential local supporters and massive reserves of manpower. As the cycle of conquest and assimilation gathered momentum, Roman armies ranged farther and farther. By the early third century BCE, they were threatening the Greek colonies of southern Italy. That, as you'll recall, is when King Pyrrhus and his war elephants showed up.

I take it Pyrrhus lost. How did the Romans defeat him?

The Roman legions (and the allied units that marched beside them) consisted primarily of heavy infantry armed with javelins and short swords. On the battlefield, they deployed in groups of 60 or 120, arranged in loose formations that could accommodate rough terrain—or engulf Macedonian-style phalanxes like Pyrrhus's. After three hard battles, Pyrrhus retreated with the remains of his army. By way of a victory lap, the Romans absorbed the rest of southern Italy, pushing the Republic's frontiers toward the wealthy and far-flung Carthaginian Empire.

Nice foreshadowing. So where did the Carthaginians come from?

The city of Carthage, located in what is now Tunisia, was founded by settlers from Phoenicia (modern Lebanon). Growing rich on maritime trade, the Carthaginians created a substantial empire that included much of the North African coast, southern Spain, and western Sicily. For centuries, relations between Rome and Carthage had been friendly. Once their political interests clashed in Sicily, however, a confrontation was inevitable.

What happened when the Romans and Carthaginians finally clashed?

The brutal, decades-long conflict we call the First Punic War. For our purposes, all that matters is the result: the Romans won, building their first navy and gaining Sicily—their first province—along the way.

When did Hannibal show up?

Hannibal was the son of Carthage's best general during the First Punic War. After the war, this general—according to Roman tradition—raised his gifted son to be an implacable enemy of the Republic. In 218 BCE, Hannibal launched the Second Punic War, marching east from the Carthaginian province in Spain with an army that included thirty-seven war elephants. He led his platoons and pachyderms over the snowbound Alps and almost immediately began to defeat Roman armies on a scale that left the Republic reeling. At Cannae, the greatest of his victories, fifty thousand Romans and allies were killed.

Why didn't the Republic collapse after these disasters?

The Roman aristocracy refused to surrender, and most of Rome's allies remained loyal. Fabius Maximus, a veteran general and statesman, advised the Romans that the only way to defeat Hannibal was to wear his army down through attrition. This strategy was adopted, and slowly confined Hannibal to southern Italy. In the meantime, a young Roman general named Scipio took the offensive, capturing the Carthaginian possessions in Spain and sailing to attack Carthage itself. Hannibal hurried home and was defeated at the Battle of Zama. The Carthaginians were stripped of their empire, and the Romans became masters of the western Mediterranean. Over the following half-century, the Roman Republic won war after war, particularly in the east, where the legions repeatedly humiliated the great Hellenistic kingdoms. The culmination came in 146 BCE, when both Greece and the Carthaginian heartland became Roman provinces.

If the Republic was so successful, why did it become so unstable in the following century?

In part because it expanded too rapidly for its own good. The provinces were mismanaged by an elite much more interested in getting rich than in governing well. The emergence of large slave-worked estates and other factors drove thousands of impoverished peasant farmers into the city of Rome and into the legions, where—without land or resources of their own—they were reliant on the rewards their commanders could give them. In a crisis, unsurprisingly, these men tended to be more loyal to their generals than to the Republic itself. The civil wars of the following century would thus be waged by what amounted to private armies.

What were those civil wars fought over?

They were nothing more and nothing less than the rivalries of leading men, played out on an empire-wide scale and at the cost of tens of thousands of lives.

How did Julius Caesar and Pompey appear on the scene?

Pompey was a military hero, famous for clearing the Mediterranean of pirates and bringing most of the Near East under Roman control. Julius Caesar made his name as a champion of the people in Roman politics. Caesar's popularity helped to win him a consulship. But his rapid rise had left him with powerful enemies and dangerous debts. To protect himself from both, he allied himself with Pompey and the immensely wealthy senator Crassus. The alliance made Caesar an unstoppable force in Roman politics and secured for him the governorship of Rome's small province in southern Gaul. From this base, he provoked conflicts with the tribes to the north and proceeded to conquer all of Gaul (roughly modern France) in a series of brilliant and bloody campaigns. Then he turned his attention back to Italy, where war threatened with Pompey.

Why did Pompey and Caesar go to war?

Mutual distrust. Recognizing that Caesar's power and reputation were eclipsing his own, Pompey aligned himself with Caesar's enemies in the Senate. Another civil war ensued. Caesar's hardened veterans defeated Pompey's forces at the Battle of Pharsalus, and Pompey himself was killed shortly thereafter. Although Caesar would spend the next three years suppressing revolts led by Pompey's supporters, he was now the master of the Roman world. He had the Senate declare him dictator for life and embarked on a series of visionary schemes. But he tried to change too much too quickly, and was assassinated by a cabal of senators.

Let me guess—another civil war followed?

Naturally. In his will, Caesar adopted his great-nephew Octavian, a sickly nineteen-year-old student. With the magic of Caesar's name and an unflinching willingness to destroy anyone who stood in his way, Octavian made himself a leading figure in Roman politics. After initial conflicts, he allied himself with his only real rival, Caesar's former lieutenant Mark Antony. For the better part of a decade, the two men divided the Roman world between them. Octavian was supreme in Italy and the western provinces. Antony ruled the east, where he became romantically involved with Cleopatra, the alluring queen of Egypt. Eventually and predictably, strained peace gave way to open war. Octavian met Antony and Cleopatra at the epochal Battle of Actium and won. Egypt was added to the Roman Empire, and Octavian, now unchallenged, returned to Rome in triumph. Soon after, he asked the Senate to crown his glory with a new title: Augustus.

Augustus was the first Roman emperor, right?

He was indeed. Remembering that Caesar had gotten himself killed by exercising power too blatantly, Augustus made a show of consulting the Senate, kept a modest house on the Palatine Hill, and called himself "first citizen" of a restored republic. But behind the facade of continuity, he and his advisers established an absolute monarchy, supported by a large standing army and represented in the provinces by deputized senators. Although there were weaknesses in the system—succession was a perennial problem, and the relationship between the emperors and the legions was potentially explosive—it proved enduring. Roman emperors would reign for the next millennium and a half.

How long did Augustus's family rule the Roman Empire?

For about a half-century after the death of Augustus himself. They were a motley crew. Augustus's adopted son and successor Tiberius had little patience for politics and withdrew to a villa on Capri. Caligula, the next emperor, was a megalomaniac. His bookish successor Claudius conquered most of Britain as a publicity stunt before marrying his niece, who had a teenage son—Nero—from a previous marriage.

Why is Nero so infamous?

Like any bad emperor worth his salt, he was murderous—in his immediate family alone, he executed his mother and forced his first wife to commit suicide. We tend to remember Nero, however, for his delusions. Convinced that he was a skilled athlete and actor, he insisted on competing at public festivals and finally in the Olympic Games, where the intimidated judges awarded him first prize in every event he entered. His extravagance was equally impressive: after a fire destroyed much of Rome, Nero built the Golden House, a gargantuan pleasure villa in the center of the city. Finally, the Senate and the legions turned on him. Nero committed suicide, lamenting, "what an artist dies in me!"

What happened after Nero's death?

A civil war, of course. The year after Nero's suicide, 69 CE, is known as the Year of the Four Emperors. For three of those emperors, the year ended very unpleasantly. But the fourth, an experienced general named Vespasian, managed to establish a new dynasty. Vespasian's older son was universally beloved. The younger son was not, and ended up assassinated. He was replaced by the first in a series of talented rulers, sometimes called the Five Good Emperors, who took the Roman Empire to the peak of its power and prosperity.

When did the Roman Empire reach its greatest size?

Under Trajan, the second "good emperor." After conquering Dacia (modern Romania), Trajan launched an invasion of Parthia, the vast eastern kingdom centered on what are now Iraq and Iran. He conquered the ancient cities of Mesopotamia and sailed down to the Persian Gulf, dreaming of following in Alexander's footsteps to India. Rebellions in his rear, however, foreclosed that fantasy, and his successor Hadrian withdrew from the new eastern territories.

How long did the imperial apogee last?

Through the late second century, the Roman Empire seemed unstoppable. The two thousand cities of the provinces prospered. Legionaries repelled raids in Scotland and Sudan. Roman coins flooded the markets of southern India. Scholar-officials at the Han Chinese court wrote reports about the mighty kingdom that ruled the Western Sea.

And then?

Pestilence and barbarians, in that order. During the reign of Marcus Aurelius, a terrible plague (probably smallpox) arrived from the east, killing millions. Then marauding Germanic tribesman breached the northern frontier. Marcus launched a series of campaigns into the forests and mountains of central Europe. Before the tribes had been fully pacified, however, he died, leaving the empire to his worthless son Commodus.

I gather that Commodus was not an especially good emperor.

He was not. Abandoning the northern war, Commodus returned to Rome, where he indulged gladiatorial fantasies. After twelve years of misrule, he was strangled by his personal trainer. A civil war ensued. The eventual winner, a general from North Africa, was harsh but effective. The later members of the dynasty he founded were less prepossessing. One killed his brother and obsessively imitated Alexander the Great. Another devoted most of his time to an orgiastic sun cult. All confirmed the tightening relationship between imperial authority and the legions, which would culminate in fifty years of military anarchy and usher in a new era of Roman history.

LATE ANTIQUITY

Why did the Roman Empire suddenly get so anarchic?

Domestically, the chief problem was a crisis of imperial legitimacy. Emperor after emperor was proclaimed by the legions, none lasting long enough to establish a dynasty, each compelled to placate the troops with currency-ruining raises and bonuses. The domestic crisis was worsened, and largely driven, by developments beyond the frontier. In the east, the shambolic Parthians were replaced by the aggressive and expansionist Sassanid Dynasty. To the north, unprecedentedly large and well-organized tribal confederations swept over the frontiers. The empire seemed to be on the verge of collapse. Athens was sacked by marauding raiders. One emperor was massacred with his army in a Bulgarian swamp; another was captured by the Sassanids and spent the rest of his life in captivity (when he died, it was rumored, his body was embalmed and set up in a temple). For more than a decade, the empire split into three parts: a breakaway Gallic Empire in the west, an east dominated by a dynamic Syrian queen, and a central block still governed from Rome.

How did the Romans recover?

The tide was turned by a series of emperors from the ranks of the legions, who reunified the empire, restored the frontiers, and effectively replaced the pseudo-republican Augustan system with overt military autocracy. The most successful of these reforming emperors was an officer from the Balkans named Diocletian. Over the course of his twenty-year reign, Diocletian made the imperial government more bureaucratic and thus (according to the bureaucrats) more efficient. He also instituted the tetrarchy, a college of four co-emperors intended to maximize the imperial presence on the increasingly precarious frontiers. The system was also designed to avoid succession crises. There were two senior and two junior emperors; at regular intervals, the senior emperors retired and were succeeded by the junior emperors. The freshly promoted emperors would then appoint a new set of junior emperors, and so on.

Interesting idea. Did it work?

Not really. The habit of hereditary succession was too strong. Barely a year after Diocletian and the other senior emperor retired, one of the new senior emperors died, and his army, ignoring Diocletian's rules, proclaimed his son Constantine emperor. Over the next two decades, Constantine campaigned against each of his co-emperors and finally emerged as the sole ruler of the Roman world. It was just before the critical battle with the first of his rivals that the young emperor instructed his soldiers to paint Christian symbols on their shields. He won that battle, issued an edict of toleration for Christianity shortly thereafter, and became the first Christian Roman emperor.

Before this, the Romans had persecuted the Christians, right?

Only occasionally. Although Christianity grew up within the Roman Empire—Jesus of Nazareth, after all, had been crucified as a rebel against imperial authority—two centuries of emperors and senators knew little and cared less about the new religion. There were Christians in most of the empire's major cities by the end of the second century, particularly in the eastern provinces. These communities, however, tended to be too small and socially humble to attract much attention. The emperors only began to systematically oppose the church during the crises of the third century. There were three empire-wide persecutions, the last and most severe taking place under Diocletian. In each case, Christians were attacked as enemies of the state who refused to take part in communal religious rituals or offer sacrifice for the emperors. Although the persecutions caused enormous trauma, they also created martyrs, whose sufferings became a source of inspiration.

Why did Constantine found Constantinople?

He wanted a capital from which he could easily reach the Danube and Persian frontiers. He chose a magnificent site on the Bosporus, garnished it with boulevards and monumental churches, and proclaimed his city the new Rome. It almost immediately became one of the most important cities in the empire and would be one of Constantine's most enduring legacies.

What happened after Constantine's death?

Constantine intended his three sons to rule the empire jointly with two of their cousins. But his sons killed their cousins, the youngest son killed the oldest son, and then the youngest son himself was murdered, leaving Constantine's middle son the sole ruler of the Roman world. Desperate for help in the endless process of shoring up the frontiers, he made one of his few remaining relatives, a studious youth named Julian, his co-emperor and stationed him on the Rhine frontier. Julian had no political or military experience. But he did have enough ability to win an important victory against the latest round of barbarian raiders, and enough ambition to rule as sole emperor after his cousin's death. On assuming the throne, Julian revealed himself to be a pagan and attempted to undo the Christianization of the empire. In this, he failed—partly because his reign was short and partly because much of the ruling class had already converted. He would be remembered as Julian the Apostate, and the Roman Empire would never again have a non-Christian ruler.

When did the Roman Empire begin its terminal decline?

At least in retrospect, by the end of the fourth century. Theodosius I, a devout Christian and competent general, was the last man to rule the entire Roman world. When he died in 395, he left the western half of the empire to one of his sons and the eastern half to the other. The division proved permanent. During the course of the fifth century, the Eastern and Western Empires would both face serious pressure from external enemies. The East would survive; the West fell.

Why were the fates of the Eastern and Western Roman Empires so different?

There were several reasons. First, despite the generally low caliber of its fifth-century emperors, the Eastern Empire managed to avoid serious civil wars. The Western Empire emphatically did not. The Eastern Empire, second, was more urbanized and prosperous, and thus had a much easier time paying its soldiers and buying off barbarian hordes. Finally, and perhaps most fundamentally, the richest and most powerful men in the Eastern Empire—the people, in other words, whose support the emperors needed most—were usually high officials in the imperial bureaucracy and thus invested in the government's success. The great notables of the Western Empire, by contrast, were the magnates of the Roman Senate. These men tended to be much more interested in their vast landholdings than in service to the state. They found it correspondingly easy to envision a world without emperors.

Why were barbarians able to conquer the Western Empire so quickly?

Because the western government was so dysfunctional. Take, for example, the Vandals, a relatively unimportant tribe that crossed the frozen Rhine during the winter of 406–407. After burning and looting their way across Gaul and Spain, the Vandals settled in the rich provinces of North Africa. Establishing their capital at the ancient city of Carthage, they created a pirate fleet that terrorized the western Mediterranean. Not quite a half-century after they first straggled over the Rhine, they sacked Rome itself. The Vandals probably never had more than twenty thousand or so warriors, yet they were able to rampage at will through most of the Western Roman Empire and steal its richest province.

Their success was largely a matter of being in the right place at the right time. At a series of critical moments—when they first crossed the Rhine, when they entered Africa, and when they seized Carthage—the imperial government was too distracted by civil wars and court intrigues to effectively oppose them.

Which parts of the Western Empire collapsed first?

First Britain (never a profitable province) was abandoned. Then a large chunk of southwestern Gaul was given to the empire's barbarian allies. Around the time the Vandals seized North Africa, Roman control of Spain began to be eroded by another Germanic tribe. By the middle of the fifth century, the Western Empire had been reduced to Italy, southern Gaul, and a sliver of Spain; without the revenues of Africa, even this rump state found it difficult to pay its soldiers. The Western Empire enjoyed a final moment of glory when it teamed up with some of its barbarian allies to fight Attila the Hun to a draw. But then the victorious Roman general, the Western Empire's last really gifted commander, was murdered by the emperor, the emperor was murdered by the general's former bodyguards, and the court descended again into chaos.

How did the Western Empire finally fall?

During the last twenty years of the empire's existence, a series of short-lived rulers came and went, most little more than puppets of the German generalissimo of the imperial armies. The end came in 476, when a barbarian general deposed the latest imperial nonentity (a child with the poignant name of Romulus Augustulus) and declared himself king of Italy. Notice was sent to the Eastern court in Constantinople, which politely acknowledged the fact that the Western Roman Empire had ceased to exist.

How significant was the collapse of the Western Roman Empire?

Life went on. Many former provinces had long been, and continued to be, devastated by marauding rebels and barbarians. In other parts of the former Western Empire, however, the collapse of the imperial order went almost unnoticed. The Germanic peoples now ruling the West usually were willing to cooperate with the old Roman aristocracies, whose members continued to collect taxes and live on their estates. Latin was still spoken, though its regional dialects began to diverge more quickly, and only the Vandals (who adhered to a heretical branch of Christianity) persecuted their subjects for religious reasons. Continuity was especially visible in Italy, where a German king sympathetic to Roman culture sent polite letters to the Senate and held games in the Colosseum. On the surface, at least, a working relationship had been established between conquerors and conquered. But the aristocracies of the west still remembered when the world had been Roman. So did the eastern emperors.

Did the eastern emperors ever attempt to reconquer the West?

Justinian, greatest of the eastern Roman emperors, came to power a half-century after the Western Empire's collapse. His driving ambition was to restore the Roman Empire to its ancient power and grandeur—and for a few years, it looked as though he might succeed. He presided over the definitive codification of Roman law. He built the church of Hagia Sophia, the greatest monument of late Roman architecture. And he sent his gifted general Belisarius to reconquer the lost provinces of the west. Roman armies occupied Carthage, reclaimed North Africa, stormed Sicily, and crossed into Italy. Within a few years, almost the entire peninsula was Roman again. Then bubonic plague arrived from the east, killing as much as a quarter of the empire's population. The tide of conquest rolled back, and Justinian's generals spent the remainder of his long reign trying to protect the far-flung frontiers.

What happened to Justinian's empire?

About fifty years after Justinian's death, a generation-long war with Sassanid Persia nearly destroyed the empire. The Romans prevailed but at a terrible cost: the Balkan provinces were lost, and most of the remaining provinces were ravaged. Before they could recover, a new threat appeared. Far to the south, in the backwater caravan city of Mecca, Muhammad had united the warring Arab tribes under the banner of Islam. Only a few years after the Prophet's death, in a battle fought during a blinding sandstorm, a Muslim force shattered the Roman armies of Syria. Within a decade, Roman Egypt, Palestine, and Syria had fallen. Within a century, the Muslims controlled an empire that stretched from Spain to Pakistan.

When did late antiquity end?

Any date is of course arbitrary. By the early eighth century, however, the Eastern Roman Empire had been reduced to Anatolia (modern Turkey), coastal Greece, and a few fragments of Italy. This attenuated state, transformed by a century of warfare, was profoundly different from the empires of Justinian and Constantine. In the half-ruined city of Constantinople and in islets of learning from the monasteries of Ireland to the pleasure gardens of Damascus, the classical tradition endured. But at this point, we can reasonably say that the Mediterranean world had entered the Middle Ages, and take our leave of antiquity.

Further Reading

$\mathcal{F}$or each question, I've tried to provide a few reasonably accessible English-language books. As a general reference to all things ancient Greek and Roman, you can't do better than the redoubtable *Oxford Classical Dictionary*.

CHAPTER 1

Liza Cleland, Glenys Davies, and Lloyd Llewellyn-Jones, eds., *Greek and Roman Dress from A to Z* (Routledge, 2007).
Alexandra Croom, *Roman Clothing and Fashion* (Amberley, 2010).

CHAPTER 2

Diana E. E. Kleiner, *Roman Sculpture* (Yale University Press, 1992).
G. M. A. Richter, *The Portraits of the Greeks*, abridged and rev. R. R. R. Smith (Cornell University Press, 1984).

CHAPTER 3

Donald W. Engels, *Classical Cats: The Rise and Fall of the Sacred Cat* (Routledge, 1999).
Iain Ferris, *Cave Canem: Animals and Roman Society* (Amberley, 2018).

Kenneth F. Kitchell Jr., *Animals in the Ancient World from A to Z* (Routledge, 2017).

CHAPTER 4

Angus Mclaren, *A History of Contraception from Antiquity to the Present Day* (Blackwell, 1990).

J. M. Riddle, *Contraception and Abortion from the Ancient World to the Renaissance* (Harvard University Press, 1992).

CHAPTER 5

Guido Maino, *The Healing Hand: Man and Wound in the Ancient World*, 2nd ed. (Harvard University Press, 1991).

Susan P. Mattern, *The Prince of Medicine: Galen in the Roman Empire* (Oxford University Press, 2013).

Vivian Nutton, *Ancient Medicine*, 2nd ed. (Routledge, 2013).

CHAPTER 6

Andrew Dalby, *Siren Feasts: A History of Food and Gastronomy in Greece* (Routledge, 1996).

Andrew Dalby, *Empire of Pleasures: Luxury and Indulgence in the Roman World* (Routledge, 2000).

Sally Grainger, *Cooking Apicius: Roman Recipes for Today* (Prospect Books, 2006).

CHAPTER 7

James Davidson, *Courtesans and Fishcakes: The Consuming Passions of Classical Athens* (HarperCollins, 1997).

Stuart J. Fleming, *Vinum: The Story of Roman Wine* (Art Flair Publications, 2001).

Jancis Robinson and Julia Harding, eds., *The Oxford Companion to Wine*, 4th ed. (Oxford University Press, 2015).

CHAPTER 8

Bonnie Blackburn and Leofranc Holford-Strevens, *The Oxford Companion to the Year* (Oxford University Press, 1999).

Robert Hannah, *Greek and Roman Calendars: Constructions of Time in the Classical World* (Duckworth, 2005).

CHAPTER 9

Kyle Harper, *The Fate of Rome: Climate, Disease, and the End of an Empire* (Princeton University Press, 2017).

Tim Parkin, *Old Age in the Roman World: A Cultural and Social History* (Johns Hopkins University Press, 2004).

CHAPTER 10

Peter Garnsey, *Food and Society in Classical Antiquity* (Cambridge University Press, 1999).

Estelle Lazer, *Resurrecting Pompeii* (Routledge, 2009).

CHAPTER 11

Kenneth W. Harl, *Coinage in the Roman Economy, 300 B.C. to A.D. 700* (Johns Hopkins University Press, 1996).

Sitta Von Reden, *Money in Classical Antiquity* (Cambridge University Press, 2010).

CHAPTER 12

Gregory S. Aldrete, *Daily Life in the Roman City: Rome, Pompeii and Ostia* (Greenwood Press, 2004).

Paul Erdkamp, ed., *The Cambridge Companion to Ancient Rome* (Cambridge University Press, 2013).

Wilfried Nippel, *Public Order in Ancient Rome* (Cambridge University Press, 1995).

CHAPTER 13

Keith Bradley, *Slavery and Society at Rome* (Cambridge University Press, 1994).
Peter Garnsey, *Ideas of Slavery from Aristotle to Augustine* (Cambridge University Press, 1996).
Henrik Mouritsen, *The Freedman in the Roman World* (Cambridge University Press, 2011).
Thomas E. Wiedemann, *Greek and Roman Slavery* (Croom Helm, 1981).

CHAPTER 14

Sarah B. Pomeroy, *Families in Classical and Hellenistic Greece: Representations and Realities* (Oxford University Press, 1997).
Beryl Rawson, ed., *Marriage, Divorce, and Children in Ancient Rome* (Oxford University Press, 1991).
Susan Treggiari, *Roman Marriage: Iusti Coniuges from the Time of Cicero to the Time of Ulpian* (Oxford University Press, 1991).

CHAPTER 15

Kenneth Dover, *Greek Homosexuality*, 3rd ed. (Bloomsbury, 2016).
Kyle Harper, *From Shame to Sin: the Christian Transformation of Sexual Morality in Late Antiquity* (Harvard University Press, 2013).
John G. Younger, *Sex in the Ancient World from A to Z* (Routledge, 2005).

CHAPTER 16

John Boardman, *Greek Art*, 5th ed. (Thames & Hudson, 2016).
Nancy H. Ramage and Andrew Ramage, *Roman Art: Romulus to Constantine*, 6th ed. (Pearson, 2015).
Caroline Vout, *Classical Art: A Life History from Antiquity to the Present* (Princeton University Press, 2018).

CHAPTER 17

Mary Beard, John North, and Simon Price, *Religions of Rome* (Cambridge University Press, 1998).

Simon Price, *Religions of the Ancient Greeks* (Cambridge University Press, 1999).

Tim Whitmarsh, *Battling the Gods: Atheism in the Ancient World* (Knopf, 2015).

CHAPTER 18

John Cherry, ed., *Mythical Beasts* (British Museum Press, 1995).

D. Felton, *Haunted Greece and Rome: Ghost Stories from Classical Antiquity* (University of Texas Press, 1999).

Sarah Iles Johnston, *Restless Dead: Encounters between the Living and the Dead in Ancient Greece* (University of California Press, 1999).

CHAPTER 19

Radcliffe G. Edmonds III, *Drawing down the Moon: Magic in the Ancient Greco-Roman World* (Princeton University Press, 2019).

Fritz Graf, *Magic in the Ancient World*, trans. Franklin Philip (Harvard University Press, 1999).

Philip Matyszak, *Ancient Magic: A Practitioner's Guide to the Supernatural in Greece and Rome* (Thames & Hudson, 2019).

CHAPTER 20

Jan Bremmer, ed., *The Strange World of Human Sacrifice* (Peeters, 2008).

Dennis D. Hughes, *Human Sacrifice in Ancient Greece* (Routledge, 1991).

CHAPTER 21

William J. Broad, *The Oracle: Ancient Delphi and the Science behind Its Lost Secrets* (Penguin, 2006).

Sarah Iles Johnston, *Ancient Greek Divination* (Blackwell, 2008).

Michael Scott, *Delphi: A History of the Center of the Ancient World* (Princeton University Press, 2014).

CHAPTER 22

Gillian Clark, *Christianity and Roman Society* (Cambridge University Press, 2004).

Johannes Geffcken, *The Last Days of Greco-Roman Paganism*, trans. Sabine MacCormack (North Holland, 1978).

A. D. Lee, ed., *Pagans and Christians in Late Antiquity: A Sourcebook* (Routledge, 2000).

CHAPTERS 23–24

M. I. Finley and H. W. Pleket, *The Olympic Games: The First Thousand Years* (Chatto & Windus, 1976).

Donald G. Kyle, *Sport and Spectacle in the Ancient World*, 2nd ed. (Wiley Blackwell, 2015).

David Potter, *The Victor's Crown: A History of Ancient Sport from Homer to Byzantium* (Oxford University Press, 2011).

CHAPTER 25

Lionel Casson, *Ships and Seamanship in the Ancient World* (Princeton University Press, 1971).

Lionel Casson, *Travel in the Ancient World*, 2nd ed. (Johns Hopkins University Press, 1994).

CHAPTER 26

Nathan T. Elkins, *A Monument to Dynasty and Death: The Story of Rome's Colosseum and the Emperors Who Built It* (Johns Hopkins University Press, 2019).

Keith Hopkins and Mary Beard, *The Colosseum* (Profile, 2005).

CHAPTER 27

Jerry Toner, *The Day Commodus Killed a Rhino* (Johns Hopkins University Press, 2014).

J. M. C. Toynbee, *Animals in Roman Life and Art* (Thames & Hudson, 1973).

CHAPTER 28

Roger Dunkle, *Gladiators: Violence and Spectacle in Ancient Rome* (Pearson, 2008).

Fik Meijer, *The Gladiators: History's Most Deadly Sport*, trans. Liz Waters (Thomas Dunne, 2004).

CHAPTER 29

John M. Kistler, *War Elephants* (Praeger, 2006).

Adrienne Mayor, *Greek Fire, Poison Arrows, and Scorpion Bombs: Biological and Chemical Warfare in the Ancient World* (Overlook, 2003).

CHAPTER 30

Duncan B. Campbell, *Besieged: Siege Warfare in the Ancient World* (Osprey, 2006).

Duncan B. Campbell, *Greek and Roman Siege Machinery 399 BC–AD 363* (Osprey, 2003).

Tracey Rihll, *The Catapult: A History* (Westholme, 2013).

CHAPTER 31

N. J. E. Austin and N. B. Rankov, *Exploratio: Military and Political Intelligence in the Roman World from the Second Punic War to the Battle of Adrianople* (Routledge, 1995).

Frank Russell, *Information Gathering in Classical Greece* (University of Michigan Press, 1999).

Rose Sheldon, *Intelligence Activities in Ancient Rome* (Routledge, 2004).

CHAPTER 32

Adrian Goldsworthy, *The Complete Roman Army* (Thames & Hudson, 2003).
Pat Southern, *The Roman Army: A Social and Institutional History* (Oxford University Press, 2007).
Peter S. Wells, *The Battle That Stopped Rome: Emperor Augustus, Arminius, and the Slaughter of the Legions in the Teutoburg Forest* (W. W. Norton, 2003).

CHAPTER 33

Amanda Claridge, *Rome: An Oxford Archaeological Guide*, 2nd ed. (Oxford University Press, 2010).
Richard Krautheimer, *Rome: Profile of a City, 312–1308* (Princeton University Press, 1980).
Peter Llewellyn, *Rome in the Dark Ages* (Faber, 1971).

CHAPTER 34

Penelope J. E. Davies, *Death and the Emperor: Roman Imperial Funerary Monuments, from Augustus to Marcus Aurelius* (Cambridge University Press, 2000).
Nicholas J. Saunders, *Alexander's Tomb: The Two-Thousand Year Obsession to Find the Lost Conqueror* (Basic Books, 2006).

CHAPTER 35

James Clackson, *Language and Society in the Greek and Roman Worlds* (Cambridge University Press, 2015).
James Clackson and Geoffrey Horrocks, *The Blackwell History of the Latin Language* (Wiley Blackwell, 2007).
Geoffrey Horrocks, *Greek: A History of the Language and Its Speakers*, 2nd ed. (Wiley Blackwell, 2010).

CHAPTER 36

Morris L. Bierbrier, "Modern Descendants of Byzantine Families," *Genealogists' Magazine* 20 (1980–1982): 85–96.

Nathaniel L. Taylor, "Roman Genealogical Continuity and the 'Descents from Antiquity' Question: A Review Article," *American Genealogist* 76 (2001): 129–36.

Acknowledgments

*W*riting a book, even an odd little one like this, is a daunting process. But thanks to my friends and family, it was much less agonizing than it could have been. Janet Dant, Martha Dowling, Emily Ho, Blake Nicholson, Cait Stevenson, Kelly Williams, and Steven Yenzer read drafts of individual answers. Along with Anya Helsel, Emily and Kelly also provided sorely needed guidance through the labyrinth of social media. My siblings Courtney, Conor, Quinn, and Austin were constant sources of encouragement (and agreed, along with my brother-in-law Rich and sister-in-law Shannon, to appear in a promotional video on ancient drinking games). I also was lucky enough to have the support of my grandparents Adrian and Marianne Ryan and Joe and Shirley Dowling (special thanks to my grandmother Shirley for her proofreading help). Finally, I have to thank Jean and Garrett Ryan, my parents, for tolerating their unemployable son as he wrote something ridiculous in the backyard. This book is dedicated to them, with deepest gratitude.

Notes

A NOTE ABOUT THE NOTES

*W*henever possible, I've cited primary sources. Thanks to the magic of the internet, the works of every major classical author are only a few keystrokes away, often in good (and free) English translations. Do yourself the favor of exploring them.

The citations are couched in the arcane abbreviations beloved of classicists. But fear not! Wherever possible, they follow the conventions of the Oxford Classical Dictionary, which are helpfully listed online: https://oxfordre.com/classics/page/abbreviation-list/#1.

CHAPTER 1

1. Lethal brooch pins: Hdt. 5.87.
2. Elagabalus: Hdn. 5.3.6. Nero's dye sting: Suet., *Ner.* 32.3. Purple silk legislation: *Cod. Iust.* 4.40, 11.9.3; *Cod. Theod.* 10.21.3. Caligula's outfits: Suet., *Calig.* 52. Commodus: Hdn. 1.14.8; Cass. Dio 73.17.4. Persians and pants: e.g., Eur., *Cyc.* 182; Ar., *Vesp.* 1087. Romans on northern barbarians: e.g., Ov., *Tr.* 4.6.47.
3. On the emergence of breeches in the Roman army, see Graham Sumner, *Roman Military Dress* (History Press, 2009), 177–87. Pants and wig: Hdn. 4.7.3.
4. Pants ban: *Cod. Theod.* 14.10.2–3. Senators wearing pants: Const. Porph., *De admin. imp.* 91; cf. Joh. Lydus, *Mag.* 1.17.
5. Swimsuit: Mart. 3.87.3. Bikini: e.g., Mart. 7.67.4. Theodora: Procop., *Anec.* 9.20–21. Undertunic: Mart. 11.99. Large breasts unattractive: e.g., Sor.,

Gyn. 2.15. Flattening breasts: Ter., *Eun.* 313–17; Mart. 14.66; cf. Ovid, *Ars am.* 3.274. Teasing husband: Ar., *Lys.* 931–32. Breast-bands as pockets: Ovid, *Ars am.* 3.621 (letters); Ap. Rhod., *Argon.* 3.867–68 (poison). Headache cure: Plin., *HN* 28.76.

6. Speedo: Mart. 7.35.1. Toga loincloth: e.g., Asc., *Scaur.* 25. Flashing the saint: Sulp. Sev., *Dial.* 3.14.

CHAPTER 2

1. Hadrian trying to cover acne scars: SHA, *Hadr.* 26.1.
2. Nero's beard: Suet., *Nero* 12.
3. Mustaches illegal in Sparta: Plut., *Cleom.* 9. Alexander introducing fashion for shaving: Ath. 13.565A (Alexander was also said to have made his men shave: Plut., *Thes.* 5.4).
4. Laws against shaving beards: Ath. 13.565C–D. Beard-loving philosopher: Arr., *Epict. diss.* 1.2.29. Philosopher visiting city: Dio Chrys., *Or.* 36.17.
5. Scipio shaving: Plin., *HN* 7.211. Caesar: Suet., *Caes.* 45. Augustus: Suet., *Aug.* 79.
6. Customers puffing cheeks: Ar., *Thesm.* 218–21. Barbers drawing blood: e.g., Mart. 11.84. Cobwebs: Plin., *HN* 29.14.
7. Tyrant's nutshells: Cic., *Tusc.* 5.20.
8. Shaving legs before date: Ov., *Ars. am.* 3.194. Bikini wax: e.g., Ar., *Eccl.* 65–67; Plin., *HN* 29.26. Dionysus the plucker: Clem. Alex., *Protrep.* 2.37.
9. Otho: Suet., *Otho* 12. Philosophical disapproval of shaving: e.g., Dio Chrys. 33.63; Arr., *Epict. diss.* 3.1.26–9. Debate on hair removal: Philostr., *VS* 536. Armpits, not legs: Sen., *Ep.* 114.14. Armpit plucking in the baths: Sen., *Ep.* 56.2; Juv. 11.156–58.

CHAPTER 3

1. Reinhold Merkelbach and Josef Stauber, *Steinepigramme aus dem griechischen Osten* (Teubner, 2004), no. 18/01/28. The sarcophagus can be visited in the Antalya Archaeological Museum.
2. Dog chariot: SHA, *Heliogab.* 28.1. Indian dogs descended from tigers: Arist., *Hist. an.* 8.27. Maltese as cure for indigestion: Plin., *HN* 30.43.
3. Missy's painting: Mart. 1.109. Historian's greyhound: Arr., *Cyn.* 5.1–6. Peritas: Plut., *Alex.* 61.3. Faithful dog: Plin., *HN* 8.144–45.

4. Philosopher and dog: Lucian, *Merc. Cond.* 32–34. Neutering dogs: Varro, *Rust.* 3.9.3. Mange cure: Arr., *Cyn.* 9.2. Lifespan of dogs: Arist., *Hist. an.* 6.20.

5. Lynched soldier: Diod. Sic. 1.83.

6. Philosopher's goose: Ael., *NA* 7.41. Partridge: Porph., *Abst.* 3.4. Historian's parrot: Phot., *Bibl.* 80. Hailing Caesar: e.g., Plin., *HN* 10.42. Drunken parrots: Arist., *Hist. an.* 8.14; Plin., *HN* 10.117. Never teach a parrot to swear: Apul., *Flor.* 12.

7. Tiberius's snake: Suet., *Tib.* 72. Alexander's mom: Plut., *Alex.* 2.6. Snakes on shoulders: Mart. 7.87.7. Snakes on the dinner table: Sen., *Ira* 2.31. Python in Rome: Plin., *HN* 8.37. Pet monkeys wreaking havoc: e.g., Cass. Dio 50.8.

8. Lion-killing senator: Cass. Dio 67.14. Scimitar: Cass. Dio 79.7. Party lions: SHA, *Heliogab.* 21, 25. Lions expensive to feed: Juv. 7.75–77. Goldflake and Innocence: Amm. Marc. 29.3.9. Bears at banquets: Lactant., *De mort. pers.* 21.5–6. A chicken named Roma: Procop., *Vand.* 3.2.25–26. Puppies and piglets: SHA, *Alex. Sev.* 41.5. Animals in the Golden House: Suet., *Nero* 31.1. Later emperor's menagerie: SHA, *Gord.* 33.1.

CHAPTER 4

1. Properties of silphium: Diosc., *Mat. Med.* 3.82–84; Plin., *HN* 19.38–46, 22.100–106; Sor., *Gyn.* 1.63.

2. Sperm spoiling milk: e.g., Sor., *Gyn.* 2.12.19.

3. Pisistratus: Hdt. 1.61. Holding breath: Sor., *Gyn.* 1.20.

4. Rinds and sponges: e.g., Sor, *Gyn.* 1.62. Berries and resin: Pliny, *HN* 24.11, 18.

5. Copper ore: Hippoc., *Mul.* 1.76. Mule testicles: Aët 16.17. Spider head: Plin., *HN* 29.85. Frog spell: *PGM* 36.320.

6. Cold water and sneezing: Sor, *Gyn.* 1.20. Beaver testicles: Diosc., *Mat. Med.* 2.24. Biting off said testicles: Ael., *NA* 6.34.

7. Bumpy rides: Plin., *HN* 7.42. Jumping: Hippoc., *Nat. puer.* 13. Abortion illegal: *Dig.* 48.8.8.

8. Infants in Sparta: Plut., *Lyc.* 16.1.

CHAPTER 5

1. This episode is in all the standard accounts of Alexander's career: e.g., Arr., *Anab.* 6.10–11; Plut., *Alex.* 63.

2. Elephant dissection: Gal., *AA* 7.10; *UP* 4.9. Dissecting barbarians: Gal., *Comp. Med. Loc.* 13.604K.

3. Cold water cure: Plin., *HN* 29.10. Doctors poisoning each other: Gal., *Praen.* 14.623K. Festival at Ephesus: *IvE* 1162. Gang of doctors: Plin., *HN* 29.11.

4. Pus extractor: Heron, *Pneum.* 2.18. Mandrake as sedative: Plin., *HN* 25.150. Unmoved by screams: Celsus, *Med.* 7. Pref. 4. Resin on wounds: Plin., *HN* 24.35. Long-eared hare: Gal., *Fasc.* 18A.777K.

5. Medics in Homer: e.g., *Il.* 4.219f. Spoon of Diocles: Celsus, *Med.* 7.5.3. Dog blood: Plin., *HN* 29.58. Sling bullets: Celsus, *Med.* 7.5.4; Paul. Aeg. 6.88. Iron claw: Plin., *HN* 7.104–5. Soldier shot through neck: Procop., *Goth.* 6.2.

6. Cicero's varicose surgery: Cic., *Tusc.* 2.53. Breast reduction: Paul. Aeg. 6.46. Liposuction: Plin., *HN* 11.213.

7. Trepanation procedure: Celsus, *Med.* 8.3. Ears plugged with wool: Paul. Aeg. 6.90.5. Plaster over brain: Gal., *Meth. Med.* 6.6.

8. Marcus's son: SHA, *Marc.* 21.3. Bladder stone emperor: Joh. Eph., *HE* 3.6. Disemboweled gladiator: Gal., *UP* 4.9. Removing breastbone: Gal., *AA* 7.13. Undertaker doctor: Mart. 1.30.

CHAPTER 6

1. Pollio's moray pit: Plin., *HN* 9.77; Sen., *Ira* 3.40.2. Pollio eating said morays: Tert., *De pall.* 5.6. Pet morays: e.g., Ael., *NA* 8.4.

2. Bread for slaves: *CIL* IV.5380.

3. Pheasant as delicacy: e.g., Clem. Alex., Paed. 2.1.3. Copaic eels sacrificed to the gods: Ath. 297D. For a useful discussion of fish prices in Classical Athens, see James Davidson, *Courtesans and Fishcakes* (HarperCollins, 1997), 186–90.

4. Nero's rotunda: Suet., *Nero* 31. Smothering guests: SHA, *Heliogab.* 21. Name in bushes, floating dishes: Plin., *Ep.* 5.6.35, 37.

5. Tombstone of a head chef: *CIL* VI.8750. Banquet in novel: Petron., *Sat.* 40, 49, 59, 60. Belching polite: e.g., Mart. 10.48.10. Spitting acceptable: Clem. Alex., Paed. 2.7. Doctor advocating flatulence: Mart. 7.18.9–10. Gluttons purging: e.g., Suet., *Claud.* 33, *Vit.* 13.

6. Poisoned sow's womb: SHA, *Verus* 11.2. Elephant trunk: Plin., *HN* 8.31. Elephant heart: Gal., *AA* 7.10. Mullet worth more than cook: Pliny, *HN* 9.67. Kissing mullets: Ael., *NA* 10.7.

7. Million sesterce dinners: Sen., *Ep.* 95.41. Lavish dinner for twelve: SHA, *Verus* 5.1–5. Gift of a Eunuch: SHA, *Heliogab.* 21.7. Vitellius's platter: Suet., *Vit.* 13.

CHAPTER 7

1. Drunken souls: Pl., *Resp.* 363D. Spartans bathed in wine: Plut., *Lyc.* 16.2. Opiated wine: Gal., *Ant.* 1.1. Wine shipment to Troy: Hom., *Il.* 7.467–71. Wine ration: see Johnathan Roth, *The Logistics of the Roman Army at War* (Brill, 1999), 40. St. Augustine's mother: August., *Conf.* 9.8. Alexander: Arr., *Anab.* 4.8; Plut., *Alex.* 50.

2. Pompeii tavern prices: *CIL* IV.1679.

3. Cheese in Homeric wine: *Il.* 11.638. Italian wines kept for centuries: Plin., *HN* 14.55. Artificial aging: Columella, *Rust.* 1.6.20.

4. Wine consumption: André Tchernia, *Le Vin de l'Italie romaine: essai d'histoire économique d'après les amphores* (École française de Rome, 1986), 21–27. A pint of wine: Hor., *Sat.* 1.1.74. Socrates: Pl., *Symp.* 214A. Man who impressed Tiberius: Plin., *HN* 14.144.

5. Flammable wine: Plin., *HN* 14.62; cf. Ath. 10.429F. Criticizing neat wine drinkers: e.g., Mart. 1.11, 6.89. Gauls invading Italy for wine: Livy 5.33. The crime of unmixed wine: Ael., *VH* 2.37. Spartan king: Hdt. 6.75, 84. Drowned semen: Arist., [*Pr.*] 3.4. Premature aging: Plut., *Quaest. conv.* 652F. Tomb inscription: *SEG* 27, 571.

6. For a collection of sources on mixing water and wine, see Ath. 10.426 B–F, 430A–31F. On Scythian drinking habits: Hdt. 4.26, 64–65, 70; Pl., *Leg.* 637E.

7. Ailments cured by wine: Plin., *HN* 23.45–49. Drinking to purge: Ath. 11.483F–84B. Drinking to drunkenness: Pseudo-Hippocrates, *De Victus Ratione in Morbis Acutis* 3.

8. Plato on getting drunk: *Leg.* 775B. Hellenistic king: Ath. 199A–B.

9. Hierarchical wine service: e.g., Plin., *Ep.* 2.6. Women resistant to wine: Plut., *Mor.* 650A–E. A woman who knew how to have fun: *CIL* VI.19055. Spanish dancing girls: Juv. 11.162–64; Mart. 5.78.26–28. Readings at banquets: e.g., Mart. 3.44, 5.78. Entertainers: Suet., *Aug.* 74; Plin., *Ep.* 1.15, 9.17; Petron., *Sat.* 53. Gladiators: e.g., SHA, *Verus* 4.9.

10. Ideal of moderation: Xenophanes, Fr. 2 (West). Three kraters: quoted by Ath. 2.36B–C. Weaponized chamber pots: Aesch., Fr. 180; Soph., Fr. 565. Sinking ship: Ath. 2.37B–E.

11. Ten cups: Mart. 1.26. Antony vomits into his toga: Cic., *Phil.* 2.63. Antony's pamphlet: Plin., *HN* 14.148. Nero in the streets: Tac., *Ann.* 13.25.

12. Alexander: Ath. 10.434A; Plut., *Alex.* 75.5 (who claims that the story is false). Fatal drinking contest: Ath. 10.437B. Verus's crystal cup: SHA, *Verus* 10.9. Jester drinking: SHA, *Aur.* 50.4. Drinking by dice: Plin., *HN* 14.140. Drinking by letter: Mart. 1.71, 8.51, 11.36, 14.170.

13. For literary references to the game of kottabos, see Ath. 15.665–68. Courtesan with cup: St. Petersburg, State Hermitage Museum inv. 644.

14. Donkey riddle: Plut., *Mor.* 150F. For an extensive collection of ancient Greek riddles (many originally devised for Symposia), see the fourteenth book of the *Greek Anthology*. The coin-spinning game (*chalkismos*) is briefly described by Pollux, *Onom.* 9.118. Emperor who wrote book on dice: Suet., *Claud.* 33.2.

15. *Symposiarch*'s penalties: Lucian, *Sat.* 4. Hanging game: Ath. 4.155E.

16. Ivy and Myrtle: Ath. 15.674–75; cf. Plut., *Mor.* 647C–D. Honey: Ath. 11.784B. Cabbage: Ath. 1.34C–E. Almonds: Plut., *Mor.* 624C. Amethysts: Plin., *HN* 37.124. Rolling in mud: Plin., *HN* 14.140. Hair of the dog: Plut., *Mor.* 127E.

CHAPTER 8

1. Augustus's sundial inaccurate: Plin., *HN* 36.71. Elaborate water clocks: e.g., Vitr., *De arch.* 9.8.5–15. Seneca: Sen., *Apocol.* 2.

2. Nero's month: Suet., *Nero* 55. Domitian: Suet., *Dom.* 13.3. Commodus: Cass. Dio 72.15.3.

3. Roman calendrical incompetence: e.g., Censorinus, *DN* 20.6. Caesar's calendar: e.g., Suet., *Iul.* 40; Cass. Dio 43.26.1; cf. Plut., *Caes.* 59.6.

4. Although one historian suggested, in the interests of neatness, that the city of Rome had also been founded in 776 BCE (*FGrH* 97), the Roman scholar Varro definitively assigned that event to 753 BCE. By 248 CE, when the Roman emperor Philip celebrated Rome's thousandth birthday with great fanfare (SHA, *Gord.* 33.1–3), Varro's date was firmly established as the beginning of Roman history.

5. Names of planets: Diod. Sic. 2.30.3. Gods as planets: e.g., Firm. Mat. 1.14. Spread of the seven-day week: Joseph., *Ap.* 2.282; Cass. Dio 37.18–19.

6. Criticizing Sabbath: e.g., Juv. 14.104–5. Lecturing on Saturdays: Suet., *Tib.* 32.2.

7. Christians respecting Sunday: e.g., Tert., *De orat.* 23. Constantine: *Cod. Iust.* 3.12.2. Farm workers: *Cod. Theod.* 2.8. Killjoy emperor: *Cod. Iust.* 3.12.10.

CHAPTER 9

1. For a handy list of elderly ancient Greeks, see [Lucian], *Macr.*

2. Census returns: Roger Bagnall and Bruce Frier, *The Demography of Roman Egypt*, 2nd ed. (Cambridge University Press, 2006). Ulpian's life table: *Dig.* 35.2.68 pr. Grim implications: Bruce Frier, "Roman Life Expectancy: Ulpian's Evidence" *HSCP* 86 (1982): 213–51.

3. For ancient speculation on the origins of new diseases, see Plut., *Mor.* 731A–34C. The advent of leprosy: Lucr. 6.1112; Plin., *HN* 26.1. Bubonic plague: Oribasius, *Coll. Med.* 44.14. The suggestion that the Plague of Cyprian may have been a form of Ebola was made by Kyle Harper, "Pandemics and Passages to Late Antiquity: Rethinking the Plague of c. 249–70 Described by Cyprian," *JRA* 28 (2015): 223–60.

4. Longevity in the hills: Plin., *Ep.* 5.6.6.

5. The severity of this epidemic is debated by scholars (as is the question of whether smallpox became endemic afterward). The academic consensus, however, is that the Antonine Plague really was disastrous. On the scale of its impact, see R. P. Duncan-Jones, "The Impact of the Antonine Plague," *JRA* 9 (1996): 108–36.

6. No rich foods: [Lucian], *Macr.* 23. Centenarian and Augustus: Plin., *HN* 22.114. Old men not pleasant to watch: Pl., *Resp.* 452B. Walking and ball playing: Plut., *An seni* 16. Vigorous massage: Gal., *San. Tu.* 6.329. Nude stroll: Plin., *Ep.* 3.1.8.

7. For a convenient list of stereotypes about the elderly, see Arist., *Rh.* 2.13. Sardinians: *FGH* 566, F. 64.

8. Rufilla's epitaph: Warren J. Moulton, "Twelve Mortuary Inscriptions from Sidon," *AJA* 8 (1904): 286.

CHAPTER 10

1. Maximinus anecdotes: SHA, *Max.* 6.5, 8–9; 28.8–9.

2. Giants in Rome: Plin., *HN* 7.74–75; Columella, *Rust.* 3.8.2. Man two feet tall: Suet., *Aug.* 43.3. Courtier: Plin., *HN* 7.75. Augustus: Suet., *Aug.* 73, 79.2. Legionary height requirements: Veg., *Mil.* 1.5; cf. Suet. *Nero* 19.2. Late antique height requirement: *Cod. Theod.* 7.13.3. One testicle: *Dig.* 49.16.4.

3. On the skeletons, see Sara Bisel and Jane Bisel, "Health and Nutrition at Herculaneum. An Examination of Human Skeletal Remains," in *The Natural History of Pompeii*, ed. Wilhelmina Jashemski and Frederick Meyer (Cambridge University Press, 2002), 451–75.

4. On the average height of men in Roman central Italy, see Monica Giannecchini and Jacopo Moggi-Cecchi, "Stature in Archaeological Samples from Central Italy: Methodological Issues and Diachronic Changes," *American Journal of Physical Anthropology* 135 (2008), 284–92. For a survey of the Greek evidence, see Sitta van Reden, "Classical Greece: Consumption," in *The Cambridge Economic History of the Greco-Roman World*, ed. Walter Scheidel, Ian Morris, and Richard Saller (Cambridge University Press, 2007), 388–89.

5. Gauls mocking Caesar's men: Caes., *BG* 2.30.3. Tall Gauls: e.g., Livy 5.44.4. Gallic women: Amm. Marc. 15.12.1.

CHAPTER 11

1. The estimate of three obols a day comes from Xen., *Vect.* 3.9. It seems to be corroborated by the fact that poor Athenian citizens who were unable to work received two obols a day from the city as a sort of disability payment ([Arist.], *Ath. Pol.* 49.4). One scholar has estimated that a Classical Athenian family of four needed four obols a day to eat well but could make do with less (Takeshi Amemiya, *Economy and Economics of Ancient Greece* [Routledge, 2006]: 75–78).

2. In early imperial Italy, a family of four would probably spend about two hundred denarii (eight hundred sesterces) each year on food (Kenneth Harl, *Coinage in the Roman Economy, 300 BC to AD 700* [Johns Hopkins University Press, 1996], 279). Additional expenses—rent, clothing, fuel, and so forth— were likely to add at least another one hundred denarii/four hundred sesterces (see Walter Scheidel, "Real Wages in Early Economies: Evidence for Living Standards from 1800 BCE to 1300 CE," *Journal of the Economic and Social History of the Orient* 53 [2010]: 433–35). The bare subsistence wage for an individual was much lower, especially in parts of the provinces; one estimate is 115 sesterces (Keith Hopkins, "Taxes and Trade in the Roman Empire [200 BC–AD 400]," *JRS* 70 [1980]: 118–19).

3. Pompeian job paying four sesterces and bread: *CIL* IV.6877. Laborers outside Athens: *IG* II² 1673.

4. The evidence for pay rates is contradictory and disputed. Here, I follow a popular interpretation (based i.a. on Thuc. 3.17, 6.8.31).

5. On the pay of Roman officers, I follow M. Alexander Speidel, "Roman Army Pay Scales," *JRS* 82 (1992): 100–103.

6. Eighteen thousand drachmas: Lys. 29.6. Earning cap for Roman lawyers: Tac., *Ann.* 11.7. Cicero's loan: Gell., *NA* 12.12. Paid in kind: Mart. 12.72.

7. Donor to Athens: *IG* II/III² 374. Twelve thousand every year: Hdt. 3.131. Doctor to the emperors: Plin., *HN* 29.7–8. Cold bath doctor: Plin., *HN* 29.22.

8. Expensive courses in public speaking: e.g., Dem. 35.15.42; Isoc. 13.3; Plut., *Mor.* 839F. Roman professor: Suet., *Gram.* 17. Two thousand sesterces: Juv. 7.217. Salaried posts: Juv. 7.186.

9. Courtesan: Gell., *NA* 1.8. Roscius: Cic., *QRosc.* 23. Augustus: Tac., *Dial.* 12.6. Lyre players: Suet., *Vesp.* 19. Retired gladiators: Suet., Tib. 7.1. Champion charioteer: *ILS* 5287.

10. Crassus: Plut., *Crass.* 2. Seneca: Cass. Dio 62.2.

11. Largest Athenian fortune: Lys. 19.48. Crassus: Plin., *HN* 33.134–35. Worth four hundred million: Cass. Dio 60.34; Sen., *Ben.* 2.27. Pompey: App., *Mith.* 116; Plin., *HN* 37.16.

12. Caligula: Suet., *Calig.* 42. Nero's heap: Cass. Dio 61.6. Nero's gifts: Tac., *Hist.* 1.20. Budget of Roman army: Richard Duncan-Jones, *Money and Government in the Roman Empire* (Cambridge University Press, 1994), 45–46 (his numbers are disputed, but so are those of every other grand-scale guesstimate of the imperial budget).

13. Expensive tables: Plin., *HN* 13.92. Statuette: Plin., *HN* 35.156. Commissioning a statue for thirty thousand sesterces HS: *CIL* VI.3.23. Cicero's house: Cic., *Fam.* 5.6.2. Neighboring house: Plin., *HN* 36.103. Athenian estate: Lys. 19.29. Caligula's wife: Plin., *HN* 9.117. Buying the throne: Cass. Dio 74.11.

CHAPTER 12

1. Collapsing *insulae*: Juv. 3.193–98; Cic., *Att.* 14.9. Rental procedures: e.g., *ILS* 6035. Homeless: Mart. 12.32.

2. Spiked sandals: Arist., *Fr.* 84 (I assume that this trick was also used in Rome). Festival crime sprees: Suet., *Aug.* 43.1.

3. Aristocratic slapper: Gell., *NA* 20.1.13. Searching senators: Cass. Dio 58.18. Murderous senators: Tac., *Ann.* 4.22, 13.44; cf. Tac., *Ann.* 14.42, Plin., *Ep.* 3.14. Guilds: Suet., *Aug.* 32.1; cf. Varro, *Rust.* 1.69.4.

4. Ambitious prefects: Hdn. 5.2.2. Bribes: Tert., *De fuga in persecutione* 13.

5. Doorkeeper gods: August., *De civ. D.* 4.8.

6. Papal election: Amm. Marc. 27.3.11–13. Alexandria riot: SHA, *Trig. Tyr.* 22.3. Ephesus: Philostr., *VA* 1.16. Beating civilians: Hdn. 2.4.1. Urban cohorts fighting praetorians: Cass. Dio 73.12; Hdn. 1.12. Battling mob: Hdn. 7.11–12; SHA, *Max.* 20.

7. Burning of Colosseum: Cass. Dio 79.25. Water and vinegar: *Dig.* 1.15.3, 33.9.3.

8. Catapults: Suet., *Nero* 38. Beating culprits: *Dig.* 1.15.3. Fire insurance: Mart. 3.52.

9. Civilian volunteers: Suet., *Claud.* 18.1. Great Fire: Tac., *Ann.* 15.38–40. Nero's rebuilding: Tac., *Ann.* 15.43. Altars: *ILS* 4914.

10. Massive floods: e.g., Cass. Dio 55.22.3. Caesar's scheme: Suet., *Caes.* 58.8. River commission: Tac., *Ann.* 1.79.

11. Romans on lead poisoning: Vitruv. 8.6.10–11.

12. Latrine dinner invitation: Mart. 11.77.

13. Octopus story: Ael., *NA* 13.6.

CHAPTER 13

1. Slave workshops: e.g., shields (Lys. 12.8) and shoes (Aeschin., *In Tim.* 97). Humorous impressions: *ILS* 5225. Brushing teeth: Plin., *Ep.* 8.18.9. Expensive cupbearer: Mart. 3.62. Twins: Plin., *HN* 7.56. Scholar: Plin., *HN* 7.128. Nine clever slaves: Sen., *Ep.* 27.5–7. Chippendales: Plin., *Ep.* 7.24.

2. Cicero and Tiro: e.g., Cic., *Fam.* 16.16.1. Sending slave to Egypt: Plin., *Ep.* 5.19. Constantine outlawing the dissolution of slave families: *CJ* 3.38.11.

3. Augustus breaking slave's legs: Suet., *Aug.* 67. Crucifying slave: Plut., *Mor.* 207B; cf. Gal., *Aff. Dig.* 4. Laws against castration: Suet., *Dom.* 9. Prostitutes: *Dig.* 48.18.3. Gladiators: *Dig.* 48.8.11. Burned alive: *Dig.* 48.19.28. Being sold to another master: e.g., *Dig.* 1.6.2.

4. Natural slavery: Arist., *Pol.* 1252a31–34. Plato objecting to slavery of Greeks: Pl., *Resp.* 469c. Plato sold into slavery (possibly an unreliable tradition): Diog. Laert. 3.19–20. Stoics on slavery: e.g., Sen., *Ep.* 47. Christians criticizing sexual abuse: e.g., Lactant., *Div. Inst.* 6.23. Eight thousand slaves: Pall., *Hist. Laus.* 61.5.

5. Runaway insurance: Ar., [*Oec.*] 1352b33–53a4. Cicero's librarian: Cic., *Fam.* 5.9, 5.10a, 13.77.3.

6. Vespasian's lover: Suet., *Vesp.* 3. Antoninus Pius: SHA, *Ant. Pius* 8.9. Marcus Aurelius: SHA, *Marc.* 29.10. Orator: Ath. 13.590D.

7. Freedman with 4,116 slaves: Plin., *HN* 33.135.

8. On the fascinating case of Musa, see Emma Strugnell, "Thea Musa, Roman Queen of Parthia," *Iranica Antiqua* 43 (2008): 275–98.

CHAPTER 14

1. Quintus and Pomponia: e.g., Cic., *Att.* 5.1, 14.13.

2. Purpose of marriage: e.g., *Dig.* 1.1.1.3. Minimum age: *Dig.* 23.2.4.

3. Anus radish: Ar., *Nub.* 1083–84. Spiny fish: e.g., Juv. 10.317. Gallant Athenian: Isae. 2.7–12. Spartan king: Hdt. 5.39. Pericles: Plut., *Per.* 24.5. Spartan bigamy: Plut., *Lyc.* 15.6–10. Athenian bigamy: Gell., *NA* 15.20.6. Epitaph: *CIL* VI.37965. First Roman divorce: Gell, *NA* 4.3.2.

CHAPTER 15

1. On Hadrian and Antinous, see e.g., SHA, *Hadr.* 14.5–7 and Cass. Dio 69.11.

2. Prometheus myth: Phdr. 4.16. It should be noted that the approach to ancient homosexuality sketched in this paragraph, though the prevalent academic view, is not universally accepted.

3. Pederasty as population control: Arist., *Pol.* 1272a22–26. Father of Oedipus: Ath. 13.602F. Spartan pederasty: e.g., Plut., *Lyc.* 17.1. Sacred Band: Plut., *Pel.* 18–19 (The existence of the Sacred Band has occasionally been called into question, but I think it more likely than not that a unit at least broadly like what Plutarch describes existed).

4. Lamb blood: Plin., *HN* 30.41. Tiberius: Suet., *Tib.* 44.1. Nero: Suet., *Nero* 28.1.

5. Plato: *Leg.* 835b–842a. Debate: [Luc.], *Am.* 19–51. Roman criticism: e.g., Sen., *Ep.* 122.7–8. Marcus: M. Aur., *Med.* 1.17.

6. Graffito: *IG* I2.924. Handsome youth: Plut., *Demetr.* 24.2–3. Ban on boy-lovers: *SEG* 27.261 (although this inscription is exceptional, men were often excluded from boys' gymnasia: e.g., Aeschin., *In Tim.* 9–12).

CHAPTER 16

1. On the mutilation of the reliefs, see R. R. R. Smith, "Defacing the Gods at Aphrodisias," in *Historical and Religious Memory in the Ancient World*, ed. R. R. R. Smith and Beate Dignas (Oxford University Press, 2012), 283–326.

2. Greek reflections on athletic nudity: Thuc. 1.6; Pl., *Resp.* 452C. Runner who lost his loincloth: Paus. 1.44.1–2. Legend about runner tripping: *Scholia B* and *T* to *Iliad* 23.683. Why Olympic trainers are naked: Paus. 5.6.7–8.

3. For a useful discussion of the many roles that nudity could play in Classical Athenian art, see Jeffrey M. Hurwit, "The Problem with Dexileos: Heroic and Other Nudities in Greek Art," *AJA* 111 (2007): 35–60. On Nikostratos of Argos, see Diod. Sic. 16.44.3.

4. On Phryne, see Ath. 13.590 D–F.

5. Seen naked by son: Plut., *Cat. Mai.* 20.5; Cic., *Off.* 1.129. No nude sculpture in early Rome: Plin., *HN* 34.18.

6. *Ithyphalloi*: Dem., *Or.* 54.14. On the retraction of the genitals (largely due to the action of the cremaster muscle), see Waldo Sweet, "Protection of the Genitals in Greek Athletics," *The Ancient World* 11 (1985): 43–46.

7. On the connection between small genitals and good breeding, see, e.g., Ar., *Nub.* 1010–14, where it is (jokingly) asserted that a proper education ensures a small penis. Disgust with circumcision: e.g., Hdt. 2.37; Mart. 7.82. Gangrene: Celsus, *Med.* 6.18.2. Hadrian's ban: SHA, *Hadr.* 14.2. Epispasm: Celsus, *Med.* 7.25.1–2.

8. One hundred and eighty feet long: Ath. 5.201E. For a full-length (so to speak) portrait of Priapus, consult the graphic poems of the Roman *Carmina Priapea*.

CHAPTER 17

1. Greek gods as Egyptian gods: e.g., Apollod., *Bibl.* 1.6.3. Jehovah as Dionysus: Plut., *Mor.* 671C–72C.

2. On the chronology of myth, see, e.g., *Marm. Par.* A1, 1–27.

3. Illiterate Greeks and Romans knew the myths through oral traditions and art (e.g., Dio Chrys., *Or.* 12.44). Figures of myths in dreams: Artem. 4.49. Emperor Agamemnon: Syn., *Ep.* 148. Epitaph: *Bulletin archéologique du Comité des travaux historiques et scientifiques* 1928–1929, p. 94.

4. Few took the myths seriously: e.g., Paus. 8.8.2–3; Plut., *Mor.* 1104B–1105B. Gods as human kings: Euseb., *Praep. evang.* 2.2 (the origin of the term "euhemerism"). Myths as instrument of control: *DK* 88 B25. Plato on the myths: *Resp.* 2.377d–79a. Aristotle: *Metaph.* 12.1074b.

5. One Greek historian claimed that the Romans consciously rejected the Greek myths (Dion. Hal., *Ant. Rom.* 1.18–20). On Roman (elite) skepticism, see, for example, Plin., *HN* 2.17. Marcus Aurelius: e.g., *Med.* 4.23. Epicurean philosopher: Lucian, *Iupp. Trag.*

6. For this conception of demons, see Plut., *De def. or.* 15.

7. Pagan catechism: Sallustius, *De diis et mundo* 4.

8. Pagan gods as demons: e.g., Lactant., *Div. Inst.* 2.15; Sulp. Sev., *V. Mart.* 22. Gods as ancient men: e.g., August., *De Civ. D.* 7.27. Moral lessons: e.g., Basil, *Hom.* 22.

9. Few believed: e.g., August., *Ep.* 16.1. Homeric Olympus as mountain in northern Greece: e.g., *Il.* 14.225–30. Homeric Olympus as the sky: e.g., *Il.* 8.19–26. Later descriptions of Olympus: e.g., Ap. Rhod., *Argon.* 3.158–63; Sen., *Herc. Oet.* 1907.

10. Stoics on the gods: e.g., M. Aur., *Med.* 7.9. Platonists: e.g., Pl., *Leg.* 10.899b. Epicureans: e.g., Lucr. 5.146–47. The calm on Olympus: Solin. 8.6.

CHAPTER 18

1. The source for this anecdote is Plin., *Ep.* 7.27.5–11, embellished here with a great deal of picturesque detail.

2. Loving an undead maiden: Phlegon, *Mir.* 1. Alexander's ghost: Cass. Dio 79.18.1–3. Whispering to victims: Apul., *Met.* 9.30. Achilles: Philostr., *Her.* 56.

3. Bathhouse: Plut., *Cim.* 1.6. Marathon: Paus. 1.32.4. Tomb robber: Joh. Moschus 77. Snakes: Ael., *NA* 1.51.

4. Ouija board: Amm. Marc. 29.1.30–31. Homer's birthplace: Plin., *HN* 30.18.

5. Democritus: Diog. Laert. 9.38; Lucian, *Philops.* 32. Augustine: August., *De cura pro mortuis gerenda* 12–15. Little doubt: e.g., Plut., *Dion* 2.3–6.

6. Gold-digging ants: Hdt. 3.102–5.

7. Basilisk: Plin., *HN* 8.78. Basilisk skin: Solin. 17.53. Catoblepas: Plin., *HN* 8.77. Catoblepas attack: Ath. 5.221B–E. Fanged Tyrant (a cheerfully tendentious translation of the Greek *odontotyrannos*): Pall., *Epistola de Indicis gentibus et de Bragmannibus*, 10.

8. Werewolf: Petron., *Sat.* 62. Wolf festival: Paus. 8.2.6.

9. Vampire story: Philostr., *VA* 4.25. Regulus and the dragon: e.g., Val. Max. 1.8.

10. Sulla's satyr: Plut., *Sull.* 27.1–2. Canaries: Paus. 1.23.5–6. St. Antony: Jer., *Vita Pauli* 8.

11. Spanish Triton: Plin., *HN* 9.10. Pickled Triton: Ael., *NA* 13.21; Paus. 9.20.5. Centaur: Phlegon, *Mir.* 34–35; Plin., *HN* 7.35.

12. Finding the remains of heroes: e.g., Paus. 8.29.4. Bones of Orestes: Hdt. 1.67–68. Orion: Plin., *HN* 7.73. Tooth: Phlegon, *Mir.* 43. Boar: Paus. 8.46.1, 8.47.2. Sea monster: Plin., *HN* 9.11.

13. Ant hides: Strabo 15.1.44. Ant horns: Plin., *HN* 11.111. Winged pig: Ael., *NA* 12.38; cf. Plin., *HN* 8.81. Impossibility of the centaur: Gal., *UP* 3. Wonders cloaked in lies: Paus. 8.2.7.

14. Ancient UFOs: Richard Wittmann, "Flying Saucers or Flying Shields," *CJ* 63 (1968): 223–26.

15. Extra planets: e.g., Plut., *De def. or.* 22–30; Plin., *HN* 2.3. Souls on the moon: e.g., Plut, *De fac.* 28–30.

CHAPTER 19

1. This is a suitably lurid retelling of Luc. 6.507–830.

2. Snake attack: Luc. 9.607–949 (some scholars see rich symbolism in this episode, but I will never be convinced that it is good poetry). Magicians as frauds: Pl., *Leg.* 933a–e; M. Aur., *Med.* 1.6. Effectiveness of magic accepted: e.g., Plin., *HN* 28.9.

3. Iamblichus: Eunap., *VS* 5.2.7. Snake charming: Celsus, *Med.* 5.27.3. Shadow puppets: Hippol., *Haer.* 4.35.1–2. Demons and beards: Tert., *Apol.* 22. Making statues smile: Eunap., *VS* 7.2.7–10. Breathing fire: Diod. Sic. 34/35.2.5–7.

4. Roman prince: Tac., *Ann.* 2.69. Lizard doll: Lib., *Or.* 1.249.

5. Healing broken bone: Cato, *Agr.* 160. Boar: Theoph. Cont. 379. Summoning Cronus: *PGM* IV.3086–3124. Demons and sacrificial smoke: e.g., Orig., *Mart.* 45.

6. Language of the dead: this may be merely a literary flourish (e.g., Luc. 6.686–91), but I suspect that late antique magicians actually employed such theatrics. Licking the leaf: *PGM* IV.785–89.

7. Wolf beard and snake teeth: Hor., *Sat.* 1.8.42–43. Nail from sunken ship: *PGM* VII.462–66. Attaching scroll to dead criminal: *PGM* IV.2145–240.

8. Love charm: *PGM* IV.1390–1495. Summoning demon: *PGM* XII.14–95. Chariot race: for some interesting examples, see John G. Gager, ed., *Curse Tablets and Binding Spells from the Ancient World* (Oxford University Press, 1999), 42–77.

9. Commentary: Paulus, *Sent.* 5.23. Imperial edicts: *Cod. Theod.* 9.16.6–7. Witch hunts: Amm. Marc. 28.1.1–45; 29.1.1–3.5.

10. Christian view of magic: e.g., August., *De doctrina christiana* 2.36–38.

CHAPTER 20

1. This vignette is founded on Plut., *Quaest. Graec.* 38.

2. Probably the most famous description of a Greek sacrifice is Hom., *Od.* 3.430–63. On Roman sacrifice, see, e.g., Dion. Hal., *Ant. Rom.* 7.72.

3. October horse: e.g., Plut., *Quaest. Rom.* 97. Priapus: Ov., *Fast.* 6.319–48. Patrae: Paus. 7.18.12–13.

4. Carthage: Diod. Sic. 20.14.6. Wicker men: Caesar: *BGall.* 6.16. Germans: Strabo 7.2.3. Taurians: Hdt. 4.103.

5. Achilles: Hom., *Il.* 23.175–77. Fish and onion: Plut., *Numa* 15.5–10. Planks: Paus. 9.3.3–8. Tiber puppets: Ov., *Fast.* 5.621–32.

6. Themistocles: Plut., *Them.* 13.2–3. Skepticism: e.g., Dennis Hughes, *Human Sacrifice in Ancient Greece* (Routledge, 1991), 111–14. Mt. Lykaion: Pl., *Resp.* 8.565d; Porph., *Abst.* 2.27.2.

7. Catiline: Cass. Dio 37.30.3. Augustus: Suet., *Aug.* 15. Sacrifice of Greeks and Gauls: Plut., *Quaest. Rom.* 83. Human sacrifice banned: Plin., *HN* 30.12.

8. For a concise discussion of the *pharmakoi* and their religious significance, see Walter Burkert, *Greek Religion* (Blackwell, 1985), 82–84. Flying *pharmakos*: Strabo 10.2.9.

9. Roman scapegoating: Lydus, *Mens.* 4.49. Pompey sparing captives: App., *Mith.* 117. Zenobia: SHA, *Tyr. Trig.* 30.27. Generals surrendering life: e.g., Livy 10.28–29. Blood poured over Jupiter: e.g., Justin, Apol. 2.12.5; Lactant., *Div. Inst.* 1.21.3 (Since the evidence for this festival comes from early Christian authors who obviously had an ax to grind, many scholars are dubious).

10. King of the Grove: esp. Strabo 5.3.12. Speculation: Paus. 2.27.4. Caligula: Suet., *Cal.* 35.3.

CHAPTER 21

1. Croesus and the Oracle: Hdt. 1.53.
2. Sheepskin: Paus. 1.34.5. Cave oracle: Paus. 9.39.9–13.
3. Fortune: e.g., Cic., *Div.* 2.41. Egypt: Dio Chrys., *Or.* 32.13. Fish oracle: Ael., *NA* 8.5; Plin., *HN* 32.17. Virginity snake: Ael., *NA* 11.16. Masked snake: Lucian, *Alex.* 15–16. Skull: Hippol, *Haer.* 4.41. Fire oracle: Cass. Dio 41.45.
4. Alexander at Delphi: Plut., *Alex.* 14.6–7. Frenzy: Plut., *De def. or.* 51.
5. Scythians: Hdt. 4.74; cf. 1.202. References to cannabis: e.g., Oribasius, *Coll. Med.* 4.20, 31. Oracle origin story: Diod. Sic. 16.26.2–4; Plut., *De def. or.* 42 (a more restrained version). Geographer: Strabo 9.3.5. Vapor shortage: Plut., *De def. or.* 50. Ruined spring: Paus. 3.25.8.
6. For a survey of the literary evidence and its drawbacks, see Joseph Fontenrose, *The Delphic Oracle* (University of California Press, 1978), 197–203.
7. For a summary of the skeptical case, see Daryn Lehoux, "Drugs and the Delphic Oracle" *CW* 101 (2007): 41–56.

CHAPTER 22

1. The destruction of the Serapeum is described by Ruf., *HE* 11.22–30.
2. Marcia: Hdn. 1.17.
3. For a useful survey, see Frank Trombley, "Overview: The Geographical Spread of Christianity," *The Cambridge History of Christianity I: Origins to Constantine* (Cambridge University Press, 2006), 302–13.
4. Mandating baptism: *Cod. Iust.* 1.11.10. Burning: Malalas 491.18–20.
5. John of Ephesus: Joh. Eph., *HE* 3.36–37. Tree worship: Greg., *Ep.* 8.19. Sardinian pagans: Greg., *Ep.* 4.25–27. Pagan shepherds: Const. Porph., *De admin. imp.* 50.

6. Heliopolis and Edessa: Joh. Eph., *HE* 3.27–28. On the history of Harran, see *The Encyclopaedia of Islam*, 2nd ed. (Brill, 1960–2005), s.v. "Harran."

7. On the direct conversion of temples to Christian shrines, see Timothy Gregory, "The Survival of Paganism in Christian Greece: A Critical Essay," *AJP* 107 (1986): 237–39. The story of "Saint Demetra" is told in George Mylonas, *Eleusis and the Eleusinian Mysteries* (Princeton University Press, 1961), 11–12.

8. End of Lupercalia: Gelasius, *Adv. Andromachum*. Criticizing Maioumas: Joh. Chrys., *Hom. in Matth.* 7.6.

CHAPTER 23

1. Dance of Spartan girls: Ar., *Lys.* 77–82. Wrestling match: Schol. Juv. 4.53.

2. Single chariot finished: Pind., *Pyth.* 5.49–51. Jockeyless horse: Paus. 6.13.5.

3. Torn entrails: Paus. 8.40.3. Two days: Dio Chrys., *Or.* 28.7.

4. Lion hunter: Paus. 6.5.5. Finger tipper: Paus. 6.4.2. Victorious corpse: Paus. 8.40.2.

5. Three hundred chariots: Diod. Sic. 13.82. Fighting beside king: Plut., *Mor.* 639E. Athenian cash prizes: Plut., *Sol.* 23.3. Thirty thousand drachmas: Dio Chrys., *Or.* 66.11. Cloaks as prizes: Pind., *Ol.* 7.83.

6. Free agents: e.g., Paus. 6.13.1, 6.18.6.

7. The headquarters of the association: *Inscriptiones graecae urbis Romae* 237. Crown: *PLondon* 3.1178.

8. Trajan: Plin., *Ep.* 10.40.2. Sulla: App., *B. Civ.* 1.99. Nero at the Olympics: Suet., *Nero* 24.2. Nero's Greek games: Suet., *Nero* 12.3–4. Sand from Egypt: Plin., *HN* 35.168. Every prize in advance: Tac., *Ann.* 16.4.

9. Cakes from heaven: Stat., *Silv.* 1.6.9–50. Pipes: e.g., Sen., *Ep.* 90.15. T-shirt cannons: e.g., Cass. Dio 66.25.5; Suet., *Nero* 11.2.

10. A horse named winner: *ILS* 5288.

11. Boar dung: Plin., *HN* 28.237.

12. Outfits: Juv. 5.143–44. Tombstone: *CIL* VI.9719. Swallows: Plin., *HN* 10.71. Dung: Gal., *MM* 4.6. Caligula: Cass. Dio 59.14. Nero: Plin., *HN* 33.90. Caracalla: Hdn. 4.6.

13. Funeral pyre: Plin., *HN* 7.186. Gilded busts: Mart. 5.25.10. Crescens: *ILS* 5285. Diocles: *ILS* 5287.

14. Tunics: Procop., *Anec.* 7.12–13. Mullets: Procop., *Anec.* 7.10. Nika rebellion: Procop., *Pers.* 1.24.

CHAPTER 24

1. Milo's feats: Paus. 6.14.6–7. Milo at war: Diod. Sic. 12.9. Milo's appetite: Ath. 10.412F. Chicken gizzards: Plin., *HN* 37.144. Milo training with cow: Quint., *Inst.* 1.9.5.

2. Roman author's advice: Cels., *Med.* 1.1–2. Restoring health: Plin., *HN* 28.53–54.

3. Galen on exercise: *San. Tu.*, esp. 1.8. Small ball: Gal., *De parvae pilae exercitio.* Hangover: Philostr., *Gym.* 54.

4. Alexander: Plut., *Alex.* 39.5. Augustus: Suet., *Aug.* 83. Trajan: Plin., *Pan.* 81.1–3. Hadrian: SHA, *Had.* 2.1. Marcus Aurelius: SHA, *Marc.* 4.9. Sparring: SHA., *Had.* 14.10; *Comm.* 2.9. Swimming: SHA, Alex. Sev. 30.4. Jogging: e.g., Auson., *Grat. act.* 14.

5. Olympic champion: Plut., *Dem.* 6.2. Roman jogger: Mart. 7.32. Ultra-runners: Plin., *HN* 7.84.

6. Liver: Gal., *San. Tu.* 2.10–11. Weights in Roman baths: e.g., Sen., *Ep.* 56.1; Mart. 14.49.

7. Bronze ball: Jer., *in Zach.* 3.12. Gym rock inscription: *CIL* III.12924. Boulder at Olympia: *IVO* 717. Boulder at Thera: *IG* XII.3.449. Stringing bow: Paus. 6.8.4.

CHAPTER 25

1. The song of the colossus: e.g., Paus. 1.41.3. The inscriptions on the statue's legs are collected in André Bernand and Etienne Bernand, *Les inscriptions grecques et latines du Colosse de Memnon* (Imprimerie de l'institut français d'archéologie orientale, 1960).

2. Merchant who made seventy-two voyages: *CIG* 3920.

3. Plutarch's well-traveled friends: Plut., *De def. or.* 2, 18.

4. Shipwrecked author: Jos., *Vit.* 15.

5. Speed of ships: Lionel Casson, *Ships and Seamanship in the Ancient World* (Princeton University Press, 1971), 284–88. Destination times: Plin., *HN* 19.3–4. Sailing season: Veg., *Mil.* 4.39.

6. Swivel seats in carriage: SHA, Pert. 8. Gaming boards: Suet., Claud. 33. Alexander's carriage: Diod. Sic. 18.26–27.

7. Professional runners: Plin., HN 7.84. Carriage making twenty-five miles per day: e.g., Hor., Sat.1.5.86. Caesar's sprint: Suet., Caes. 57. Two hundred miles: Plin., HN 7.84.

8. Robbers taking over inns: Cyp., *Ep.* 68.3. Leg-hacking brigand: Gal., *UP* 2.188K. Crucifying highwaymen: e.g., *Dig.* 48.19.28.

9. Human flesh: Gal., *Alim. Fac.* 6.663K; *SMT* 12.254K. Roadside lodges: e.g., Cic., Att. 10.5.3, 11.5.2.
10. Biting and gouging: Paus. 3.14.10. Endurance contest: Plut., *Lyc.* 18.1. Tour guides at Delphi: Plut., *De Pyth. or.* 2. Tourists visiting the statue of Zeus at Olympia: e.g., Arr., *Epict. diss.* 1.7.23. Thumb of Colossus: Plin., *HN* 34.41. Promethean clay: Paus. 10.4.4. Helen's breast: Plin., *HN* 33.81.
11. Erotic pottery: [Luc.], *Am.* 11.
12. Alexander's tomb: e.g., Strabo 17.1.8.
13. Climbing the Great Pyramid: Plin., *HN* 36.76. Shooting the rapids: Aristid., *Or.* 36.47–51. Etched message: J. Baillet, *Inscriptions grecques et latines des Tombeaux des Rois ou syringes* (Imprimerie de l'Institut français d'archéologie orientale, 1920–6), no. 602.

CHAPTER 26

1. We don't know exactly how long it took to build the Colosseum, but it must have been less than ten years. The single textual reference to the construction process (*Chronograph of 354 AD* [*MGH Chronica Minora* I, 146]) tells us only that Vespasian began the project and his son Titus finished it. This is echoed by Suetonius (*Vesp.* 9; *Tit.* 7).
2. Hadrian's python: Cass. Dio 69.16.
3. On these skilled slave builders, see, e.g., Frontin., *Aq.* 2.116–17 and Sen., *Ep.* 90.25–26.
4. It has been estimated that the construction of the Baths of Caracalla involved up to 13,100 men (J. DeLaine, "The Baths of Caracalla," *Journal of Roman Archaeology* [1997]: 193).
5. On ancient construction cranes, see Vitr. 10.2.1–10 and Heron, *Mechanica* 3.1–10.
6. Dedication of the Colosseum: Cass. Dio 66.25.

CHAPTER 27

1. Senators in sunhats: Cass. Dio 59.7.8.
2. Crucifixion and disemboweling: Mart., *Spec.* 9. Man dropped into cage of bears: Mart., *Spec.* 10. Orpheus: Mart., *Spec.* 24–25. Amazons: Mart., *Spec.* 8. Elephant and bull: Mart., *Spec.* 20, 22. Polar bear: Mart., *Spec.* 17.
3. On the rhinoceros, see Mart., *Spec.* 11. Bear vs. bull: Sen., *Ira* 3.43.2 (one of several examples). Bull vs. elephant: Mart., *Spect.* 20. Lion vs. tiger: Mart., *Spec.* 21.

4. Bear-hunting centurion: *CIL* XIII.8174.

5. Running down ostriches: Ael., *NA* 14.7. Bison hunt: Paus. 10.13.1–2. Capturing big cats: Opp., *Cyn.* 4.77–111, 212–29, 320–53. Catching tigers: Plin., *HN* 8.66. Mirror method: Claudian, *Rapt. Pros.* 3.263.

6. This rule only applied to animals scheduled to appear in the emperor's games (*Cod. Theod.* 15.11.2).

7. Inscriptions: *CIL* VI.8583, *AE* 1971 181, *CIL* 10209. Sculptor and leopard: Plin., *HN* 36.40. Crocodiles in Rome: Strabo 17.1.44. On the evidence for Rome's primary *vivarium*, see George Jennison, *Animals for Show and Pleasure in Ancient Rome* (Manchester University Press, 1937), 174–76.

8. Lion tricks: Mart., *Spec.* 12; Stat., *Silv.* 2.5.25–27. Monkeys: Juv. 5.153–55.

9. Tiger and goat: Plut., *De soll. an.* 20. Prisoners fed to the animals: Suet., *Calig.* 27.1. Sick crocodiles: Symm., *Ep.* 6.43, 9.132.

10. Elephant heart: Gal., *AA* 7.10. Ostrich brains: SHA, *Heliogab.* 30. Nutritional value of arena meat: Gal., *Alim. Fac.* 6.664. Tokens for arena meat: Mart. 8.78.7–12. Public hunt: SHA, *Prob.* 19.

CHAPTER 28

1. On the gladiator's skull, see Fabian Kanz and Karl Grossschmidt, "Head Injuries of Roman Gladiators," *Forensic Science International* 160 (2006): 207–16.

2. Six fighting styles: *CIL* VI.631. Statue of doctor: *CIG* 1106. Galen: Gal. 13.600K.

3. Barley boys: Plin., *HN* 18.72. Pork diet: Gal. 6.661K. Acorn fed: Philostr., *Gym.* 43. Goat meat: Ath. 402C. Three pounds of meat: Gal. 8.843K.

4. Weight gain theory: see Sandra Lösch et al., "Stable Isotope and Trace Element Studies on Gladiators and Contemporary Romans from Ephesus," *PLOS ONE* 9 (2014): 1–17.

5. Gladiators described as muscular: e.g., Cyp., *ad Don.* 7. Soft bodies: Gal. 6.529. Vulnerable: Gal., *Protrep.* 4.

6. Gladiator advertisements: e.g., *CIL* IV.7992. Programs: Cic., *Phil.* 2.97.3. Portraits: Plin., *HN* 35.52. Moonstone: Plin., *HN* 36.162. Amber: Plin., *HN* 37.45.

7. Olympic bribery: Paus. 5.21.3–5. Fixed wrestling match: *POxy.* 79.5209.

8. Long duel: Hor., *Epist.* 2.2.98.

9. Gladiator lease money: *ILS* 5163.45–46. Caesar's battle: Suet., *Caes.* 39.3. British town: Suet., *Claud.* 21.6.

10. Claudius's knives: Suet., *Claud.* 34.2.

11. Fan clubs: *IvE* 2905. Shouting advice: Tert., *Ad Mart.* 1.2. Stoned monk: Theod., *HE* 5.26. By the book: Petron., *Sat.* 45.12. Bride's hair: Plut., *Quaest. Rom.* 87. Epilepsy: Plin., *HN* 28.4. Sand: Plin., *HN* 15.19; 28.50.

12. Eleven gladiators: *ILS* 5062. Fight for his life: *AE* 1971, 430–31. Bloodless combats: Suet., *Nero* 12.1. Marcus: Cass. Dio 71.29. Commodus: Cass. Dio 72.17.

13. On the gladiator code, see M. J. Carter, "Gladiatorial Combat: The Rules of Engagement," *CJ* 102 (2006–2007): 97–114. Always wins, never kills: Mart. 5.24.

14. Gladiator with 150 victories: *CIL* IV.2451.

CHAPTER 29

1. On the Battle of the Hydaspes/Jhelum, see Diod. Sic. 17.88 and Arr., *Anab.* 5.15–17.

2. Corral trick: Arrian, *Indica* 13. Elephants saving trapped comrades: Plin., *HN* 8.24; Ael., *NA* 6.61. Driving herd into valley: Plin., *HN* 8.24. Walking backward off ship: Plin., *HN* 8.6. Bulls behaving badly: *HN* 8.27. Elephant diet: Ael., *NA* 10.10.

3. Elephant breath: Ach. Tat. 4.4. Elephant saving driver: Plut., *Pyrrh.* 33.4–5.

4. Subjected to volleys of stones: [Caes.], *BAfr.* 27.

5. Special rafts: Polyb. 3.46. Elephant sleds: Livy 44.5.

6. Polyb. 5.84–85 describes an elephant duel.

7. Elephants terrifying Gauls: Lucian, *Zeuxis* 8–11. Wounded elephant: Plin., *HN* 8.20.

8. Bishop summoning gnats: Theod., *HE* 2.30. Model elephants: Polyaenus, *Strat.* 4.21.

9. Anti-elephant corps: Polyaenus, *Strat.* 4.21. Anti-elephant knights: Veg., *Mil.* 3.24. Anti-elephant "tanks": Dion. Hal., *Ant. Rom.* 20.1.6–7. Flaming pigs supposedly scattered the entire elephant corps of one Hellenistic king and helped the Romans defeat another (Ael., *NA* 1.38, 16.36).

10. Mother elephant: Dion. Hal., *Ant. Rom.* 20.12.14. Double-edged weapon: Livy 27.14. Common enemy: App., *Hisp.* 46.

11. Moving colossal statue: SHA, *Hadr.* 19.12. Elephants as private mounts: e.g., Cass. Dio 49.7. Performing troupe: Ael., *NA* 2.11; Plin., *HN* 8.5.

CHAPTER 30

1. On the subterranean skirmish, see Simon James, "Stratagems, Combat, and Chemical Warfare in the Siege Mines of Dura-Europos," *AJA* 115 (2011): 69–101.

2. For a description of a very castle-like late Roman fortified villa, see Venatius Fortunatus, *Carm.* 3.2.

3. Patroclus: Hom., *Il.* 16.698–711.

4. Pirates at Rhodes: Diod. Sic. 20.82–83. Alesia: Caes., *BG* 7.69–74.

5. Human pyramid: Caes., *BG* 7.47. Determining the height of a wall: Veg., *Mil.* 4.30. Balloon ladder: Heron, *Pneum.* 2.

6. Catapulted head: Frontin., *Str.* 2.9.5. Jerusalem: Joseph., *BJ* 5.270. Thunderbolt: Anon., *de rebus bell.* 18. Man's head: Joseph., *BJ* 3.257. Pinioned barbarian: Procop., *Goth.* 1.23.4–12. Crusher: Josh. Styl. 53.

7. Roman architect: Vitr. 10.15. Mega-ram: Diod. Sic. 20.95.1.

8. Roman siege tower: Veg., *Mil.* 4.17. Additional stories: Veg., *Mil.* 4.19. Screaming prisoners: Diod. Sic. 20.54.2–7. Fire hoses: Apollodorus, *Poliorcetia* 174.2–7.

9. Salamis tower: Diod. Sic. 20.48. Rhodes: Diod. Sic. 20.91; Plut., *Demetr.* 21; Vitr. 10.16.4.

10. Caesar: Caes., *BG* 7.24. Masada: Joseph., *BJ* 7.306–7.

11. Bronze shield, bees and wasps: Aen. Tact. 37.3–7. Burning feathers: Livy 38.7. Bears: App., *Mith.* 78. Scorpion pots: Hdn. 3.9. The wolf: Veg., *Mil.* 4.23. Rhodians and the city taker: Diod. Sic. 20.96–97. Sewage: Vitr. 10.16.7.

12. On the siege of Amida, see Amm. Marc. 19.1–9.

CHAPTER 31

1. This anecdote is inspired by Amm. Marc. 15.3.7–9.

2. Pillow talk: Polyaenus, *Strat.* 5.13.

3. Reading senators' mail: SHA, *Hadr.* 11.4–6. Hunting Christians: Euseb., *HE* 6.40.2–3. In disguise: Arr., *Epict. diss.* 4.13.5.

4. Retired agent: Innocent, *Ep.* 38 (*PL* XX, 605B).

5. Loose horse: Frontin., *Str.* 1.2.1. King's head: *AE* 1969/70, 583. German chieftain: *AE* 1956, 124.

6. Arcani: Amm. Marc. 23.3.8. Sahara, Sudd: Plin., *HN* 5.14–15, 6.181. Remote islands: Plut., *De def. or.* 18.

7. Britain: Caes., *BG* 4.21. Mountains of Armenia: Amm. Marc. 18.6–7. Enemy fleet: Procop., *Vand.* 1.14.1–5.

8. Spies in Persia: Procop., *Anec.* 30.12. Spies as merchants: Amm. Marc. 26.6.4–6; Anon., *Strat.* 42.7. Disguised as soldier: Procop., *Pers.* 1.15.5. Man in Roman uniform: Amm. Marc. 18.6.17. Plot to assassinate Trajan: Cass. Dio 68.11.3. Disloyal official: Amm. Marc. 18.5.1–3.

9. Methods of sending coded messages: Aen. Tact. 31; Front., *Strat.* 3.13. Bureaucratic script: *Cod. Theod.* 9.19.4. Purple ink: *Cod. Iust.* 1.23.6.

10. Poison garden: Plut., *Demetr.* 20.2. Mithridates: e.g., Cass. Dio 37.13.

11. Locusta: Suet., *Nero* 33.2–3; Tac., *Ann.* 12.66. Chieftain: Tac., *Ann.* 2.88. Poison needles: Cass. Dio 67.11.6, 73.14.4.

12. *Frumentarii* as assassins: e.g., SHA, *Sev.* 8.1–2; *Did. Iul.* 5.8. Lion hunter: Cass. Dio 73.14.1–2. Fatal accident: Tac., *Ann.* 11.19. Marcus Aurelius: Cass. Dio 71.14. Kidnapping: e.g., Amm. Marc. 29.7.7; Joh. Eph., *HE* 3.40–41. Banquet strategy: e.g., Amm. Marc. 29.6, 30.1.18–23. Attila: Priscus, Fr. 11.1.

CHAPTER 32

1. For an overview, see Siegmar von Schnurbein, "Augustus in Germania and His New Town at Waldgirmes East of the Rhine," *JRA* 16 (2003): 93–108.

2. Executed for setting aside swords: Tac., *Ann.* 11.18. Licensed prostitutes: this interpretation is based on understanding *lixa cohortis* as "cohort prostitute" as opposed to "cohort servant." Epitaph: *Bulletin archéologique du Comité des travaux historiques et scientifiques* 1928–1929, 94.

3. The most famous description of a Roman army on the march is Joseph., *BJ* 3.115–26. For a description of how to set up an imperial-era marching camp, see Ps.-Hyginus, *De Munitionibus Castrorum*.

4. Britons: Tac., *Agr.* 29–37. Nomads: Arr., *Acies contra Alanos* 12–31. Danube: Cass. Dio 71.7.

5. Bridge: Cass. Dio 68.13. Auxiliaries swimming Danube: *CIL* III.3676. Soldier freeing captives: Cass. Dio 71.5.

6. The Roman view of Germany: Caes., *BG* 6.21–24; Tac., *Germ.*

7. Caesar's bridges: Caes., *BG* 4.17–18, 6.9.

8. The most complete ancient account of the battle is Cass. Dio 56.18–22.

9. Small fort: Arr., *Peripl. M. Eux.* 9.3

10. Chieftains coming to dinner: e.g., Amm. Marc. 21.4. Settling tribes on Roman soil: e.g., *CIL* XIV, 3608.

11. On Germans using Roman coins, see, e.g., Tac., *Germ.* 5. Roman-style houses in Germany: e.g., Amm. Marc. 17.1.7.

12. Exploding cows: Pompon. 3.53. Incestuous natives: Strabo 4.5.4. Snakes: Solin. 22.3.

13. Ambitious governor: Tac., *Agr.* 24. Coins: Peter Crawford, "The Coleraine Hoard and Romano-Irish Relations in Late Antiquity," *Classics Ireland* 21–22 (2014–2015): 41–118.

CHAPTER 33

1. Constantius's visit: Amm Marc. 16.10.14–16. There are two late antique lists of Rome's buildings: the *Notitia* and the *Curiosum*. The numbers given here are taken from the *Curiosum*. Elagabalus and the cobwebs: SHA, *Elag.* 26.6.

2. Vandals stripping tiles: Procop., *Goth.* 1.5. Pedestal: *CIL* VI.1658. Statues: Procop., *Goth.* 1.22.

3. Greg., *Dial.* 2.15.3.

4. Apartment buildings as tourist destination: Tert., *Adv. Valent.* 7. Floods destroying apartments: *Liber pontificalis* (Duchesne) I, 399; cf. Gregory of Tours, *Hist.* 10.1.

5. Forests of statues: Procop., *Goth.* 4.21.12–14. Statues stolen in the night: Cassiod., *Var.* 7.13. Constans pillaging: *Liber pontificalis* (Duchesne) I, 363. Shipwreck with Constans's scrap: R. Coates-Stephens, "The Byzantine Sack of Rome," *Late Antiquity* 25 (2017): 207–9. Pile of statues: Rodolfo Lanciani, *The Destruction of Ancient Rome: A Sketch of the History of the Monuments* (Macmillan, 1899), 196.

6. Pope supervising destruction: *Liber pontificalis* (Duchesne) I, 503.

7. On the busy contractor, see Rodolfo Lanciani, *The Ruins and Excavations of Ancient Rome* (Macmillan, 1897), 375.

8. Palace statues stripped: *Chron. min.* 1.336. Marble quarry: Magister Gregorius, *De mirabilibus urbis Romae* 17.

CHAPTER 34

1. For a sober summary of the rumors, see A. B. Bosworth, *Conquest and Empire: The Reign of Alexander the Great* (Cambridge University Press, 1988), 171–73. Aristotle: Plut., *Alex.* 77.3–4.

2. Alexander's tomb: Strabo 17.1.18.

3. Augustus: Cass. Dio 51.16.5. Alexander's breastplate: Suet., *Cal.* 52; Cass. Dio 59.17.3. Caracalla's obsession: Cass. Dio 78.7–8; *Epit. de Caes.* 21.4. Caracalla at the tomb: Hdn. 4.8.9.

4. Palace Quarter devastated: Amm. Marc. 22.16.15. Tsunami: Amm. Marc. 26.10.15–19. Continued existence: Lib., *Or.* 49.11–12. Rhetorical question: Joh. Chrys., *Hom. in Ep. II ad Cor.* (*PG* 61, 581).

5. Autopsy on body of St. Mark: Leonardo Manin, *Memorie storico-critiche intorno la vita, traslazione e invenzioni di S. Marco Evangelista*, 2nd ed. (G. B. Merlo, 1835), 24–25.

6. Pyre of Septimius Severus: Hdn. 4.2.6–9. Galerius: Ivana Popovic, "Sacred-Funerary Complex at Magura," in *Felix Romuliana—Gamzigrad*, ed. I. Popovic (Arheološki Institut, 2011), 141–58.

7. Funeral of Augustus: Suet., *Aug.* 100; Cass. Dio 56.42.

8. Agrippina: *CIL* VI.886. Urn: Rodolfo Lanciani, *Pagan and Christian Rome* (Macmillan, 1892), 182.

9. Assos limestone: Plin., *HN* 36.131.

10. Nero and the haunted walnut tree: Giacomo Alberici, *Historiarum sanctissimae et gloriosissimae virginis deiparae de populo almae urbis compendium* (Rome, 1599), 2–8. In case you're wondering, Nero wasn't actually buried on the future site of Santa Maria del Popolo; his family tomb was elsewhere.

11. Maximian: *Chronicon Novaliciense*, App. 11 (*MGH, Scriptores* 7:126–27). My thanks to Ray Van Dam for informing me of this source. Constantius: *Flores historiarum*, a. 1283, ed. H. R. Luard, in *Rerum britannicarum medii aevi scriptores* 95 (London, 1890), 59. Preserved Roman woman: Rodolfo Lanciani, *Pagan and Christian Rome* (Macmillan, 1892), 295–301. Body of Justinian: Niketas Choniates, *Historia* 648.

12. For a vivid description of the discoveries beneath Santa Petronilla, see Rodolfo Lanciani, *Pagan and Christian Rome* (Macmillan, 1892), 200–205. On the identification of the bodies, see Mark Johnson, *The Roman Imperial Mausoleum in Late Antiquity* (New York, 2009), 171–74. Piso: Katherine Bentz, "Rediscovering the Licinian Tomb," *The Journal of the Walters Art Gallery* 55/56 (1997/1998): 63–88. Sarkamen: I. Popovic and M. Tomovic, "Golden Jewelry from the Imperial Mausoleum at Sarkamen (Eastern Serbia)," *Antiquité Tardive* 6 (1998), 287–312.

13. On the burials in Holy Apostles, see Philip Grierson, "The Tombs and Obits of the Byzantine Emperors (337–1042)," *DOP* 16 (1962), 3–63.

14. Body of Alexius: Alexander van Millingen, *Byzantine Churches in Constantinople: Their History and Architecture* (Macmillan, 1912), 147–48.

15. Varnakova tombs: Anastasios Orlandos, Η Μονή Βαρνάκοβας (Athens, 1922), 11–16. Tomb of Andronicus II: Theodore Macridy, "The Monastery of Lips and the Burials of the Palaeologi," *DOP* 8 (1964): 271.

CHAPTER 35

1. Spanish Latin: e.g., Cic., *Arch.* 10; Mart. 12.21.3–6.

2. The epitaph actually describes the languages (respectively) as *usus francisca, vulgari et voce latina*. The modern names (and national connotations) of French and Italian are much later inventions.

3. Classicists will notice that I've played a little fast and loose with my ancient (i.e., more or less Koine) Greek example for the purpose of accentuating parallels with Modern Greek. The most common word for book in Classical Greek was βίβλος, not the diminutive βιβλίον, and the possessive construction I used here (τὸ βιβλίον μου) really means "some book of mine" as opposed to the more emphatic τὸ ἐμὸν βιβλίον (my own book). Peccavi; ex toto corde paenitet me.

4. On Tsakonian, see Geoffrey Horrocks, *Greek: A History of the Language and Its Speakers*, 2nd ed. (Wiley Blackwell, 2010), 88, 274.

CHAPTER 36

1. For the pedigree collapse example, see Kenneth Wachter, "Ancestors at the Norman Conquest," in *Statistical Studies of Historical Social Structure*, ed. K. W. Wachter, E. A. Hammel, and P. Laslett (Academic Press, 1978), 153–61. Common ancestor: Douglas Rohde, Steve Olson, and Joseph Chang, "Modelling the Recent Common Ancestry of All Living Humans," *Nature* 431 (2004): 562–66. European inbreeding: Peter Ralph and Graham Coop, "The Geography of Recent Genetic Ancestry across Europe," *PLoS Biol* 11, no. 5 (2013): e1001555. https://doi.org/10.1371/journal.pbio.1001555.

2. Zeus as ancestor: e.g., Pl., *Alc.* 121A. Historian in Egypt: Hdt. 2.143. Bishop: Syn., *Ep.* 113.3. Roman elite: e.g., Jerome, *Ep.* 108.1–4; Symm., *Ep.* 1.2.4.

3. Sosius Priscus: *ILS* 1104.

4. Sindelinda: S. J. B. Barnish, "Transformation and Survival in the Western Senatorial Aristocracy, c. A.D. 400–700," *PBSR* 56 (1988): 154.

5. Most notably, a French genealogist named Christian Settipani (e.g., *Les ancêtres de Charlemagne*, 2nd ed. [Oxford University Press, 2014]) has attempted to trace Charlemagne's descent back to the fourth-century Gallic notable Flavius Afranius Syagrius via Arnulf of Metz.

6. Morris Bierbrier, "The Descendants of Theodora Comnena of Trebizond," *The Genealogist* 12 (1998): 60–82.

7. D. M. Nicol, *The Immortal Emperor: The Life and Legend of Constantine Palaiologos, Last Emperor of the Romans* (Cambridge University Press, 1992), 109–28.

Index